STATISTICS
FOR
TEACHERS

STATISTICS FOR TEACHERS

ESTELLE S. GELLMAN

Harper & Row, Publishers
New York, Evanston, San Francisco, London

I am indebted to the literary executor of the late Sir Ronald A. Fisher, F.R.S., to Dr. Frank Yates, F.R.S., and to Oliver & Boyd, Edinburgh, for permission to reprint Tables III and IV from their book *Statistical Tables for Biological, Agricultural and Medical Research*.

STATISTICS FOR TEACHERS

Standard Book Number: 06-042289-0

LIBRARY OF CONGRESS CATALOG CARD NUMBER: 72-13121

CONTENTS

Although statistical methods have long been used in educational research, statistics is an area that has been greatly neglected in the education of classroom teachers. This situation is being remedied, and a growing number of schools are now specifying proficiency in statistics as a requirement for a degree in education. Unfortunately, however, most of the statistics texts now available are directed at the educational researcher rather than at the classroom teacher. The focus of these texts is on the use of statistical methods in research, and the application of these methods to the classroom situation is largely ignored. Since most teachers do not have the level of sophistication in mathematics and research design that these texts assume, they find the material to be irrelevant and unusually difficult to master. Consequently, if statistics is to be appropriately taught to teachers, there is a need for a statistics text that is specifically designed for teachers. Thus this book is specifically designed for use in pre-service and in-service teacher training programs.

The emphasis of this book is on the application of statistics in describing classroom performance and in testing hypotheses relevant to the classroom situation. The material on inferential statistics is directed toward giving the student competence to critically read the research reported in the professional journals and to use statistical methods in analyzing and interpreting data that might be collected in the school situation.

This book is designed for a one-semester course and thus includes only the most commonly used statistical methods. The material on inferential statistics is quite thorough, however, and should provide the student with enough background so that more advanced methods can be mastered easily.

Since most students of education do not have a substantial background in mathematics, the text assumes a minimum of competence in this area. No mathematical preparation beyond elementary algebra is required for a complete understanding of the material. Mathematical derivations have been completely omitted, and explanations are given in "everyday" language.

Great Neck, New York   Estelle S. Gellman

STATISTICS
FOR
TEACHERS

STATISTICS AND THE TEACHER 1

It is a rare teacher who looks forward to studying statistics. For most, statistics is surrounded by an aura of fear. Most teachers do not have extensive training in mathematics and are apprehensive about their ability to comprehend a subject which is, in fact, a branch of mathematics. The truth of the matter is, of course, that statistics is no more difficult than many other subjects, and that it may be quite adequately understood without any mathematical preparation beyond elementary algebra. It is actually the fear of the subject, rather than the subject matter itself, that causes most of the difficulty. Our first task, then, is to dispel this fear. Let us begin by examining the nature of the subject, for with familiarity will come the knowledge that statistics need not be a source of fear. To the contrary, a knowledge of statistics can provide the teacher with a much greater understanding of educational data.

What is Statistics?

Usually, when we think of statistics, our thoughts turn toward numbers. When a statistician thinks of a statistic, however, he is referring not to just any number, but to a computed value that tells him something about a set of numbers. Assume that we have a set of scores on a spelling test, as listed in Table 1.1. Now, suppose that the principal of our school asks how the group did on the spelling test. We could tell him that Mary had a score of 100, John had a score of 60, Michael had a score of 90, and so forth. By the time we get down to Walter, however, it is highly unlikely that he will remember what we said about Mary. Furthermore, the principal probably is not interested in the scores obtained by particular students but merely wants a general idea of the performance of the class as a whole.

Instead of listing all the students and their scores, however, we could give the principal the average score for the group. The scores are averaged by first finding the sum of the scores, and then dividing this sum by the number

Table 1.1. Scores of Ten Students on a Spelling Test

Student	Score
Mary A.	100
John B.	60
Michael C.	90
Robert D.	100
Nancy E.	70
Barbara F.	50
Sally G.	60
Henry H.	80
Linda I.	70
Walter J.	70

of students. If we follow this procedure, as we do next, we would find the average score to be 75.

Finding the Average Score

1. Sum the individual scores:

   $100 + 60 + 90 + 100 + 70 + 50 + 60 + 80 + 70 + 70 = 750$

2. Divide the sum of the scores by the number of students:

   $$\frac{750}{10} = 75$$

This average score is a statistic that succinctly describes the scores of the ten students. It is a computed value that tells us something about this set of numbers. The particular average that we have just computed is a statistic which is called the *mean.* The mean is one of several different measures of typical or average performance that may be computed to describe a set of scores.

Averages, however, are not the only type of statistic that we may compute. Statistics may also be computed that tell us the degree to which our scores differ from each other, or the degree to which different sets of scores are similar or related. As with the mean, these other statistics are simple to compute. They are all computed values that summarize the information in a set of data.

Now that we have some idea of what statistics are, we should begin to see that statistics is not difficult. However, we must make a distinction between applied and theoretical statistics. *Applied statistics* is the use or application of various statistics in a particular discipline. Using the mean to describe a set of test scores, for example, is an application of this statistic in the discipline of education. If we were to use the mean to describe the salaries of unskilled laborers, we would be applying the statistic to the field of economics. In applied statistics, then, we are concerned with the use of statistics in a particular discipline.

Theoretical statistics, on the other hand, is the study of the derivation and nature of the statistic itself. A theoretical statistician would not necessarily be concerned with how we use the mean to describe our educational data but would be concerned with the mathematical properties of the statistic. Obviously, then, the theoretical statistician must be trained in mathematics. For the person studying applied statistics, however, advanced training in mathematics is not a necessity. In applying statistics to a particular discipline, we must know what the statistic tells us, and when the statistic is appropriately used. In order to find the mean score on a test, for example, we do not have to know why the mean is computed in the way that it is. We need only know when it is appropriate to use this statistic, how it is computed, and what it can tell us about a set of scores. Although the use and interpretation of a statistic is, of course, limited by its mathematical properties, one can learn the limitations of a statistic without an extensive background in mathematics.

Thus we see that the study of theoretical statistics is quite difficult for a teacher who is untrained in mathematics. Moreover, it would be equally difficult for a teacher to apply statistics to an unfamiliar discipline. When we study the application of statistics to education, however, the teacher has nothing to fear. All that is needed in the way of mathematics is the ability to add, subtract, multiply, and divide, and enough background in elementary algebra to enable one to solve simple algebraic equations.

Why Should the Teacher Study Statistics?

Now that we have considered what the study of statistics involves, let us turn to the question of why a knowledge of statistics is important for the teacher. The teacher who has a knowledge of statistics not only can make use of the appropriate statistics in describing the performance of his class to others but is also in a position to better understand the information he receives. When you stop to think of the extent to which a student's career is determined by his grades in class and the scores he receives on standardized achievement and aptitude tests, you can see how important it is that such information be properly evaluated by the teacher. Without a knowledge of statistics, however, such evaluation can be quite difficult, if not impossible.

When standardized achievement tests are given in the schools, the scores are often reported to the teacher in the form of *standard scores* or *percentile ranks*. But what does it mean if Mary gets a standard *T*-score of 50 in reading? When one has become accustomed to grading on a percentage system in which 65 is the passing grade, one usually thinks of 50 as being rather low. When one is dealing with standard *T*-scores, however, a score of 50 is neither high nor low, but average for the group. A *T*-score is a statistic that is commonly used in reporting test scores, and it is just as commonly misinterpreted. When the teacher has had training in statistics, however, such misinterpretations are less likely to occur.

A knowledge of statistics also helps the teacher evaluate course grades and the differences in ability represented by different grades. Even if John received grades of 80 in arithmetic and 95 in reading, for example, he has done relatively better in arithmetic if the percentage of students in the class who scored below 80 in arithmetic happened to be higher than the percentage who scored below 95 in reading. The study of statistics enables the teacher to make such evaluations.

In addition to the use of statistics in describing student performance, a knowledge of statistics is a necessity if one is to critically read the professional journals in education. Statistical methods are widely used in educational research, and the results of the research studies usually are reported in the language of statistics. Let us assume that a study has been reported in which, after comparing two methods of teaching arithmetic, the author concludes that one method produces superior problem-solving ability to the other. In order to determine whether the author's conclusion is warranted, we might look at how he compared the two methods and examine the results of the comparisons. Let us assume, then, that the author gave a problem-solving test to students who learned under the two methods, and that the scores of the two groups of students were then compared by a *t*-test. If this were the case, the author might report that *t* was equal to 5.53, which was significant at the .01 level of significance, and that the null hypothesis was therefore rejected. Was his conclusion warranted? How can the teacher who does not know what "*t*" is, or what it means for "*t*" to be significant, decide? One could, of course, just skip that section of the article and read only the author's conclusions. It is obvious, however, that such a procedure would put the teacher in the precarious position of having to put all his trust in the judgment of the author. And although educational researchers usually can be trusted, such interpretation of results is not an exact science. Consequently, one must understand the meaning of the results before one can critically evaluate conclusions based on these results. When important decisions such as which teaching method to use are going to be based on what the teacher reads in the journals, it becomes a matter of serious concern that the teacher be able to evaluate what he is reading.

Although most teachers are more concerned with the results of research done by others than with doing research of their own, there are many instances in which the teacher might also become involved in a research project. The teacher might want to see whether her methods have different effects on students of different backgrounds or, perhaps, whether students do better when they are allowed to work on projects with their friends. Or the teacher may be requested to participate in a study comparing the performance of different classes within a school, or different schools within a school district. Here, too, a knowledge of statistics is essential. Let us assume, for example, that the IQ scores of students in two schools have been compared, and that the average IQ score in Westside School was found to be 110, whereas the average in Eastside School was only 100. On the basis of these data, the teacher untrained in statistics might conclude that, on the average, the students in Westside School have more scholastic promise than do those in Eastside School. It may well be, however, that a difference of only 10 points is so minute a difference as to be attributed to chance. That is, if we were to give a similar test a week later, it would be just as likely for the students in Eastside School to perform better than those in Westside School as for the reverse to occur. How do we know whether the difference reflects a true difference in ability? We can never know for sure, but statistics provide a tool for evaluating such differences and for determining the likelihood that the differences are not due merely to chance.

A one-semester course in statistics cannot provide the teacher with the skill to plan a complex statistical analysis. What a teacher can gain from such a course, however, is the ability to apply the basic statistical techniques in evaluating educational data. As we have seen, this basic knowledge is a necessity if the teacher is to properly evaluate student performance and to critically read the professional journals in education.

CLASSIFICATION OF EDUCATIONAL DATA 2

We now know that statistics is concerned with numbers, and that when we apply statistics to education, we must consider the types of numbers that are of interest to the teacher. For the most part, the teacher is concerned with numbers that represent scores on tests. These tests are designed to measure various abilities, and a score represents the level of ability attained by the student. These scores may also be used to rank students in terms of their ability, in which case the numerical rank of a student is another number that is of interest to the teacher. There are times, however, when numbers are assigned merely to differentiate one group of students from another. For example, the teacher may decide to divide a class into five groups, each of which will work on a different aspect of a class project. Then, in order to differentiate among the groups, he may assign a different number to each group. In this case, the numbers merely serve as names and do not give any information about the relative performance of the students in the different groups.

In each of these cases we are concerned with numbers, but each of these numbers provides a different type of information about our students. In order to use our statistics correctly, we must know the type of number we are dealing with. Therefore, before we go on to using statistics, let us consider the different types of numbers to which our statistics may be applied.

What is a Variable?

When we are dealing with numbers such as test scores, the scores represent the different values of our *variable*. A variable is any dimension on which persons or things may differ. A variable may take on different values for different persons or things, and these different values are called the *variate values*. Test scores are variables because different students may receive different scores on a test. The different scores a student may receive are the variate values. Similarly, we may be interested in a variable such as course grades. If our students may be assigned grades of A, B, C, D, or F, these

7

different letter grades are the variate values. We may even be concerned with a variable that is as non-numerical as language preference. If, for example, we wanted to know whether our students preferred to study French or Spanish, the two languages would be the variate values.

Although test scores, letter grades, and language preference could all be classified as educational variables, these variables differ in a number of ways.

Discrete and Continuous Variables

The first distinction we make among variables is the distinction between *discrete* and *continuous* variables. When a variable may take on any value within a range of values, we have a continuous variable. Weight, for example, is a continuous variable. The weight of a student may be anywhere from, let's say, 50 pounds to 250 pounds. There is no weight within this range that is excluded; one student may weigh 90 pounds, another 85.5 pounds, and another 72.75 pounds. Although it is unlikely that we would report a student's weight as being 72.74931 pounds, even this number is a possible value within our range of weights. We would not report a value such as this, not because the value does not exist, but because our scale is not fine enough to measure with such a high degree of precision.

Let us assume that our weights are being read from the scale shown in Figure 2.1. When a student steps onto the scale, the indicator stops at a point on the line that corresponds to the weight of the child. Note that even though the line from which the values are read is marked only at specified intervals, the line is *continuous*. The indicator may stop not only at the marked values, but at any point along the line. The indicator may stop at the point which is equivalent to a weight of 72.4931 pounds but, if this were the case, we would

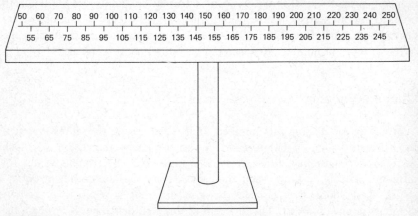

Figure 2.1.

probably report the weight as 72.5 pounds. The child can actually weigh 72.4931 pounds, but, because the scale is not fine enough for us to make accurate distinctions between ten-thousandths of a pound, we would report the weight to the nearest half pound. Nevertheless, since it is possible for the child to be any weight within our range, our variable is continuous.

When our variable may take on only certain specified values, and no values other than those specified, we have a *discrete* variable. Sex, for example, is a discrete variable. A student may be male or female; the student cannot be anything between these two specified variate values. In this case, the variate values cannot be visualized as forming a continuous straight line, but a dotted line, with each dot representing one of the possible values.

Although non-numerical variables such as sex are obviously discrete, numerical values may also be discrete. Consider the variable of class size. Even if we have no restrictions on the number of students allowed to enroll in a particular class, the number of students in a class is limited to certain specified values. We cannot have 25.5 students in a class, nor can we have 15.67. The variate values are limited to whole numbers. Since this limitation is not imposed by a lack of precision in our measurement instrument but by the nature of the variable itself, we have a discrete variable.

Now that we have considered the distinction between continuous and discrete variables, we must also consider the problems that occur when we are dealing with any set of actual data. Actual data, such as test scores, are always discrete. We may, for example, give a 100-item arithmetic test to measure the extent to which our students have mastered a unit in arithmetic. If we allow 1 point for each problem correct, and if we do not allow any partial credit, our scores are limited to the whole-number values ranging from 0 to 100. A student cannot possibly get a score of 82.7965, nor can he get a score of 70.25. In this case, however, even though our scores are discrete, we would treat the data as if they were continuous. We would treat the data in this manner because we can assume that the variable being measured, arithmetic ability, is a continuous variable, and that the data are discrete only because our measurement instrument, the test, is limited in the precision with which it can measure the variable.

To illustrate the distinction between a discrete variable and discrete data for a continuous variable, let us consider how the values on discrete and continuous variables are interpreted. To illustrate the interpretation of values on a continuous variable, refer again to the scores on our arithmetic test, and consider all of the students who received scores of 70. Even if we could assume that our test was perfectly reliable, we could not assume that all of the students with scores of 70 had mastered the unit to the same extent. Some might have had the degree of mastery equivalent to a score of 70.25; others might have mastered the material only to the degree equivalent to a score of 69.95. Degree of mastery is continuous, and students may have any degree of mastery. The test, however, is not sensitive enough to enable us to distinguish between the degree of mastery equivalent to a score of 70.25, and the degree equivalent to a score of 69.9. Thus students with these differing degrees of mastery would receive the same score, and we would not know whether a student who has a score of 70 has the degree of ability that corresponds exactly to a score of 70. Similarly, even when two students receive the same score, we do not know that they have exactly the same amount of ability. When we have a continuous variable, then, we do not interpret a score as representing one discrete value but as representing a range of values. With a discrete variable, however, our interpretation is somewhat different.

To illustrate the interpetation of values on a discrete variable, consider again the values for the variable of class size. As with scores on a test, the values on this variable are also limited; if our classroom has only 100 seats, we cannot have a class with more than 100 students. When we have a class size of 70, however, we know that the class in question has exactly 70 students. The class cannot have 70.25 students, nor can it have 69.95 students. Similarly, if two classes are the same size, they have exactly the same number of students. We can interpret our values as being exactly what they are because, with a discrete variable, the variable itself can only take on these specific values. The data are discrete because of the nature of the variable and not because of a lack of precision in our measurement technique.

In actual practice, then, it is the nature of the underlying variable that determines whether the data are treated as discrete or continuous. Even though our data may be discrete, we treat them as being continuous if we can assume that the trait or ability that we are measuring is continuous, and that the discontinuity of our data is imposed merely by the lack of precision in our measurement instrument.

Levels of Measurement

In addition to the distinction between discrete and continuous variables, we may further classify our variables according to the type of scale on which they are measured. Some variables may be measured only on rather gross scales; other variables may be measured on scales that provide more precise information. Depending upon the type of information that the scale can provide, the scale may be classified as a nominal, an ordinal, an interval, or a ratio scale.

When the measurement scale is such that the different values on the scale differ only in kind, rather than in amount, we have a *nominal scale*. For example, we may have a variable such as language preference, and the variate values may be French, Spanish, and German. These values differ in name only, not in amount. One can say only that French is different from German, not that it is any greater or less than German. If we were to use a nominal scale to measure the performance of two students, we could determine only whether our students had the same or different values on the variable being measured. If, for example, we were to compare the language preferences of John and Michael, our nominal scale would provide only enough information for us to determine whether their preferences were the same or different. It would be meaningless to state that John's language preference was any higher or lower than Michael's.

In the case where language preference is our variable, our variate values are non-numerical. It is possible, however, to have a nominal scale even though our variate values are numbers. For example, we might divide a class into five groups and arbitrarily assign different numbers to the different groups. These numbers would serve merely as labels or names. If we knew that Mary was a member of group 1 and that Alice was a member of group 2, we would know only that the girls were in different groups. We would not know whether Mary's group was any higher or lower than Alice's; we would know only that they were different.

Sometimes, however, the scale values can indicate whether one student did better or worse than another. This is the case when we have an *ordinal scale,* that is, a scale on which the values may be ordered from highest to lowest. Assume for example, that a teacher has assigned grades of Excellent, Good, Satisfactory, and Unsatisfactory to a set of English papers. These values may be ordered from highest to lowest, with Excellent at the top of the scale of values and Unsatisfactory at the bottom. If we know that Mary received a grade of Excellent and that Alice received a grade of Satisfactory, we not only know that the girls' grades were different, but we know that Mary did better than Alice.

Even though our ordinal scale provides us with enough information to determine whether Mary's grade was higher or lower than Alice's, this type of scale does not indicate how much better Mary did than Alice. It might have been that all of the papers were very close in quality, and that the difference in quality between an Excellent and a Satisfactory paper was insignificant. On the other hand, there might not have been much difference between the Excellent and Good papers, but the good papers might have been substantially better in quality than were the Satisfactory ones. Since our scales do not tell us how much of a difference there was between the grades, we cannot say how much higher or lower one student was than another. All ordinal scales limit us in this same way; although the values on an ordinal scale may be ordered from highest to lowest, each successive value does not necessarily differ from the next highest value by the same amount.

This limitation becomes particularly apparent when we look at *ranks* or *rank orders.* Assume that we have just given a spelling test to ten students, and that the students had the following number of words correct:

Student	Number of Words Correct
Mary A.	98
John B.	90
Michael C.	84
Robert D.	85
Nancy E.	100
Barbara F.	83
Sally G.	65
Henry H.	70
Linda I.	69
Walter J.	75

On the basis of these scores, we could order the students from highest to lowest, assigning a rank of 1 to the student with the highest score, a rank of 2 to the student with the next highest score, and so on. The students would thus be assigned the following ranks:

Student	Score	Rank
Nancy E.	100	1
Mary A.	98	2
John B.	90	3
Robert D.	85	4
Michael C.	84	5
Barbara F.	83	6
Walter J.	75	7
Henry H.	70	8
Linda I.	69	9
Sally G.	65	10

This process of assigning ranks is called *ranking,* and the ranks are values on an ordinal scale.

If a teacher who was not familiar with the original scores was informed that Nancy had a rank of 1, and that John had a rank of 3, he would know that Nancy had more words correct than John. He would not know how many more words Nancy had correct than John. Similarly, if he was informed that Robert had a rank of 4, and that Barbara had a rank of 6, he would know that Robert had more words correct than Barbara. Note that the difference in rank between Nancy and John is the same as the difference in rank between Robert and Barbara. If we now look back to the number of words which each student had correct, however, we can readily see that the equal differences in rank do not correspond to equal differences in the number of words correct. Whereas the difference of two ranks between Nancy and John reflects a ten-word difference in the number of words correct, the same difference of two ranks between Robert and Barbara reflects only a two-word difference in the number of words correct. As you can see, then, equal differences in rank do not necessarily correspond to equal differences in the variable being measured.

When we have a scale on which equal differences between scale values do correspond to equal differences on the variable, we then have an *interval scale*. Interval scales provide us with enough information to determine not only whether one student did better or worse than another, but how much better or worse that student did.

We rarely if ever have true interval scales when we are dealing with educational variables. With most educational variables, we have no way of determining whether equal differences between our scale values correspond to equal differences on the variable. To illustrate an interval scale, therefore, let's consider the weather, and let's assume that we are measuring the temperature on a Fahrenheit scale. When our scale reads 75°, we know that it is 5° hotter than when our scale reads 70°. Similarly, when our scale reads 100°, we know that it is 5° hotter than when the scale reads 95°. Furthermore, we also know that the difference in heat between 95 and 100° is exactly the same as the difference between 70 and 75°. That is, anywhere along our scale, equal increments in our scale values correspond to equal increments of heat. Thus it takes exactly as much heat to raise the temperature from 95 to 100° as it does to raise it from 70 to 75°; it takes twice as much heat to raise it from 70 to 80°, and it would take one-fifth as much heat to raise it from 70 to 71°. With an interval scale, then, equal differences between scale values correspond to equal differences in the variable being measured.

When we turn to most of our educational variables, however, we have no way of knowing whether equal differences between scale values correspond to equal differences in the variable. Consider a variable such as intelligence. We generally measure intelligence with an IQ test, and we assume that equal increments in IQ score anywhere along the scale of IQ values correspond to equal increments in intelligence. We assume that the difference between the IQ scores of 70 and 75 corresponds to the same amount of difference in intelligence as does the difference between the scores of 130 and 135. In other words, if Mary's IQ score is 135, John's is 130, Robert's is 75, and Alice's is 70, we assume that Mary is as much more intelligent than John as Robert is than Alice. In actual fact, however, we have no way of knowing whether the difference between the IQ scores of 70 and 75 represents the same difference in intelligence as does the difference between the scores of 130 and 135. Whereas we know that it takes the same amount of heat to raise our thermometer from 70 to 75° as it does to raise it from 95 to 100°, it may well be that it takes a greater increment in intelligence to raise a score 5 points at the upper end of the scale than it does at the lower end of the scale. Or it may well be that just the opposite is true. Since we have no way of knowing what the truth is, it is customary to assume that equal increments in score values anywhere along the scale represent equal increments in intelligence. Only if we accept this assumption, however, can we then think of IQ scores as forming an interval scale.

If our values did meet the requirements necessary for an interval scale, then our scale values would provide us with enough information to determine the degree to which students differed from each other. We could then say that John and Mary differed to the same extent as did Robert and Alice. In addition, we could make ratio statements comparing these differences. That is, if we knew that John and Mary differed by 5 points, and that George and Susan differed by 10 points, we could say that the difference between John and Mary and the difference between George and Susan are in the ratio of 1:2. In other words, the difference in intelligence between George and Susan is twice as great as the difference between John and Mary. Note, however, that although we may make ratio statements about the differences between students, we cannot make ratio statements about the score values.

Assume, for example, that we have the following scores:

Student	Score
Nancy	120
Michael	90
Henry	60

If IQ scores form an interval scale, we can say that the difference in intelligence between Nancy and Henry is twice as great as the difference between Nancy and Michael. We cannot say, however, that Nancy is twice as intelligent as Henry. We cannot make this statement because an interval scale does not have a true *zero point*. That is, we do not have a value on our scale of IQ values which corresponds to zero intelligence. Thus, if a child received an IQ score of zero, it would not mean that he had zero intelligence. Similarly, if a child received a score of zero on an arithmetic test, it would not mean that he had zero arithmetic ability. A score of zero merely means that the child's ability, however low it may be, is not measurable on our scale. If we were to give him an easier test, he would probably get another score.

Before we can say that one student has three or four times as much of a particular ability as does another, we must know that the first child's score is three or four times as far from the true zero point for that ability. If we do not know what value is equivalent to the true zero point, we cannot make statements of this nature. It may well be that on our IQ test, for example, zero intelligence would be equivalent to a score of −50. If this were so, a score of 120 would certainly not be twice as far as a score of 60 from the zero point for intelligence. Therefore, a child with a score of 120 could not be said to be twice as intelligent as a child with a score of 60. In actual fact, we do not even know how to define zero intelligence, much less assign it a point on a scale. Without this information, however, we cannot make meaningful ratio statements concerning the intelligence of our students.

The limitation imposed by the lack of a true zero point occurs with all interval scales. Even on our Fahrenheit scale, 0° does not represent the absence of heat; when the temperature is 40°, it is not twice as hot as when it is 20°, nor is it half as hot as when it is 80°. With an interval scale, then, we can determine whether our students are the same or different, whether one student did better or worse than another, and, in addition, the extent to which the students differed. When a trait is measured on an interval scale, however, we cannot determine the ratio of one student's ability to another's. We cannot say that one student has five times as much, or one-third as much ability as another.

When we have a scale that has all of the properties of an interval scale and, in addition, does have a true zero point, we have a *ratio scale.* Values on variables such as height, weight, age, or number of spelling words correct may form ratio scales. For each of these variables we can specify a true zero point that indicates the absence of the variable. If a child spells zero words correct on a spelling test, for example, we have an absence of any words correct. Note, however, that we do not have an absence of spelling ability. We do not have a true zero point for spelling ability, only for the number of words correct. The scale values indicating the number of words correct would form a ratio scale for measuring the number of words correct, but they would form only an interval scale for measuring spelling ability. We could say, then, that John had twice as many words correct as Mary, but we could not say that he has twice as much spelling ability. Similarly, a ratio scale allows us to say that one child is twice as tall, twice as old, or weighs twice as much as another.

Now that we have examined the four types of measurement scales, we can see that as we go from a nominal scale to a ratio scale, the scale values provide us with increasingly more information about the variable being measured. Whereas nominal scales can indicate only whether people are the same or different on the variable being measured, ordinal scales can tell us whether one person's value on the variable is greater or less than another's, interval scales can tell us how much greater or less, and ratio scales can tell us how many times greater or less.

In view of the fact that so many important decisions in a student's career are based on his scores on various measurement scales, it is most important that the teacher be able to distinguish among the scales and be aware of the limitations in interpretation that are imposed by each. It is all too often that we see misinformed teachers attribute equal differences in ability to equal differences in rank. If John's rank on a test is 80, Mary's is 70, and Alice's is 60, it may very well be that the difference in performance between Mary and John is three times the difference between Mary and Alice. If we use ranks as the basis for forming special instruction groups, we must be very sure that we are not falsely assuming that substantial differences in rank reflect equally substantial differences in ability. Frequently, large differences in rank reflect insignificant differences in test performance. One must be particularly aware of such discrepancies when interpreting the results of standardized achievement and aptitude tests.

With most of the widely used tests, the teacher may never see the raw score or the number of items a child had correct; he is merely told the child's percentile rank. *Percentile ranks* are a form of ordinal data that indicate the percentage of students having scores lower than that of the child in question. In the middle ranges, from about the fortieth to the sixtieth percentile, large differences in percentile ranks often reflect rather minor differences in ability. This discrepancy occurs because most of the students fall in the middle range of ability, and a difference of only a few points can account for a great number of students. Assume, for example, that 100 students took a 100-item arithmetic test, that 10 students had scores lower than 50, and that 40 had scores between 50 and 55. If this were the case, then a student with a score of 50 would have a percentile rank of 10. A student with a score of 55, however, would have done better than $50/100$ of the students and would have a percentile rank of 50. As you can see, then, a difference of only 5 score points would account for a difference of 40 percentile ranks. Unfortunately, however, many teachers are not aware that percentile ranks are ordinal data, and that large differences in rank do not necessarily reflect large differences in ability. Consequently, one frequently sees a teacher treating a child with a percentile rank of 40 on a test as being quite inferior in ability to the child with a percentile rank of 60. Although the child may, in fact, have considerably less ability, our percentile ranks do not provide enough information on which to base such a judgment.

Other instances of misinterpretation occur when teachers attribute to interval scales the properties of ratio scales. If Alice receives 50 in arithmetic, while Mary receives 75 and John receives 100, one cannot assume that Alice has only half as much arithmetic ability as John or two-thirds as much ability as Mary. One must even be tentative in assuming that the difference in ability between Alice and Mary is equivalent to the difference between Mary and John. Although we frequently assume that we are measuring abilities on an interval scale, we must also remember that all too often we have no way of knowing whether equal differences in scale values really reflect equal differences in ability. Assumptions that cannot be proven may be made for purposes of practicality, but if we are to make meaningful interpretations of our data, we must be aware that these assumptions are not always met.

As you can see, it is important that the teacher understand the limitations inherent in the data which he receives. The teacher must be aware of the assumptions underlying the various scales, and the level of information that they provide. Only then can he be sure that he is not reading into a score more information than it provides. The consideration of continuity and of level of measurement is important not only in interpreting particular score values, however, but also in determining how to analyze a set of data. Certain statistics can be used only with a continuous variable; others are appropriate only when the variable is discrete. Analyses that are appropriate with interval data are not necessarily appropriate when we are dealing with nominal or ordinal data. Furthermore, as we will see in the next chapter, different types of data are even tabulated in different ways. Thus as we progress further into the analysis of our data, we will see more clearly the extent to which the questions of continuity and level of measurement limit the analyses that may be performed.

PRACTICE PROBLEMS

1. For each of the following examples, (1) identify the variable being measured, (2) indicate the type of scale on which the variable is being measured, and (3) indicate whether the variable is continuous or discrete:
   a. Percentage of items correct on a test of scholastic aptitude.
   b. Class standing in high school.
   c. Number of words correct on a spelling test.
   d. Report-card grades in conduct.
   e. Classification of first graders as to ethnic background.
   f. Number of absences per academic year.
2. Given the following scores on a language aptitude test, which of the conclusions given below are warranted?

Student	Percentile Rank
Alice	95
Barbara	90
Charles	90
Dorothy	80
Edward	75
Frank	60
George	45

   a. Barbara has twice as much mathematical ability as George.
   b. Barbara and Charles have exactly the same amount of ability.
   c. The difference in ability between Dorothy and Edward is the same as that between Barbara and Charles.
   d. Barbara and Charles had the same scor᾽ on the test.
   e. There were twice as many students between Frank and Dorothy as between Dorothy and Charles.
   f. Charles had twice as many items right as George.

ORGANIZATION AND PRESENTATION OF DATA 3

Now that we have considered the scales on which our variables may be measured, let us turn our attention to the analysis of the data that our measurements yield. If we record our measurements as they occur, we usually end up with a mass of unorganized data from which it is difficult to extract the information that we desire. Therefore, our first step is to organize the data in such a way that the information is more readily available. Assume, for example, that the following data represent the recorded foreign language preferences of a group of students:

French, Spanish, French, French, German, Spanish, Spanish, French, French, Spanish, German, Spanish, French, German, German, Spanish, French, Spanish, French, Spanish, French, French, German, French, Spanish, German, French, Spanish, French, French.

Which language was most often preferred? Was French preferred over Spanish? Or was Spanish preferred over both French and German?

Although the data provide all the information necessary to answer these questions, the information would be much easier to extract if the data were more meaningfully organized.

Frequency Distributions

Although data may be organized in any number of ways, the most usual procedure is to construct a table in which each possible value of the variable is listed along with the number of times that each value occurred in the data. Such a table is called a *frequency distribution,* and is illustrated in Table 3.1.

Note how the trends in the data become so much more apparent when the data are presented in this manner. One glance at the table indicates that French was the preferred language, and that Spanish was preferred to German. The frequency distribution does not provide us with any new

Table 3.1. Foreign Language Preferences of 30 Students

Language	Number of Times Preferred
French	14
Spanish	10
German	6

information, but it facilitates the task of finding the information that we want.

Now that we see the advantage of presenting our data in a frequency distribution, let us consider the various steps involved in the construction of such a table. The first step always is to decide upon a title. This step is sometimes glossed over as being self-evident, but it is all too often forgotten. Consider, for example, the following data:

Test Score	Frequency
160	1
150	2
140	2
130	4
120	8
110	10
100	15
90	10
80	5
70	3

It is obvious that scores of 110 appeared in the data twice as frequently as did scores of 80, and that more than half the scores fell below a score of 110. But scores on what? And for whom? It might have been obvious to the person who constructed the table, but if he constructed three tables for three different sets of scores, it is highly unlikely that he would remember which scores were which for very long. In order to identify our data, then, it is important that we give each table a title. The title should be concise, and it may be written in telegraphic language, but it must indicate the variable that was measured, and on whom the measurements were made. The foregoing data, for example, might be identified by the title, "IQ Scores of 60 High-School Students."

Once we have decided on the title, we can then consider the body of the table itself. As in the frequency distribution illustrated in Table 3.1, we will have one column in which we list the values of the variable, and a second column in which we indicate the frequency with which each value occurred. As may also be noted in Table 3.1, each of these columns has a heading. It is customary to use the name of the variable as the heading for the column of variate values but, in some cases, the letter X is substituted. The letter X is often used to represent the value of a variable, and the practice of

Table 3.2. Distribution of Grades Received by 15
Students on an English Assignment

Grade	Frequency
Excellent	2
Good	7
Satisfactory	5
Unsatisfactory	1

substituting an X for the name of the variable is common when one is preparing a frequency distribution for one's own use in analyzing data. When one is presenting the information to others, however, it is better practice to spell out the name of the variable. Referring again to the column indicating the frequency with which each value occurred, the heading for this column usually is "Frequency" or just "f."

If we refer again to Table 3.1, we can see that each value of the variable was listed separately, and that the values were listed in the order of frequency, from most frequently occurring value to least frequently occurring value. This procedure is the same for all nominal data. With ordinal, interval, and ratio data, however, the procedure is somewhat different.

With ordinal data, as with nominal data, we would also list each of our variables. In this case, however, the variables would not be listed in the order of frequency, but in the order of value. Consider, for example, a frequency distribution of the following grades on an English assignment:

> Satisfactory, Good, Good, Satisfactory, Unsatisfactory,
> Excellent, Satisfactory, Good, Good, Satisfactory,
> Excellent, Good, Good, Good, Satisfactory.

Our values would be listed as illustrated in Table 3.2. Note that the grades are not listed in order of frequency but are ordered from highest to lowest in value.

With interval and ratio data, the values are similarly ordered from highest to lowest. Since we generally have a large range of possible values when we have interval and ratio data, however, it can become quite cumbersome to list each value separately. Assume, for example, that we wanted to make a frequency distribution of the following set of IQ scores:

> 113, 120, 117, 115, 110, 100, 96, 85, 100, 83, 94, 90, 75, 101, 105,
> 81, 130, 96, 116, 83, 105, 110, 110, 116, 121, 117, 122, 119, 93, 90,
> 107, 107, 113, 105, 112, 125, 93, 112, 124, 110, 125, 117, 125, 126,
> 95, 95, 123, 101, 111, 97, 100, 111, 117, 142, 106, 127, 121, 136,
> 131, 110, 137, 102, 107, 110, 98, 120, 103, 130, 99, 110, 142, 120,
> 124, 137, 115, 128, 118, 133, 103, 109, 114, 144, 108, 137, 106, 114,
> 117, 120, 117, 126, 117, 129, 119, 115, 134, 130, 140, 130, 142, 137,
> 100, 95, 115, 110, 115, 96, 112, 118, 83, 92, 99, 100, 99, 86, 135, 83,
> 92, 140, 126, 90.

Table 3.3. Distribution of IQ Scores Received by 120 Third-Graders

Score	Frequency	Score	Frequency	Score	Frequency
144	1	120	4	97	1
143	–	119	2	96	3
142	3	118	2	95	3
141	–	117	7	94	1
140	2	116	2	93	2
139	–	115	5	92	2
138	–	114	2	91	–
137	4	113	2	90	3
136	1	112	3	89	–
135	1	111	2	88	–
134	1	110	8	87	–
133	1	109	1	86	1
132	–	108	1	85	1
131	1	107	3	84	–
130	4	106	2	83	4
129	1	105	3	82	–
128	1	104	–	81	1
127	1	103	2	80	–
126	3	102	1	79	–
125	3	101	2	78	–
124	2	100	5	77	–
123	1	99	3	76	–
122	1	98	1	75	1
121	2				

If we were to list each possible value within the range of scores covered by our data, we would end up with the rather lengthy distribution illustrated in Table 3.3. Not only does this distribution look cumbersome, but it does not give a clear picture of the trends in the data. The values cover so wide a range of scores, that it is difficult to get an overall view of the distribution. What we need is a way of condensing the distribution so that the overall trends in performance are not hidden in the mass of separate scores. It is for this reason that we often *group* our data. That is, we divide the scores into a series of *score intervals*, each of which includes a specified range of scores. Then, rather than list each separate value in our frequency distribution, we can list the score intervals. Rather than list 100, 104, 105, 106, 107, and 108 as separate score values, we could represent these scores by two score intervals, 100-104 and 105-109.

To illustrate the process of grouping, let us now make a *grouped frequency distribution* of the IQ scores given in Table 3.3. The first step is to decide on the number of score intervals and the size of each interval. For most purposes, it is best to work with between 10 and 20 intervals. In any particular instance, however, the number of intervals to use will be determined by the data. We first look at the data, then, to determine the

Table 3.4. Distribution of IQ Scores Received by 120 Third-Graders

Score Interval	Frequency
140-144	6
135-139	6
130-134	7
125-129	9
120-124	10
115-119	18
110-114	17
105-109	10
100-104	10
95-99	11
90-94	8
85-89	2
80-84	5
75-79	1

number of score points the data cover. In our data, for example, since the highest score is 144 and the lowest is 75, our data cover a range of 70 score points. We must then determine how many score points should be included in each interval if we are to have between 10 and 20 intervals. To get an estimate, let us assume that we will have 15 intervals. Dividing the 70 score points by 15, we can see that we would have to include about 4 or 5 score points in each interval. Since it is most convenient to work with intervals which include an odd number of score points, let us settle, then, upon an interval size of 5.

Now that we have decided upon our interval size, the next step is to set up the intervals. We would start by establishing our bottom interval to include our lowest score value. Since our lowest value is 75, our bottom interval would be 75-79. Note that our bottom interval could just as well have been 71-75, 72-76, 73-77, or 74-79. The interval 75-79 was chosen, however, merely because it is conventional, when using 5-point intervals, for the lower score in the interval to be a multiple of 5. Once we have decided upon the bottom interval, we then specify each succeeding 5-point interval until we have reached the interval that includes our top score. As illustrated in Table 3.4, our top interval is 140-144.

Our last step, now, is to determine the number of scores that fell within each interval, and to enter the totals in the frequency column. In determining the frequencies, we may take one interval at a time and count the number of scores that fell within that interval. Usually, however, it is more efficient to tally the scores as they occur. That is, as each score is read from the data, a tally mark is placed next to the interval in which the score fell. Then, after all the scores are tallied, the tally marks for each interval are counted, and the totals are entered in the frequency column. To check that each score was

Table 3.5. Time Required by High-School Students
on a Speeded Reading Test

Number of Minutes	Frequency
50.0	1
49.5	3
49.0	5
48.5	9
48.0	12
47.5	15
47.0	12
46.5	11
46.0	9
45.5	5
45.0	3

included in the tally, one should always make sure that the sum of the frequencies is equal to the total number of scores.

If we now compare the grouped and ungrouped frequency distributions, we can see that it is easier to get an overall picture of the performance of the group from the grouped frequency distribution. We can clearly see from the grouped distribution that the greatest concentration of scores was in the range from 110 to 119, and that, assuming that the average IQ score for the population is equal to 100, most of the students in this group are above average in IQ. Note, however, that although the overall trends in performance are clearer in the grouped frequency distribution, there is a loss of information. We no longer know whether the score in our bottom interval was 75. It might just as well have been 76, or 78. Nor do we know how the 15 scores in the interval from 105 to 109 were distributed. They all may have been equal to 106, or they may have been equally distributed between 107 and 109. For most purposes, however, this loss of information is more than compensated for by the gain in clarity and convenience.

Once we have made a frequency distribution of our data, we are ready to begin our analysis. We might just want to inspect the data for a general picture of the trends in performance or, in some cases, we might want to do a more complex statistical analysis. We will consider various types of statistical analyses in later chapters; at this point, however, we should consider some of the assumptions that are made about the data in a frequency distribution. First, notice that there are gaps between the values that are listed in our frequency distributions. In neither the grouped nor ungrouped distribution is there a place to record a score value of 104.25. It is true that IQ scores are not recorded in fractions of a point, but remember that intelligence is a continuous variable, and that we must therefore treat the data as if they were continuous. In order to eliminate the gaps in our data, then, we assume that a

Table 3.6. Size of Classes in Northside Private Day School

Class Size (Number of Students)	Frequency
50-54	1
45-49	0
40-44	0
35-39	2
30-34	3
25-29	5
20-24	8
15-19	10
10-14	15
5-9	10
0-4	5

score of 104, for example, really represents a range of scores from 103.5 to 104.5. Similarly, a score of 100 represents a range of scores from 99.5 to 100.5, and the score interval 100-104 represents a range of scores from 99.5 to 104.5. We thus assume that each score really represents a range of values extending from the point midway between the score and the next lowest score to the point midway between the score and the next highest score. These midpoints are called the *real* or *exact limits* of the interval. If our values were as listed in Table 3.3, the exact limits of a score of 90 would be 89.5 and 90.5. If we have larger intervals, as in Table 3.4, the exact limits of the interval from 100 to 104, for example, would be 99.5 and 104.5. Note, however, what happens when the score values are not whole numbers. For the data given in Table 3.5, the lower exact limit of a score of 49.5 is equal to 49.25, while the upper exact limit is equal to 49.75. The exact limits are always the points midway between the score values that are listed. In this case, then, 49.25 is midway between the values of 49.5 and 49.0. Similarly, 49.75 is midway between 49.5 and 50.0.

By assuming, then, that each interval represents a range of scores extending from the lower to the upper exact limit, we eliminate the gaps in our data. Thus even though our data are discrete, we treat the variable being measured as if it were continuous. Even when the variable being measured is discrete, however, it is often useful to assume that the data extend from the lower to the upper exact limit of the interval. When one wishes to determine the size of an interval, for example, one need merely subtract the lower from the upper exact limit. In the frequency distribution illustrated in Table 3.6, for example, the size of each interval is equal to 5. Consider the interval from 10 to 14. If a class had 10, 11, 12, 13, or 14 students, it would fall within this interval. That is, these are the only five discrete values that fall into this interval. In other words, we are not measuring a continuous variable. Note, however, that if we subtract the lower exact limit of the interval, 9.5, from the upper exact limit, 14.5, the difference is exactly equal to the interval size. Thus, regardless of whether our variable is continuous or discrete, we may properly determine the interval size by finding the difference between the upper and lower exact limits of the interval.

There are many instances, however, in which the false assumption that the data for a discrete variable are continuous will lead to results that must be interpreted with caution. It is the false assumption of continuity that leads to such statements as the average family in the United States has 2.5 children. The number of children in a family is a discrete variable, and, quite obviously, a family cannot have 2.5 children. Since the assumption of continuity is necessary for many types of analyses, however, it is conventional to assume that the score intervals in a frequency distribution extend from the upper to the lower exact limits of the interval.

When one makes the assumption of continuity, one usually makes a second assumption regarding the distribution of the scores within the score interval. Once we have grouped our data into a grouped frequency distribution, we no longer know exactly how the scores were distributed in the data. For lack of information, then, we assume that the scores were equally distributed throughout the interval. That is, if we go half the way up the interval, we take into account half of the scores. In other words, if 10 scores fell within the interval from 100 to 104, we would assume that 5 of those scores fell between 99.5 and 102. Note, also, that the same assumption is made even when the interval size is 1. We assume, for example, that a score of 100 represents a range of scores from 99.5 to 100.5, and that those scores are equally distributed over the range of the interval.

Sometimes, however, our analyses require that we represent our score interval by a single number. When this is the case, we let the *midpoint* of the interval represent all the scores within that interval. The midpoint is the point midway between the upper and lower exact limits of the interval, and it can be found by adding half the interval size to the lower exact limit of the interval. If we wanted to find the midpoint of the interval from 100 to 104, for example, we would use the following procedure.

Finding the Midpoint of an Interval

1. Determine the interval size:

    $104.5 - 99.5 = 5$

2. Add half the interval size to the lower exact limit of the interval:

    $99.5 + \dfrac{5}{2} = 102$

As indicated, the midpoint of the interval is 102.

The midpoint is an inaccurate representation of scores to the degree that the scores within the interval are not equal to the midpoint. However, using

Table 3.7. IQ Scores Obtained by Students in
Upper- and Lower-Class Schools

	Frequency	
IQ Scores	Upper-Class Schools	Lower-Class Schools
130+	40	25
120-129	50	30
110-119	60	50
100-109	70	70
90-99	60	45
80-89	60	15
70-79	40	10
60-69	20	5

the midpoint usually does not result in any gross inaccuracies. It should be noted, though, that as the size of the interval is increased, the inaccuracy resulting from grouping the data also increases.

Thus far we have considered frequency distributions in which we have indicated either the number of times that a value occurred, or the number of scores that fell within an interval. In some cases, however, it is more useful to know the proportion of times a score occurred or, if we have a grouped distribution, the proportion of the scores that fell within a specified interval. If we are comparing two distributions in which there are different numbers of scores, for example, comparisons are facilitated if we know the proportion of times each score occurred in the separate distributions. To illustrate, consider the distributions in Table 3.7. Note that if we compared the number of students in each type of school who received scores above, say, 130, we might mistakenly conclude that, since more students in the upper-class schools received these high scores, comparatively more upper-class students receive scores this high. When one compares the proportion of students in each type of school receiving scores above 130, however, one can see that an equal proportion of the students in both schools received such scores.

When we are making comparisons between groups of unequal size, then, we have to know more than merely the number of students who fall within a particular range of scores. We have to know whether the number of students in one group who performed at a specified level was *proportionately* higher or lower than the number of students in the other group who performed at the same level. In order to find this information, we divide the number of students within the interval by the total number of students in the group. In order to find the proportion of upper-class students receiving scores equal to or above 130, for example, we follow the procedure illustrated on the next page.

Finding the Relative Frequency of a Score Interval

1. Determine the total number of students in the group:

   $$40 + 50 + 60 + 70 + 60 + 60 + 40 + 20 = 400$$

2. Divide the number of students falling within the interval by the total number of students in the distribution:

   $$\frac{40}{400} = .10$$

Since 40 upper-class students received scores equal to or above a score of 130, and since the total number of upper-class students who were in the sample was 400, the proportion of upper-class students receiving such scores is .10. Following this procedure, we can similarly determine the proportionate number of students within each group that fell within each of the score intervals. Once we have this information, we can construct a new distribution in which the proportions are recorded. Such a distribution is called a *relative frequency distribution,* and is illustrated in Table 3.8.

The relative frequency distribution is similar in form to the other distributions that have been considered. The only difference is that a relative frequency distribution indicates the proportion of scores, rather than the number of scores, that fell within each score interval. Although it requires more work to determine the relative frequencies than it does to determine the absolute frequencies, the use of a relative frequency distribution facilitates the making of comparisons between unequal groups. When we have unequal groups, and we wish to compare the proportionate number of students in each group who fell within specified score intervals, our task would be quite

Table 3.8. Proportionate Distribution of IQ Scores in Upper- and Lower-Class Schools

| | Relative Frequency | |
| | Upper-Class Schools | Lower-Class Schools |
IQ Scores		
130+	.10	.10
120-129	.12	.12
110-119	.15	.20
100-109	.18	.28
90-99	.15	.18
80-89	.15	.06
70-79	.10	.04
60-69	.05	.02

difficult if our frequency distribution provided only absolute frequencies. Each time we wanted to make a comparison, we would first have to determine whether the absolute frequencies were equivalent. When we have a relative frequency distribution, however, this task is already done, and we may proceed immediately with our comparisons.

Reviewing the material in this section, now, we can see that we use a frequency distribution merely as a means for presenting data. The frequency distribution does no more than summarize the data. It does not provide us with any new information but merely presents the data in such a way that the overall trends in performance are easier to visualize. Thus far we have considered performance only in terms of the number or proportion of students who received a specified score or fell within a specified score interval. There are times, however, when we do not want to know how many students received a specified score but how many students had scores below that score. We might want to know whether there are enough slow students to warrant a separate class for remedial reading instruction. Or we might want to know if there is a sufficient number of bright students to warrant the formation of a class for the intellectually gifted. When we want this kind of information, we are interested in a special form of frequency distribution, a *cumulative frequency distribution.*

Cumulative Frequency Distributions

Whereas the frequency distributions that we have thus far considered only indicate the frequency with which each data value occurred, a cumulative frequency distribution indicates the number of scores that fell above or below a particular score. Consider the data in Table 3.4. If we were to make a cumulative frequency distribution of these scores, our cumulative frequencies would be as indicated in Table 3.9.

Each cumulative frequency indicates the number of scores that fell below the *upper exact limit* of the interval. Thus the cumulative frequency of the bottom interval is equal to the frequency of that interval, since only the scores within that interval fell below the upper exact limit of that interval. The cumulative frequency of the second interval, however, is equal to the frequency of the second interval plus the cumulative frequency of the bottom interval. The cumulative frequency of the second interval thus reflects the fact that the total number of scores that fell below the upper exact limit of the second interval includes the scores within the second interval as well as all the scores that fell below that interval. The cumulative frequency of each succeeding interval, then, is equal to the frequency of the interval plus the cumulative frequency of the interval below. The cumulative frequency of the interval from 110 to 114, for example, is obtained by adding the frequency

Table 3.9. Cumulative Frequency Distribution of IQ Scores
Received by 120 Third-Graders

Score Interval	f	Cumulative Frequency
140-144	6	120
135-139	6	114
130-134	7	108
125-129	9	101
120-124	10	92
115-119	18	82
110-114	17	64
105-109	10	47
100-104	10	37
95-99	11	27
90-94	8	16
85-89	2	8
80-84	5	6
75-79	1	1

of the interval, 17, to the cumulative frequency of the interval below, 47. The cumulative frequency of the interval is thus equal to 64, which represents the sum of the 17 scores within the interval plus the 47 scores that fell below the interval. The cumulative frequency therefore indicates the total number of scores falling below the upper exact limit of the interval. When one reaches the top interval, then, the cumulative frequency of that interval should be equal to the total number of scores, because all of the scores in a distribution must be equal to or less than the score that was, in fact, the highest score. If the cumulative frequency of the top interval is not equal to the total number of scores, we know that we have made a mistake, and that the cumulative frequencies must be computed again.

Note that in the cumulative frequency distribution illustrated in Table 3.9, we have included the absolute frequency as well as the cumulative frequency of each interval. These absolute frequencies were included for purposes of illustration, and it is not necessary to include them in a cumulative frequency distribution. There are times, however, when both the absolute and cumulative frequencies may be of interest; we then construct a distribution that provides both types of information. A frequency distribution is constructed to present the data in a meaningful way, and it should therefore include whatever information is of interest to the person analyzing the data. Note, also, that we may construct a relative cumulative frequency distribution, as illustrated in Table 3.10. In this case, the relative cumulative frequency for each interval is determined by dividing the cumulative frequency of the interval by the total number of scores included in the

Table 3.10. Relative Cumulative Frequency Distribution of IQ Scores
Received by 120 Third-Graders

Score Interval	Cumulative Frequency	Relative Cumulative Frequency
140-144	120	1.00
135-139	114	.95
130-134	108	.90
125-129	101	.84
120-124	92	.77
115-119	82	.68
110-114	64	.53
105-109	47	.39
100-104	37	.31
95-99	27	.23
90-94	16	.13
85-89	8	.07
80-84	6	.05
75-79	1	.01

distribution. For the interval from 100 to 104, for example, we would divide the cumulative frequency, 37, by 120, which yields a relative cumulative frequency of .31. Whereas the cumulative frequency of 37 tells us that 37 students had scores equal to or below a score of 104.5, the relative cumulative frequency, .31, tells us that 31 percent of the students had scores equal to or below this score.

If we now refer to the cumulative frequencies in Table 3.9, we can see at a glance how many students fell below or above a particular score. Let's say that our school was considering a special class for slow learners, but 10 eligible students were needed before the school district would allot the funds. If slow learners are defined as students with IQ scores below 85, one can see directly from the frequency distribution whether a sufficient number of students are available. Similarly, if the schools in a district were being compared as to the proportion of students in each school with IQ scores below 85, the proportion of such students in a school could be directly determined from a relative cumulative frequency distribution as illustrated in Table 3.10.

The cumulative frequency distribution, then, is another means of presenting data. The cumulative frequency distribution goes one step beyond the other frequency distributions that were considered, however, in that it indicates not only the number or the proportion of scores that fell within a specified score interval, but also the number or the proportion of scores that fell below the upper exact limit of the interval.

Graphic Representation of Data

Although the various types of frequency distributions are commonly used as a means for presenting data, the trends in the data are sometimes easier to visualize when the data are presented graphically. There are two types of graphs that are commonly used to represent statistical data, the *frequency polygon* and the *histogram*. Each of these graphs provides the same information provided in the frequency distribution, but each represents the scores within an interval in a somewhat different manner.

The Frequency Polygon

A frequency polygon is a line graph in which each score interval is represented by a single point, the midpoint of the interval. Consider, for example, the frequency polygon illustrated in Figure 3.1. This polygon is a graphic representation of the data in Table 3.4. Note that the midpoints of the intervals are marked off along the horizontal axis, and the frequency of each interval is indicated by a point plotted above the midpoint of the interval. The first step in constructing a frequency polygon, then, is to mark off the midpoints of our score intervals along the horizontal axis, and to mark the frequencies along the vertical axis of the graph. Then, for each score interval, we plot the point indicating the frequency of that interval above the appropriate midpoint. If we were to plot the frequency of the interval from 100 to 104, for example, we would plot a point on the graph at the point

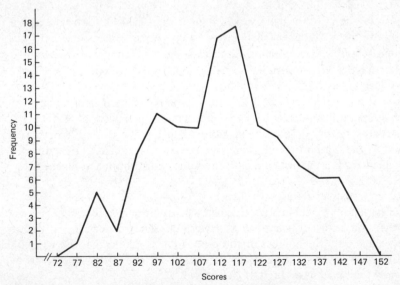

Figure 3.1 IQ scores received by 120 third-graders.

which represents the intersection of a frequency of 10 on the vertical axis and a midpoint of 102 on the horizontal axis. We would similarly plot the frequencies of each interval included in our frequency distribution. Then, when all the points were plotted, each point would be connected to the next by a straight line. Since it is conventional to "anchor" the frequency polygon to the horizontal axis, midpoints are usually marked off for the intervals above and below the top and bottom intervals included in the frequency distribution, and points indicating frequencies of zero are plotted for these intervals. When these points are connected to the other points on the graph, the frequency polygon is brought down to the horizontal axis.

The frequency polygon is the best type of graph to use when comparing data for two or more distributions. Assume, for example, that we want to compare the performance of the students in three school districts on a state-wide history test, and that the scores in each district are distributed as indicated in Table 3.11. Frequency polygons may be drawn to represent these scores (Figure 3.2), and the comparisons among the districts could be made by comparing the frequency polygons. Note that comparisons are facilitated because all three polygons can be drawn on the same set of axes. Although any number of frequency polygons may be drawn on the same set of axes, one must be sure that the lines connecting the points on the different polygons are drawn differently, and that a legend is supplied which identifies the different distributions.

However, even though the frequency polygons in Figure 3.2 are all drawn on the same set of axes, it is somewhat difficult to compare the performance of the students in District 1 with the performance of the students from the other two school districts. These comparisons are difficult because there were fewer students in District 1 and, consequently, it is difficult to determine

Table 3.11. Distribution of Scores in School Districts 1, 2, and 3 on a State-Wide History Test

	School District					
	1		*2*		*3*	
Score Interval	Fre-quency	Relative Fre-quency	Fre-quency	Relative Fre-quency	Fre-quency	Relative Fre-quency
95-99	10	.10	16	.08	14	.07
90-94	12	.12	24	.12	16	.08
85-89	15	.15	30	.15	24	.12
80-84	23	.23	50	.25	26	.13
75-79	13	.13	26	.13	50	.25
70-74	12	.12	24	.12	30	.15
65-69	8	.08	16	.08	24	.12
60-64	7	.07	14	.07	16	.08

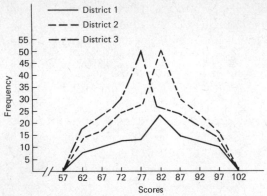

Figure 3.2. History scores obtained by students in School Districts 1, 2, and 3.

whether a lower absolute frequency for a score interval may, in fact, reflect a higher relative frequency. Even though only 10 students in District 1 had scores equal to or above a score of 90, for example, the proportion of students in District 1 receiving such scores was higher than the proportion of such students in either District 2 or District 3. What we need, then, is a way of compensating for the differences among the distributions in the number of scores.

When we discussed frequency distributions for groups of unequal size, we found it more convenient to use a relative frequency distribution. Similarly, when we compare frequency polygons for unequal groups, we can use a relative frequency polygon. A relative frequency polygon, as illustrated in Figure 3.3, is constructed in a manner similar to the frequency polygons already described. Instead of marking off the absolute frequencies along the vertical axis, however, we mark off the relative frequencies. We then plot the

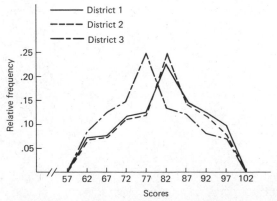

Figure 3.3. Relative frequency of history scores received by students in School Districts 1, 2, and 3.

relative frequency for each interval over the midpoint of the interval and connect the points to form the relative frequency polygon. Note that comparisons are easier among the relative frequency polygons than among the frequency polygons previously illustrated. We can see at a glance that proportionately more students in District 1 than in Districts 2 and 3 received scores equal to or above a score of 95.

When we wish to present our data graphically, then, we may use one of our frequency polygons. Graphs such as these are often used in place of frequency distributions because they are usually more "eye-catching," and because many people find it easier to visualize the trends in the data when they are presented graphically. The frequency polygon, however, is not the only type of graph that may be used to depict the data in a frequency distribution.

The Histogram

Another type of graph that is often used to present statistical data is a bar graph called a histogram. Unlike the frequency polygon, in which the scores within an interval are represented by the midpoint of the interval, the histogram represents the scores within an interval as being evenly spread out from the lower to the upper exact limits of the interval. When we construct a histogram, then, we do not mark off the midpoints of our intervals on the horizontal axis but the upper and lower exact limits of each interval. As may be noted in Figure 3.4, the upper exact limit of one interval is the same as the lower exact limit of the next interval. Consequently, there are no spaces between the bars of a histogram. As with the frequency polygon, we mark off the frequencies for the histogram along the vertical axis of the graph. In this case, however, the frequency of an interval is represented by a bar which extends from the lower to the upper exact limit of the interval, and which is

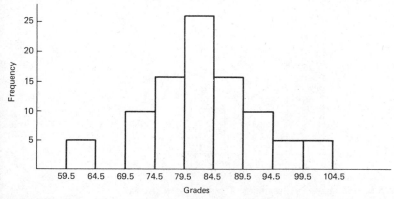

Figure 3.4. Distribution of grades on an arithmetic test.

drawn to a height equivalent to the frequency of the interval as marked on the vertical axis. Note that when the frequency of an interval is equal to zero, a space is left for that interval between the two adjacent intervals, but no bar is drawn.

Comparing the histogram and the frequency polygon, now, we can see that either type of graph may be used to picture the data in a frequency distribution. Each type of graph provides the same information, but each represents the score interval differently. In the frequency distribution the scores within an interval are represented by the midpoint of the interval, whereas in the histogram, the scores are represented as evenly distributed over the width of the interval. Note, however, that in both cases we mark off the score values on the horizontal axis in such a way that differences between score values are measurable. That is, equal differences between score values are reflected by equal distances on the axis. The difference between score values is not measurable, however, when we have nominal and ordinal data. Thus the histogram and frequency polygon are appropriate only for the representation of interval or ratio data.

When we wish to graphically present nominal or ordinal data, it is appropriate to use the ordinary bar graph. The bar graph, as illustrated in Figure 3.5, is similar to the histogram, except that there are gaps between the bars. When one is constructing a bar graph, the width of the bar and the amount of space between bars is determined by purely aesthetic considerations. The only limitation is that, for purposes of uniformity, the bars must be of equal width. With nominal data, it is customary to place the bars from left to right in order of frequency. This convention is not strictly followed, however, and the bars may be ordered differently if a different ordering seems to facilitate interpretation of the data. With ordinal data, the ordering of the bars, as illustrated in Figure 3.6, follows the order of the values on the ordinal scale.

Note that with a bar graph such as the one in Figure 3.7, two sets of data may be represented on the same set of axes. When this is the case, the bars

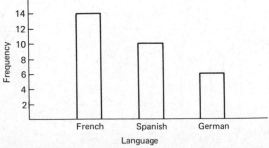

Figure 3.5. Language preferences of high school students.

Figure 3.6. Distribution of English composition grades.

representing the different data should be filled in differently, and a legend should be supplied.

As we have seen, then, the frequency polygon, histogram, and bar graph are all methods for graphically representing the data in a frequency distribution. All indicate the frequency with which the different data values occurred. As was previously noted, however, we are not always interested in the frequency with which a particular value occurred; sometimes we would rather know the number of scores that fell above or below that value. We are then concerned with the cumulative frequency of a score. In order to graphically present data of this nature, we use a special type of graph called a cumulative frequency polygon.

The Cumulative Frequency Polygon

A *cumulative frequency polygon* or a *relative cumulative frequency polygon* is used to graphically represent the data in a cumulative frequency distribution. Since the cumulative frequency of an interval indicates the number of scores that fell below the upper exact limit of the interval, we

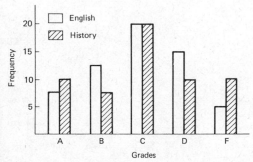

Figure 3.7. Distribution of final grades in English and history.

mark off the horizontal axis of our cumulative frequency polygon with the upper exact limits of each interval. On the vertical axis, we mark off the frequencies or, if we are constructing a relative cumulative frequency polygon, the relative frequencies of the intervals. Above the upper exact limit of each interval, then, we plot a point at the height equivalent to the cumulative frequency of the interval as marked off on the vertical axis. When the cumulative frequency of each interval is plotted, each point is connected to the next by a straight line. As may be noted in Figure 3.8, the cumulative frequency polygon is brought down to the horizontal axis on the left but not on the right.

For purposes of illustration, both the cumulative and the relative cumulative frequencies are indicated in Figure 3.8. Although this may be done, we usually present either the cumulative or the relative cumulative frequencies. If we present the cumulative frequencies, we can determine from the graph the *number* of students who had scores equal to or below a particular score. If we present the relative cumulative frequencies of the intervals, we can determine the *proportion* of the students that had scores equal to or below the score.

As we have now seen, graphs provide another way of presenting the data in a frequency distribution. We often present data graphically because many people find it easier to form an overall picture of the data when they are presented in this fashion. Thus, even though a frequency distribution and a frequency polygon provide the same information about the data, the data often seem more meaningful when a frequency polygon or histogram is presented. Meaningful organization of one's data, however, is only the first step in data analysis. Once the trends in the data are apparent, they must be interpreted. Once we know how many times a score on a test occurred, what can we than conclude about the average performance of the group? Is one class performing better than the other classes in the school? Is the performance level about the same in all subjects? Or are the grades consistently lower in one particular area? The statistics covered in the following chapters will enable the teacher to answer questions such as these.

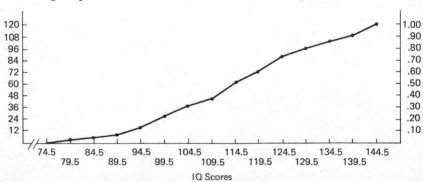

Figure 3.8. Cumulative frequency of third-grade IQ scores.

PRACTICE PROBLEMS

1. Tabulate and graph the following grades in a high school English class:

   A, A, B, F, B, F, A, C, D, A, A, A, B, B, B, F, A, A, A, C, D, C, C, A,
   B, C, B, B, C, C, C, C, F, D, D, C

2. Construct a grouped and ungrouped frequency distribution of the
   following scores on a spelling test:

   100, 90, 80, 95, 99, 70, 75, 73, 72, 71, 60, 61, 62, 90, 91, 92, 93, 95,
   93, 90, 65, 63, 87, 92, 88, 87, 96, 93, 91, 95

   What can you say about the performance on the test? Which distribution
   provides a clearer picture of the performance of the class?

3. On the same set of axes, draw a histogram and a frequency polygon of the
   grouped data in Problem 2. How do the two graphs compare?

4. Determine the relative frequency of each score interval in the following
   distributions:

   Distribution of Grades in English and History

Score Interval	Frequency	
	English	History
95-99	10	5
90-94	20	15
85-89	30	20
80-84	25	10
75-79	20	5
70-74	15	5

   In which subject did a higher proportion of the students fall in the 90s? In
   the 70s?

5. Determine the relative cumulative frequencies for the data in problem 4.
   Compare the percentage of students who had scores of 74 and below in
   English with the percentage who fell in that range in history. What
   percentage of the students had grades of 90 or above in history? In
   English? In which subject did the students do better?

MEASURES OF TYPICAL PERFORMANCE 4

Although a frequency distribution or a graph may present data in an organized and meaningful way, there are times when you may want to present the data more succinctly. If someone were to ask you how your class did on their final exam, for example, you wouldn't want to list how many students received each score; you would want to convey a general idea of the average or typical performance of the class as a whole. In doing so, you would report a measure of typical performance. Measures of typical performance are statistics that summarize the information in a frequency distribution. They are used to describe the performance of a single group or to compare the performance of several groups.

In the field of education, there are three different measures of typical performance that are used, the *mode,* the *median,* and the *mean.* Each of these statistics gives a picture of the typical performance of a group, but each differs in its definition of "typical." The mode defines the typical score as the most frequently occurring score, the median defines it as the score below which (and above which) 50 percent of the students fall, and the mean defines it as the arithmetic average. In considering which of these measures to use, then, we must consider what each statistic tells us, and which definition is most appropriate for the group whose performance we want to describe.

The Mode

The mode is very simply defined as the most frequently occurring value in a frequency distribution. If we were to refer to the distribution in Table 4.1, for example, the mode would be 85. As you can see, the mode is determined by looking at the distribution of scores and choosing that score that occurred most frequently.

There are times, however, when the most frequently occurring score is not as obvious. Assume, for example, that we have the distribution of scores on a reading test given in Table 4.2. In this case, we can see that the score interval in which most of the scores fell was the interval from 70 to 74. Since this is a

Table 4.1. Distribution of Scores on a Final Exam in History

Score	Frequency
100	1
95	3
90	5
85	12
80	8
75	7
70	2

grouped frequency distribution, however, we have no way of knowing how these scores were actually distributed. It may have been that all eight students had scores of 72, or it may have been that three had scores of 71, and five had scores of 73. In the absence of any further information as to how the scores actually were distributed, however, we call the interval in which the most scores fell the modal interval, and we designate the midpoint of that interval as the mode. In this example, therefore, the mode would be the midpoint of the interval from 70 to 74, and that would be 72.

It is interesting to note, however, that if one of the students whose score fell in the interval from 70 to 74 had received a 75 instead, and one of the students whose score was in the interval from 95 to 99 had received only a 94, the mode would have changed from 72 to 92. If these changes had occurred, the one extra person in the interval from 90 to 94 would have increased the frequency of that interval to 8, while the one score that was raised to 75 would have decreased the frequency of the interval from 70 to 74 to 7. A slight change in the scores of only two students would thus have changed the mode by 20 points. As you can see, the mode is somewhat unstable as a measure of typical performance, and it may be subject to wide changes as a result of minor changes in the scores of one or two students. Furthermore, even with a large range of scores, it is possible for the mode to be either the highest or the lowest score in the distribution. As a measure of typical performance, therefore, one may question the representativeness of the mode.

It should also be noted that a distribution may have more than one mode, and that these multiple modes need not be similar. Referring again to the distribution of scores in Table 3.2, consider what would have happened if only one of the students who had a score in the interval from 95 to 99 had received a score of 93. Had this change occurred, the intervals from 90 to 94 and from 70 to 74 would both have had a frequency of 8. There would no longer be one interval that included the highest number of scores, and we would have what is known as a *bi-modal distribution,* or a distribution in which there are two scores or score intervals with the highest frequency of occurrence. As you can see, then, a distribution can have more than one

Table 4.2. Distribution of Scores on a Reading Test

Score Interval	Frequency
95-99	3
90-94	7
85-89	5
80-84	6
75-79	5
70-74	8
65-69	4

mode. Not only can there be a bi-modal distribution, but there can also be a distribution with as many as five, or ten, or twenty modes. Such distributions are known as *multi-modal distributions,* and they can occur whenever there is a large range of possible score values. It should be noted, however, that in the extreme case where every single score occurs with the same frequency, we say that there is no mode.

Considering the fact that the mode may take on many values that may or may not be similar, and that minor changes in the scores of one or two students may result in large variations in the mode, one may question the usefulness of the mode as a measure of typical performance. The mode merely tells us which score or scores occurred most frequently, and it is really up to the teacher to decide how well that score describes the performance of her class. In cases where the mode is an extreme score, or where there are several widely different scores that have frequencies almost as high as the modal score, one may certainly hesitate in designating the mode to describe the group's performance. Because of these drawbacks, the mode is not generally used with numerical data. When one is working with nominal data or certain types of ordinal data, however, the mode may be the only measure that is appropriate. Consider the problem confronting a school that would like to offer a third foreign language to supplement offerings of French and Spanish. In trying to decide which additional language to offer, the school administrators may want to consider the preferences of the students and may decide to offer whatever language is preferred. A questionnaire may be distributed to the students, and the results may be tallied as indicated in Table 4.3.

In describing the preference of the students, the appropriate statistic to use is the mode. In this case, the mode is Russian, which was the most frequently preferred language. With data of this nature, the mode is the only measure of typical performance that can be used. It just wouldn't make sense to try to find the "middle" language or the arithmetic average of the languages. When one is dealing with numerical data that are ordinal, interval, or ratio, however, the appropriate measure of typical performance most frequently is the median or the mean.

Table 4.3. Language Preferences of High School Students

Language	Number of Times Preferred
German	50
Latin	35
Russian	107
Hebrew	86
Greek	48
Italian	97

The Median

The median is that score in a distribution above which, and below which, 50 percent of the students fall. It is the "middle" score, the score that divides the upper half of the class from the lower half. Unlike the mode, the median is not as sensitive to minor changes in one or two scores. The median is representative of the performance of the middle range of students and, except for those cases in which the scores of half the class cluster at the high or the low end of the distribution, the median will not be the highest or the lowest score in a distribution.

Calculating the Median for Ungrouped Scores

To illustrate the calculation of the median, let us now refer to some typical distributions of grades. Assume that we have the distribution of final grades reported in Table 4.4, and that we want to compare the performance in each of these classes. At first glance, the distributions appear to be very similar. Note, however, that even though the students in each of the classes had similar grades, the modes are quite different. Whereas the modal score in the German class is equal to 95, the mode of the French class is only 80. The mode does not appear to be representative of the performance of these students, and, if we used the mode in comparing the grades in each of the classes, our results would be very distorted. We want a measure of typical performance that will be more representative of the average student. In order to describe the performance in each of these classes, then, we use the median.

Since the median is the score below and above which half of the students fall, the first step in calculating the median is to determine how many students there are in each half of the class. Since there were 30 students in each of the modern language classes, we can see that in each of these classes we will be looking for the score below (and above) which 15 students fell. In the Latin class, however, there was an odd number of students, and it would be impossible to divide this class in half. Nevertheless, we will follow the same procedure and look for the score below and above which 16.5 students would have fallen.

Table 4.4. Distribution of Final Grades in Four Language Classes

	French		Spanish		German		Latin	
	LANGUAGE							
Score	*f*	*cf*	*f*	*cf*	*f*	*cf*	*f*	*cf*
95	1	30	1	30	4	30	1	33
94	2	29	2	29	2	26	2	32
93	3	27	3	27	3	24	3	30
92	3	24	3	24	1	21	2	27
91	3	21	3	21	2	20	3	25
90	1	18	1	18	1	18	2	22
89	2	17	3	17	2	17	2	20
88	1	15	1	14	0	15	2	18
87	1	14	0	13	1	15	2	16
86	1	13	1	13	2	14	2	14
85	3	12	3	12	3	12	4	12
84	3	9	2	9	2	9	2	8
83	0	6	4	7	3	7	3	6
82	1	6	1	3	2	4	1	3
81	1	5	1	2	1	2	1	2
80	4	4	1	1	1	1	1	1
N	30		30		30		33	
Mode	80.0		83.0		95.0		85.0	
Median	88.5		88.83		88.0		88.0	

Once we know the number of students that must fall in each half of the class, we then scan the cumulative frequencies. As you may remember, the cumulative frequency of an interval tells us the number of students that fell below the upper exact limit of that interval. If the cumulative frequency of an interval is 15, we know that 15 students fell below the upper exact limit of that interval. In the French class, then, we can see that 15 students fell below the upper exact limit of the interval from 87.5 to 88.5. Similarly, we know that the remaining 15 students fell above the lower exact limit of the interval from 88.5 to 89.5. Since the upper exact limit of the interval from 87.5 to 88.5 is the same as the lower exact limit of the interval from 88.5 to 89.5, this is the dividing point between the upper and lower halves of the class. The median grade in French is thus 88.5.

In the Spanish class, however, the cumulative frequency in which we are interested does not appear. What we must do, therefore, is to first determine the interval in which the fifteenth student fell. We can see that 14 students fell below the upper exact limit of a score of 88, and that 3 students fell within the next interval. We know, therefore, that the fifteenth student fell somewhere within the interval from 88.5 to 89.5. Even though we know that all of the students that fell within that interval actually received scores of 88, we cannot say that 88 was the score below which 15 students fell. We must remember that we are measuring a continuous variable, and that any one score on a continuous variable represents a range of actual ability. We assume that any score represents a range of scores extending from the lower to the upper exact limit of the score interval, and that the scores of all students falling within that interval are evenly distributed over the interval. Now if we go half-way into an interval, we assume that we have accounted for the scores of half of the students within that interval. In this case, then, since we want to find the score below which the fifteenth student fell, we must account for 1 of the 3 students whose scores fell between 88.5 and 89.5. Since we must account for one-third of the students, we must go one-third of the way into the interval. The interval size is 1, and one-third of the interval would be equal to .33 points. The score that is one-third of the way into the interval is thus equal to 88.5 plus .33, which is 88.83. We can assume, then, that 1 of the 3 students within that interval fell below a score of 88.83, and that 2 fell above. Adding that student who fell below this score to the 14 that fell below the interval, we have a total of 15 students that fell below a score of 88.83. Note, also, that if we add the 2 students within the interval who fell above this score to the 13 who fell above the interval, we also have 15 students who fell above a score of 88.83. The median grade in Spanish is thus 88.83.

Comparing the median grades in the French and the Spanish classes, now, we find that the medians are much closer than were the modes. The median is more representative of the performance of the middle range of students and, as a measure of typical performance, is more appropriate to our needs. The similarity of the median scores in these two classes appears to support our original impression that the scores in each of these classes were about the same. Let us now find the median score of the other two classes, and see whether this impression will continue to be supported.

In finding the median grade in German, we will again look for the score that divides the upper 15 students from the lower 15. Referring to the cumulative frequencies, we can see that the lower 15 students all fell below the upper exact limit of a score of 87. Note, however, that the upper 15 all fell above the lower exact limit of the score of 89. What then is the median? In each of the other cases we found that the score below which the lower half of the class fell was the same as the score above which the upper half of the class fell. In this case, however, we have a gap in which none of the students fell. In instances such as this, the median is the score that is midway between the lowest score in the upper half of the class and the highest score in the lower half of the class. Since the highest score in the lower half of the class is equal to 87.5, and the lowest score in the upper half of the class is equal to 88.5, the score that is midway between these scores is 88.0. We will thus designate 88.0 as the median grade in German.

Referring now to the grades in Latin, the median will be the score that divides the upper 16.5 students from the lower 16.5. From the cumulative frequencies, we can see that 16 students fell below the lower exact limit of the interval from 87.5 to 88.5, and that 1 student fell within this interval. The median score will therefore lie somewhere between 87.5 and 88.5. In determining exactly where the median lies, we will follow the same procedure we used for the Spanish class. In this instance, since we know that 16 students fell below a score of 87.5, we will have to account for an additional ½ student from the interval from 87.5 to 88.5. Since there is 1 student with that interval, ½ student will be equivalent to half of the students within the interval. Thus, since we must account for half of the students within the interval, we will have to go halfway into the interval. Since the interval size is 1, we will have to go .5 of a point above the lower exact limit. Adding .5 of a point to 87.5, we find that the median is equal to 88.0.

Note that this is the score of the seventeenth student; it is the score of the "middle" student in the class. Whenever there is an odd number of students in a class, and when there is one student who fell at the middle of the distribution, the median score will be the score of that middle student. In all other cases, the median may be computed as described earlier. This procedure is summarized in the following formula.

Formula for Computing the Median

$$\text{Median} = LL + \frac{\frac{N}{2} - cf\,(i)}{f}$$

Where LL = the lower exact limit of the interval in which the middle student falls

$N/2$ = the number of students in the distribution divided by two

cf = the cumulative frequency of the interval below that in which the middle student falls

f = the frequency of the interval within which the middle student falls

i = the interval size

This procedure may be used whenever the median score is needed. Remember, however, that when $N/2$ appears in the cumulative frequencies, and the frequency of the next highest interval is *not* equal to zero, the median does not need to be computed in this manner; the median is simply the upper exact limit of the interval for which the cumulative frequency is equal to $N/2$. When the next highest interval does have a frequency of zero (as in the German class), the median is the point that is halfway between the upper exact limit of the interval with a cumulative frequency of $N/2$ and the lower exact limit of the next highest interval that has a frequency greater than zero.

Comparing the performance in the four classes, now, we can see that the median scores were quite similar. In interpreting these statistics, we can say that the middle range of students in each of the classes performed at about the same level. The median, as a measure of typical performance, defines the typical performance as the performance of the middle student (or students) in the class. It may well be, however, that the middle student is not at all typical of the other students in the class. It may happen, for example, that most of the students do either very well or very poorly on a test, and that just one or two fall in the middle range. The median would then be representative of only those few students who fell in the middle, and it would not reflect the performance of the other students in the class. One must remember that the median is merely a measure of the middle range of performance, and that it says nothing about the range of actual scores.

Calculating the Median for Grouped Scores

As you may have noted, in each of the classes discussed we were working with an ungrouped distribution of scores; we knew exactly what score was obtained by each student, and we found the median by determining the score that divided the upper from the lower half of the class. When there is a large range of possible scores, however, it is generally more convenient to work with a grouped distribution. When we group our scores, however, we lose some information. We no longer know exactly which score was received by each of the students, and a median computed from grouped scores will not necessarily be the same as if it were computed from the raw scores. Let us consider, for example, how we would determine the median score in each of our classes if we had grouped the scores as indicated in Table 4.5. Note that

Table 4.5. Grouped Distribution of Final Grades in Four Language Classes

| | LANGUAGE | | | | | | | |
| | French | | Spanish | | German | | Latin | |
Score	f	cf	f	cf	f	cf	f	cf
94-95	3	30	3	30	6	30	3	33
92-93	6	27	6	27	4	24	5	30
90-91	4	21	4	21	3	20	5	25
88-89	3	17	4	17	2	17	4	20
86-87	2	14	1	13	3	15	4	16
84-85	6	12	5	12	5	12	6	12
82-83	1	6	5	7	5	7	4	6
80-81	5	5	2	2	2	2	2	2
N	30		30		30		33	
Median	$87.5 + \frac{1}{3}(2)$		$87.5 + \frac{2}{4}(2)$				$87.5 + \frac{.5}{4}(2)$	
	= 88.17		= 88.5		= 87.5		= 87.75	

we will follow the same formula we used in finding the median of the ungrouped data, but our interval size will be larger than 1.

Since the median is the score below and above which half the students fell, we must again start our calculations by determining how many students fell in each half of the class. As indicated previously, the number of students in the French, Spanish, and German classes was 30, and, in each of these classes, we are looking for the score above and below which 15 students fell. In the Latin class, we are looking for the score below which 16.5 students fell.

Looking at the cumulative frequencies for the French class, now, we find that 14 students had scores that were below a score of 87.5, and 3 had scores within the interval from 87.5 to 89.5. We know, therefore, that the median is somewhere within that interval. In determining where within that interval the median lies, we again assume that all the scores falling within an interval are evenly distributed over that interval, and we must determine how far into the interval we must go in order to account for the number of students that we need. In this case, then, since we need 1 more student to give us 15 students, we must account for 1 of the 3 students that fell within that interval, and we must go one-third of the way into the interval. The interval size is now equal to 2, so we must take into account one-third of the 2 score points that fell within that interval, or .67 score points. Adding .67 to 87.5, we find, as indicated in Table 4.5, that the median is 88.17.

In the Spanish class, now, we can see that the median will also fall somewhere within the interval from 87.5 to 89.5. In this case, however, since only 13 students fell below the interval, we will have to take into account 2 out of the 4 students that fell within that interval. Since we will thus have to account for one-half of the students falling within the interval, we will have to go halfway into the interval. One-half of a 2-point interval is equal to 1 point, and, as indicated in Table 4.5, adding 1 point to 87.5 yields a median of 88.5.

In the German class, we find that the cumulative frequency of the interval from 85.5 to 87.5 is exactly equal to 15. Since we are again looking for the score below which 15 students fell, the median of this distribution is equal to the upper exact limit of that interval. The median is thus equal to 87.5.

In the Latin class, where we are looking for the point below which 16.5 students fell, we again find that the median will lie somewhere in the interval from 87.5 to 89.5. In this case, since we need to find the point below which 16.5 students fell, and we know that 16 students fell below the interval from 87.5 to 89.5, we will have to account for an additional ½ student. Since 4 students fell within the interval containing the median, ½ a student is equal to one-eighth of the students falling within the interval. Since we must account for one-eighth of the students within the interval, then, we must go one-eighth of the way into the interval. One-eighth of a 2-point interval is equal to .25 of a point, and adding .25 of a point to the lower exact limit of the interval gives us a median of 87.75.

Table 4.6. Grades on the Midterm and Final Examinations in Chemistry

	EXAMINATION			
	Midterm		*Final*	
Scores	*f*	*cf*	*f*	*cf*
98-100	0	30	3	30
95-97	0	30	2	27
92-94	0	30	2	25
89-91	0	30	2	23
86-88	7	30	3	21
83-85	8	23	3	18
80-82	3	15	8	15
77-79	2	12	7	7
74-76	1	10	0	0
71-73	1	9	0	0
68-70	2	8	0	0
65-67	6	6	0	0
Median	82.5		82.5	

Comparing the median scores determined from the ungrouped scores with those obtained from the grouped scores, we can now see that some differences do exist. These differences are due to the loss of information that occurs when scores are grouped into intervals. In this instance, since our interval size was only 2, the loss of information was not that great. The larger the interval size, however, the greater will be the loss of information. Consequently, one would expect the difference between the median scores computed from grouped and ungrouped data to be larger when the interval size is increased.

The median, then, is another measure of typical performance. Unlike the mode, the median does not represent the most frequently occurring score, but, rather, the score of the "middle" student. As a measure of the performance of the middle range of students, the median is unaffected by the scores of the students who fall at either the lower or the upper extremes of the distribution. Consider the distribution of grades given in Table 4.6. The median score on the midterm examination is the same as on the final. In both cases, there were 30 students who took the test, and in both cases, the cumulative frequency of the interval from 80 to 82 was equal to 15. The median score on both tests was thus 82.5. Note, however, that even though the median scores were the same, the performance on each of the tests was really quite different. The class seemed to show definite improvement on the final; those who had done extremely poorly on the midterm had caught up with the rest of the class, and some had progressed so far they achieved grades that were much higher than any of those on the midterm. The median scores, however, do not reflect this improvement. The median reflects only the

Table 4.7. IQ Scores of Ten Beginning First-Graders

Student	Score
Mary	150
Robert	140
Anthony	135
Arlene	120
John	105
Arthur	105
Roberta	100
Dorothy	95
William	95
Susan	95

middle range of performance. The median is not affected by the scores of those students who are not in the middle; it does not reflect improvement at either extreme. The median would be the same whether all the scores that fell above the median were equal to 86, or whether they were all equal to 96. The lowest student in the class could have received a 0, a 10, a 38, or an 80; the median would still remain the same.

There are times, of course, when you do not want the performance of one or two extreme students to have a large effect on the measure of typical performance that is reported. If, for example, you have a class in which 34 students have scored between 85 and 92 on a test, and one student has a score of 15, you might not want the score of the lowest student to carry very much weight. In instances such as this, it is likely that the one or two extreme students have some special problems and are not really representative of the class as a whole. Consequently, you do not want the description of the performance of the other students to be dragged down because of these one or two atypical students. There are other times, however, when you do want the extreme scores to be reflected in the measure of typical performance. When you do want every single score to influence the measure that you report, there is a third measure of typical performance that is used. This measure is called the mean.

The Mean

The mean is the arithmetic average. Generally, when you hear people refer to the average, they are referring to the mean. The mean is the sum of the scores divided by the number of students.

If you had the distribution of scores in Table 4.7, for example, the mean would be computed, as indicated below, by summing the scores of the 10 students, and then dividing this sum by 10. The mean would thus be 114.

Finding the Mean

1. Sum the scores of each of the students:

$$150 + 140 + 135 + 120 + 105 + 105 + 100 + 95 + 95 + 95 = 1140$$

2. Divide this sum by the number of students:

$$\frac{1140}{10} = 114$$

Unlike the median, the mean is not necessarily the middle score in a distribution. In the foregoing example, for instance, there were four students whose scores exceeded the mean, while there were six whose scores were lower. The mean, therefore, is higher than the median. The median score would be 105, which is 9 points lower than the mean. The reason for this difference is that whereas the median does not take into account the differences between the scores, and is dependent only on the *number* of students that fell above or below a particular point, the mean is dependent on the *distance* between each individual score. As illustrated in Table 4.8, the mean is that point in a distribution such that the sum of the differences between every single score and the mean equals zero. When we sum the differences between each score and the median, however, the sum will not be equal to zero unless the median is equal to the mean. In Table 4.8 this sum is equal to 90; the sum of the differences between each score and any score other than the mean will always be larger than zero. In order that the sum of these differences between each score and the mean be minimized, each score in the distribution must be taken into account in determining the mean. In this case, then, the mean is higher than the median because the extreme scores at the high end of the distribution force the mean to move in that direction. The median, on the other hand, is unaffected by the distance of

Table 4.8. Sum of the Differences Between Each Score and the Mean and Between Each Score and the Median

Score	Difference Between Each Score and the Mean	Difference Between Each Score and the Median
150	150 - 114 = 36	150 - 105 = 45
140	140 - 114 = 26	140 - 105 = 35
135	135 - 114 = 21	135 - 105 = 30
120	120 - 114 = 6	120 - 105 = 15
105	105 - 114 = −9	105 - 105 = 0
105	105 - 114 = −9	105 - 105 = 0
100	100 - 114 = −14	100 - 105 = −5
95	95 - 114 = −19	95 - 105 = −10
95	95 - 114 = −19	95 - 105 = −10
95	95 - 114 = −19	95 - 105 = −10
	Sum = 0	Sum = 90

these scores from the other scores in the distribution, and it is not pulled in that direction.

As you can see, then, the mean is dependent on the size of the differences between the scores. For this reason, the mean is unacceptable for use with ordinal data. When we have ordinal data, as you may remember, we do not know the distance between any two score values; we know only whether one value is higher or lower than the other. Since the mean is dependent on the distances between score points, and we do not know the distance between score points on an ordinal scale, we cannot use the mean with ordinal data. When we have ordinal data, therefore, we should use the median; the mean should be used only with interval and ratio data. As mentioned in Chapter 2, however, we often assume that we have interval data when, in fact, the data are ordinal. Although it is not really proper to use the mean with such data, the mean is nevertheless used to describe ordinal data when it is assumed that these data form an interval scale.

The mean generally is symbolized as either $\bar{X}$ or μ. $\bar{X}$—read "X bar"—is usually used to represent the mean of a sample; μ—the Greek letter mu—is used to represent the mean of a population. This distinction between a sample and a population becomes very important when we are concerned with inferential statistics. For now, however, it is sufficient to say that we have a *population* when we have a score for every person within a specified group, and we have a *sample* when we have scores for only some of the members of the group. Having made this distinction, it is important to note that $\bar{X}$ is generally used to describe the mean of any score distribution, even though the scores comprise a population. In either case, the mean is computed in the same way and represents the sum of each of the scores divided by the total number of scores included in the distribution. In summarizing this procedure, the following formulas may be used.

Formulas for Computing the Mean

Mean of a population: $\quad \bar{X} = \dfrac{\Sigma fX}{N}$

Where $\quad \Sigma$ = "the sum of"

$\quad\quad\quad f$ = the number of times that each score occurred

$\quad\quad\quad X$ = the value of each score

$\quad\quad\quad N$ = the number of students in the population

Mean of a sample: $\quad \bar{X} = \dfrac{\Sigma fX}{n}$

Where $\quad \Sigma$ = "the sum of"

$\quad\quad\quad f$ = the number of times that each score occurred

$\quad\quad\quad X$ = the value of each score

$\quad\quad\quad n$ = the number of students in the sample

Each of these formulas is read as "the sum of each score multiplied by the number of times that it occurred, and divided by the total number of students." Note that these formulas outline a somewhat different procedure than that followed earlier. Whereas we previously found the mean of the scores by summing each score and dividing by the total number of scores, these formulas indicate that each score value should be multiplied by the number of times that it occurred. However, the two procedures yield identical scores. In the foregoing distribution, for example, we had 3 students who had scores of 95, and 2 who had 105. In computing the mean, therefore, we summed three 95s and two 105s. The same result could have been achieved, however, if we had summed the product of 95 X 3, and 105 X 2. In other words, rather than adding each score separately, we may multiply each score by the number of times that it occurred, and we may sum the products. In either case, the sum is to be divided by the total number of students, and the final result will be the same.

Calculating the Mean for Ungrouped Scores

Now that we know how to compute the mean, let us apply these computations to some practical situations. Assume that we have the distribution of IQ scores reported in Table 4.9, and we want to determine whether, if we put all of these students in the same class, the average IQ score

Table 4.9. Distribution of IQ Scores for 50 Transfer Students

Score (X)	Frequency (f)	Score X Frequency (fX)
110	4	440
109	3	327
108	4	432
107	5	535
106	9	954
105	8	840
104	7	728
103	5	515
102	0	0
101	1	101
100	0	0
99	0	0
98	1	98
97	1	97
96	1	96
95	1	95
	$n = \Sigma f = 50$	$\Sigma fX = 5258$

$$\text{Mean} = \bar{X} = \frac{\Sigma fX}{n} = \frac{5258}{50} = 105.16$$

in that class would be about the same as for the other classes in the school. Assuming that the mean IQ scores for the other classes ranged from 98 to 110, we want to see whether the mean of this group falls within that range. In finding the mean, we multiply each score by the number of times that it occurred, and we then divide the sum of these products by the total number of students. As indicated in Table 4.9, the mean score is 105.16, which is certainly within the range of the other classes.

Calculating the Mean for Grouped Scores

Assume, now, that we again want to compare the midterm and final chemistry grades that were reported in Table 4.6. This time, however, let us use the mean to describe the typical performance on each of the tests. By referring to Table 4.10, however, you may note that we have a grouped frequency distribution, and we do not know the frequency with which each score occurred. In determining the mean, therefore, we do not know what scores to sum. What, then, do we do? Since we have no idea of the actual frequency of each individual score, we let the midpoint of each interval represent all of the scores that fell within that interval. Then, rather than multiplying each individual score by its frequency, we multiply each midpoint by the number of scores that fell within the interval. These products are then summed, and the sum of these products is divided by the total number of students.

Table 4.10. Grades on a Midterm and Final Examination in Chemistry

Score	Midpoint (X)	Midterm f	Midterm fX	Final f	Final fX
98-100	99	0	0	3	297
95-97	96	0	0	2	192
92-94	93	0	0	2	186
89-91	90	0	0	2	180
86-88	87	7	609	3	261
83-85	84	8	672	3	252
80-82	81	3	243	8	648
77-79	78	2	156	7	546
74-76	75	1	75	0	0
71-73	72	1	72	0	0
68-70	69	2	138	0	0
65-67	66	6	396	0	0
		$n = 30$	$\Sigma fX = 2361$	$n = 30$	$\Sigma fX = 2562$

$$\bar{X} = \frac{2361}{30} = 78.7 \qquad \bar{X} = \frac{2562}{30} = 85.4$$

As indicated in Table 4.10, the mean score on the midterm examination is 78.7, while the mean on the final is equal to 85.4. Note that whereas the *median* scores on both of these exams were the same, the *mean* score on the final is higher than the *mean* on the midterm. The improved performance that was exhibited on the final exam was thus reflected in the mean. This improvement was reflected in the mean because the mean is sensitive to each of the scores in a distribution. Thus the low scores on the midterm served to pull the mean toward the low end of that distribution, whereas the high scores on the final pulled the mean toward the high end of that distribution. As you can see, then, the mean is the preferred measure of typical performance when we want every score in the distribution to affect the statistic that is used in describing the scores.

Which Statistic to Use?

We have now considered the three measures of typical performance that may be used in describing educational data. Each of these statistics summarizes the data that would appear in a frequency distribution, but each describes the data in a different way. The mode tells us the score that was most often obtained, the median tells us the score above and below which half the students fell, and the mean tells us the score about which the sum of the deviations from each of the other scores would be the lowest. Because of these differences, each of these statistics is appropriate for different situations.

Since the mode is very unstable and does not provide as much information as do the other two measures of typical performance, the mode is generally appropriate only when the other measures cannot be used. The mode is thus the appropriate measure to use in describing nominal data. Even when we have ordinal, interval, or ratio data, however, the mode may be used if we are interested in finding only the most frequently occurring score. One must remember, though, that the mode may not be representative of the general performance within a class.

Since the median is dependent only on the number of students that fell above and below a particular point and is not concerned with the distance between the scores, the median is appropriate for use with ordinal data. Since the median is not affected by the extreme scores in a distribution, however, the median is also the appropriate measure to use in describing interval or ratio data when we do not want our measure of typical performance to be affected by a few extreme scores.

The mean, on the other hand, is the measure to use when we want a measure of typical performance that is sensitive to every score in the distribution. The mean is influenced by the extent of the differences between each of the scores in a distribution, and it cannot be used with ordinal or nominal data. Thus the mean is restricted to use with only interval and ratio data. As was previously mentioned, however, the mean is used with ordinal data in those instances when the ordinal data are assumed to form an interval scale. Because it does take into account every score in the distribution, the mean is the most informative measure of typical performance and is most widely used. One must be aware, however, that the mean is sometimes used when it is not really appropriate.

In deciding which measure to use in describing the performance of a group, then, there are two things that must be considered. First, we must consider the type of data that we have. Then, once we know what statistics are appropriate for our data, we choose the statistic that will give us the information we want. Once we have described the typical performance of a group, however, there is still some additional information that we might want to know. Assume, for example, we know that the mean IQ score in three classes is equal to 100. Even though the average score in each of the classes is the same, we do not really know enough to say whether or not the ability in each of the classes is similar. It might be that in one of the classes, every student in the class received a score of 100. In the second class, the students might have been evenly split with half receiving scores of 90, and half receiving scores of 110. And in the third class, the students might have been evenly distributed with every score between 70 and 130 having been received by one student. You can see, then, that even though the three classes had the same mean, the performance in these classes may not really be parallel. Thus, in addition to a measure of the typical performance in a class, we also want some measure of how the scores within the class were distributed. Such measures are called measures of variability, and they will be discussed in the following chapter.

PRACTICE PROBLEMS

1. Find the mean, the median, and the mode of the following set of arithmetic scores:

Score	Frequency
90	15
85	10
80	5
75	5
70	5

Are all three measures of typical performance the same? Why?

2. Find the median of each of the following sets of scores:
   a. 77, 77, 77, 76, 76, 76, 76, 74, 74, 74, 74, 74, 73, 72.
   b. 77, 77, 76, 76, 76, 75, 75, 75, 75, 75, 75, 74, 74, 73, 72.
   c. 77, 77, 76, 76, 76, 76, 75, 75, 75, 73, 73, 73, 72, 72, 72.

3. Find the mean, the median and the mode of the following distribution of reading scores:

Score Interval	Frequency
95-99	30
90-94	20
85-89	10
80-84	5
75-79	5

Which measure of typical performance best describes the performance of the class? Why?

4. Assume that your class has taken a state-wide reading test, and that 40 percent of your students fell below the median. How would you explain these results to your principal?

5. Assume that you have given a final exam on which the mean was equal to 70 and the median was equal to 80. If two students who were absent take the exam at a later date, and their scores are 75 and 85, how would these scores affect the mean? How would they affect the median?

6. Assume you have given a test on which the mean was equal to 80 and the median was equal to 90. Did more students score above 90 than below? Did more score above 80 than below?

Although measures of typical performance provide a description of the average performance in a class, we need more information before we can conclude that the performance in two classes is similar. We also want to know the degree of variability within each group. That is, we want to know whether all the scores are similar, or whether there are large differences among the students.

Assume that we have the distribution of scores shown in Table 5.1. In each of these classes, the mean score is exactly the same. Looking at the distributions, however, we can see that the performance in each of the classes was not really similar. In the biology class, although most of the students performed at the mean, there were a few students at each of the extremes. In the chemistry class, the students were evenly distributed over the entire range of scores, and in the physics class, all the students fell within a very narrow range. As you can see, then, even though the mean score in each of the classes was the same, the distribution of scores was quite different. In order to reflect these differences, a measure of variability should be used.

Measures of variability indicate the degree to which scores differ from each

Table 5.1. Distribution of Test Scores in Three Science Classes

Score Interval	Frequency		
	Biology	Chemistry	Physics
95-99	2	4	0
90-94	0	4	0
85-89	0	4	0
80-84	26	6	30
75-79	0	4	0
70-74	0	4	0
65-69	2	4	0
Mean	82	82	82

other; they are measures of the degree of homogeneity within a group. Whenever a measure of typical performance is used, a measure of variability should also be reported. The *range* and the *standard deviation* are the two most commonly used measures of variability; the range is the measure of variability that is used when the mode or the median is reported, and the standard deviation is used with the mean.

The Range

The range is a statistic that tells us the number of score points that are included within a distribution. If we had the distribution of scores in Table 5.2, for example, the range would be equal to 11.

The range may be computed either by subtracting the lowest score from the highest score and adding one or by subtracting the lower exact limit of the lowest score from the upper exact limit of the highest score. If we were to use these methods to compute the range of the distribution in Table 5.2, our computations would be as follows:

Computing the Range

1. Range = highest score − lowest score + 1

   $$= 95 - 85 + 1$$
   $$= 10 + 1$$
   $$= 11$$

2. Range = Upper exact limit of highest score − lower exact limit of lowest score

   $$= 95.5 - 84.5$$
   $$= 11$$

Table 5.2. Distribution of Scores on an Arithmetic Test

Score	Frequency
95	1
94	0
93	0
92	0
91	0
90	0
89	1
88	5
87	7
86	9
85	5

Regardless of which method is used, the range is 11. Note that this is the same number we would get if we merely counted the number of score points included in the distribution. Rather than count the number of score points, then, we can more quickly compute the range by one of the methods indicated.

Even when we have a grouped frequency distribution, the range may be calculated in the same way. With a grouped distribution, however, we would either subtract the lower exact limit of the bottom interval from the upper exact limit of the top interval or add one point to the difference between the upper score limit of the top interval and the lower score limit of the bottom interval. For example, we might want to determine the range of the scores in each of the distributions in Table 5.1. In both the biology and chemistry classes, the range would be computed by subtracting 64.5 from 99.5 and it would be equal to 35. In the physics class, however, all the scores fall in the interval from 80 to 84. The range of the physics class is thus equal to the difference between 84.5 and 79.5, which is 5.

As you can see, then, the range is a measure of the degree to which the scores within a distribution are similar. The greater the heterogeneity of the scores, the higher will be the range. Referring to the distributions in Table 5.1, for example, we can see that the students in the biology and chemistry classes were more heterogeneous than were those in the physics class. Note, however, that even though the range in the biology class was the same as the range in the chemistry class, the students in these two classes did not exhibit the same degree of heterogeneity. Whereas the students in the chemistry class were spread out over the entire range of scores, most of the students in the biology class fell within a very narrow range, with just a few students at either extreme. Thus the students in the biology class actually formed three distinct groups. As you can see, then, the range tells us the number of score points that are included within a distribution, but it does not tell us how the students were distributed over those score points. It does not tell us whether all the students received different scores, or whether groups of students formed homogeneous groups at different points in the distribution.

Furthermore, since the range is merely a measure of the number of score points included within a distribution, the range may be greatly affected by one or two extreme scores. Referring again to Table 5.2, note that the scores of all but one of the students fell within the range from 85 to 89. If that one student had not been included, therefore, the range would have been 5. Including that one additional student, however, increases the range to 11. As you can see, then, the range is very sensitive to extreme scores; two distributions that were exactly alike except for one extreme score would have very different ranges. This drawback poses a very serious problem in the interpretation of the range, and, for this reason, the range as a measure of variability if often replaced by either the *interquartile range* or the *semi-interquartile range*.

The Interquartile Range and the
Semi-Interquartile Range

The interquartile range is a curtailed version of the range. Whereas the range tells us the number of score points that are included within the entire distribution, the interquartile range tells us the number of score points that are covered by the middle 50 percent of the students. The interquartile range is thus unaffected by one or two extreme scores and reflects only the degree of variability that is found within the middle range of students.

In technical terms, the interquartile range is the distance between the twenty-fifth and the seventy-fifth percentiles. A percentile is a point in a distribution below which a certain percentage of the students fell. The tenth percentile, for example, is the point in the distribution below which 10 percent of the students fell. The twenty-fifth percentile is thus the point below which 25 percent of the students fell, and the seventy-fifth percentile is the point below which 75 percent of the students fell. When we are finding the distance between the twenty-fifth and the seventy-fifth percentiles, then, we are finding the number of score points that were covered by the middle 50 percent of the students.

Let us now find the interquartile range of the distribution of scores given in Table 5.2. Since the interquartile range is equal to the number of score points covered by the middle 50 percent of the students, we must first eliminate the upper and lower 25 percent of the students. The point below which the lower 25 percent of the students fell is the twenty-fifth percentile, and it is calculated by using the same procedure that we followed in finding the median. Whereas the median is the fiftieth percentile, however, or the point below which half of the students fell, we are now looking for the twenty-fifth percentile, the point below which a quarter of the students fell. Thus, since there were 28 students included in the distribution, we will look for the point below which 7 students fell. Looking at the cumulative frequencies in Table 5.3, we can see that 5 students fell below the upper exact limit of a score of 85, and that an additional 9 students fell within the interval from 85.5 to 86.5. Since we must take into account 2 of the 9 students that fell within that interval, we must go 2/9 of the way into the interval. Adding 2/9 of the interval or .22 score points to 85.5, we find that 2 of the 9 students fell below a score of 85.72. We know, therefore, that 25 percent of the students fell below a score of 85.72; this score is thus the twenty-fifth percentile.

Once we know the score that cuts off the lower 25 percent of the students, we must then find the score that cuts off the upper 25 percent. This score will be the seventy-fifth percentile. In finding the seventy-fifth percentile, the first step is to determine how many students make up 75 percent of the group. Since we have 28 students, the seventy-fifth percentile will be the point below which 21 students fell. Looking at the cumulative frequencies in Table 5.3, we can see that 21 students fell below the upper

Table 5.3. Computing the Interquartile Range of a Score Distribution

Score	Frequency	Cumulative Frequency	
95	1	28	Twenty-fifth percentile:
95	0	27	$85.5 + \frac{2}{9}(1) = 85.72$
93	0	27	
92	0	27	Seventy-fifth percentile:
91	0	27	$87.5 + 0(1) = 87.5$
90	0	27	
89	1	27	Interquartile range:
88	5	26	seventy-fifth percentile −
87	7	21	twenty-fifth percentile
86	9	14	
85	5	5	$87.5 - 85.72 = 1.78$

exact limit of the interval from 86.5 to 87.5. Thus the seventy-fifth percentile is equal to 87.5.

Since the upper 25 percent of the students fell above the seventy-fifth percentile, and the lower 25 percent of the students fell below the twenty-fifth percentile, the difference between the twenty-fifth and seventy-fifth percentiles will give us the number of score points over which the middle 50 percent of the students were distributed. The last step in calculating the interquartile range, then, is to subtract the twenty-fifth from the seventy-fifth percentile. Subtracting 85.72 from 87.50, then, we have an interquartile range of 1.78.

As you can see, the interquartile range is a measure of variability that excludes the extreme scores in a distribution. When we want a measure of variability that gives us an indication of the degree of variability within the middle range of the group, the interquartile range is preferable to the range. Furthermore, since the interquartile range is not affected by extreme scores, it is a more stable measure than the range, and it is more likely to reflect real differences among different score distributions. For example, let us again compare the science classes whose grades were reported in Table 5.1. As was previously noted, the range in the biology and the chemistry class was the same. However, the interquartile ranges are different. Whereas the range does not reflect the differences in the distributions, these differences are reflected in the interquartile range.

To find the interquartile range of these classes, we again look for the difference between the twenty-fifth and seventy-fifth percentiles. Since there were 30 students in each of the classes, the interquartile range will reflect the number of score points over which the middle 15 students were distributed. In finding the interquartile range, then, the twenty-fifth and seventy-fifth percentiles will be the points below and above which 7.5 students fell.

Looking at the cumulative frequencies in Table 5.4, we can see that in the

Table 5.4. Computing the Interquartile Range of a Grouped Frequency Distribution

| | SCORE DISTRIBUTION IN THREE SCIENCE CLASSES | | | | | |
| | *Biology* | | *Chemistry* | | *Physics* | |
Score Interval	*f*	*cf*	*f*	*cf*	*f*	*cf*
95-99	2	30	4	30	0	30
90-94	0	28	4	26	0	30
85-89	0	28	4	22	0	30
80-84	26	28	6	18	30	30
75-79	0	2	4	12	0	0
70-74	0	2	4	8	0	0
65-69	2	2	4	4	0	0

Procedure for Finding the Interquartile Range in Each of the Classes

	Biology	Chemistry	Physics
1. Find the 25th percentile*			
a. Find the number of students in the lower 25% of the class (.25 × 30)	7.5	7.5	7.5
b. Locate the interval below the upper exact limit of which the desired number of students fell	80-84	70-74	80-84
c. Find the number of students who fell below that interval	2	4	0
d. Find the number of students within the interval that must be accounted for (a − c)	5.5	3.5	7.5

*The following formula may be used in computing any given percentile:

$$P\text{th percentile} = LL + \frac{Np - cf}{f}\ (i)$$

Where P = the percentile that is being calculated
  p = the percentage of students falling below the Pth percentile
  N = the total number of students in the distribution
  LL = the lower exact limit of the interval including the Npth student
  cf = the cumulative frequency of the interval below that which includes the Npth student
  f = the frequency of the interval including the Npth student
  i = the interval size

Table 5.4. *(continued)* *

Procedure for Finding the Interquartile Range in Each of the Classes

	Biology	Chemistry	Physics
1. e. Determine the fraction of students within the interval that must be accounted for	$\frac{5.5}{26} = .21$	$\frac{3.5}{4} = .875$	$\frac{7.5}{30} = .25$
f. Take that fraction of the score points falling within the interval	.21 X 5 = 1.05	.875 X 5 = 4.38	.25 X 5 = 1.25
g. Add needed number of score points to the lower exact limit of the interval	1.05 + 79.5 = 80.55	4.38 + 69.5 = 73.88	1.25 + 79.5 = 80.75

*Table continues p. 66.

biology class, the twenty-fifth percentile is somewhere within the interval from 79.5 to 84.5. Since only 2 students fell below this interval, we must take into account 5.5 of the 26 students within the interval. We must therefore go 5.5/26 of the way into the interval. The interval size is equal to 5, and 5.5/26 of the 5 score points falling within the interval is equal to 1.05 points. Adding 1.05 to the lower exact limit of the interval, we find that the twenty-fifth percentile is equal to 80.55. In finding the seventy-fifth percentile, now, we must look for the point below which 22.5 students fell. Again, this point will lie somewhere within the interval from 79.5 to 84.5. In this case, however, since we are looking for the point below which 22.5 students fell, we must take into account 20.5 of the 26 students that fell within the interval. Since we must take into account 20.5/26 of the students, we must therefore take into account 20.5/26 of the 5 score points that fell within the interval. Adding 20.5/26 of the 5 score points to the lower exact limit of the interval, we find that the seventy-fifth percentile is 83.45. The interquartile range of the biology class is thus equal to 83.45 minus 80.55, which is 2.90.

To find the interquartile range of the chemistry class, we again look for the points below and above which 7.5 students fell. In this case, however, the twenty-fifth and seventy-fifth percentiles will fall at different points in the distribution. Since 4 students fell below the lower exact limit of the interval from 69.5 to 74.5, and another 4 students fell within the interval, we know that the twenty-fifth percentile will be some fraction of the way into that interval. We must account for 3.5 of the 4 students that fell within that interval, and we must therefore go 3.5/4 of the way into the interval. Since the interval size is equal to 5 points, we must go 4.38 points into the interval, which brings us to a score of 73.88. In finding the seventy-fifth percentile of the chemistry class, now, we must again look for the point below which 22.5

Table 5.4. Computing the Interquartile Range of a Grouped Frequency Distribution *(continued)*

Procedure for Finding the Interquartile Range in Each of the Classes		
Biology	Chemistry	Physics
2. Find the 75th percentile*		
a. Find the number of students in the lower 75% of the class (.75 × 30)		
22.5	22.5	22.5
b. Locate the interval below the upper exact limit of which the desired number of students fell		
80-84	90-94	80-84
c. Find the number of students who fell below that interval		
2	22	30
d. Find the number of students within the interval that must be accounted for (a − c)		
20.5	.5	22.5
e. Determine the fraction of students within the interval that must be accounted for		
$\frac{20.5}{26} = .79$	$\frac{.5}{4} = .125$	$\frac{22.5}{30} = .75$
f. Take that fraction of the score points falling within the interval		
.79 × 5 = 3.95	.125 × 5 = .625	.75 × 5 = 3.75
g. Add the needed number of score points to the lower exact limit of the interval		
83.45	90.13	83.25
3. Find the interquartile range (75th percentile − 25th percentile)		
83.45 − 80.55 = 2.90	90.13 − 73.88 = 16.25	83.25 − 80.75 = 2.50

students fell. Looking at the cumulative frequencies, we can see that the seventy-fifth percentile fell somewhere in the interval from 89.5 to 94.5. Since 22 students fell below this interval, we must account for an additional 1/2 student. Since 4 students fell within the interval, 1/2 a student is equal to one-eighth of the students within the interval. If we therefore go one-eighth of the way into the interval, we will find that the seventy-fifth percentile is equal to 90.13. Subtracting 73.88 from 90.13, then, we find the interquartile range of the chemistry class is 16.25.

As you can see, then, although the range of the biology and chemistry classes was the same, the interquartile range was quite different. These differences in the interquartile range reflect the fact that the students in each of the classes performed differently. In the biology class, where most of the students fell within a very narrow range of scores, the interquartile range was relatively small. In the chemistry class, however, where the students were more spread out, the interquartile range was much larger. Also, if we look at the physics class, we will see that although the range of the physics class was much smaller than that of the other two classes, the interquartile range is very close to that of the biology class.

Looking at the physics class, then, we see that both the twenty-fifth and seventy-fifth percentiles lie within the interval from 84.5 to 89.5. Since the twenty-fifth percentile is the point below which 7.5 students fell, the twenty-fifth percentile will be 7.5/30 of the way into the interval. Similarly, the seventy-fifth percentile will be 22.5/30 of the way into the interval. With an interval size of 5, 7.5/30 of the interval is equal to 1.25 points, and 22.5/30 of the interval is equal to 3.75 points. Adding 1.25 and 3.75 to the lower exact limit of the interval, then, we find that the twenty-fifth and seventy-fifth percentiles are equal to 80.75 and 83.25. The interquartile range of the physics class is thus equal to 83.25 minus 80.75, which is 2.50 points.

Comparing the physics and biology classes, now, you can see that the interquartile range of the physics class is only .40 of a point lower than that of the biology class. Even though the range was quite different in these two classes, the interquartile range is similar. The similarity in the interquartile range reflects the fact that, except for a few extreme students in the biology class, the scores in the two classes were similarly distributed, with most of the students falling within a very narrow range of scores. If, in comparing the three science classes, we used the range as our measure of variability, the biology and chemistry classes would appear to be similar, with the physics class being the exception. When we use the interquartile range, however, the biology and physics classes appear to be similar, with the chemistry class being different. Which, then, is the correct interpretation? The answer depends on what it is you want to know. If you want to know the number of score points over which the entire class was distributed, you must use the range. If, however, you want to compare the variability among different classes, and you are not really interested in the extreme scores but are more concerned with the middle range of students, the interquartile range is preferable. As you can see, the interquartile range remains unaffected by a few extreme scores, for it is a measure of the degree of homogeneity within the middle range of scores.

In addition to the interquartile range, however, there is another measure that is also used. This measure is the *semi-interquartile range.* The semi-interquartile range is used in the same situations as is the interquartile range, and it is merely equal to half the interquartile range. If the interquartile range is equal to 10, the semi-interquartile range is equal to 5. The semi-interquartile range does not provide us with any more information than does the interquartile range, but, because it is widely reported as a measure of variability, it is an important statistic to know.

The range, the interquartile range, and the semi-interquartile range are all measures of variability which are, in essence, measures that tell us the number of score points that are covered by a particular group of students. As you have seen, we can use these measures in comparing the variability in performance among various groups. Even though we may know that the typical performance in two groups is the same, we do not necessarily know that the spread of scores in the two classes is similar. It is our measure of variability that tells us the degree to which the distributions in each of the classes were alike. Note, though, that measures of variability are not only used for purposes of comparison; they are also useful measures to consider in evaluating the performance of your class.

Assume that you must assign grades of A, B, C, D, and F to your class, and that you are basing these grades on each student's class average. If you have 30 students in your class, and the range of the class averages is equal to 35 points, you may assume that the students in your class really differed in performance and do, in fact, deserve different grades. Consider what you would do, however, if even though the range was equal to 35, the interquartile range was only equal to 2. Such an interquartile range would indicate that 50 percent of your students fell within 2 points of each other, which should certainly make you wonder whether you would be justified in giving these students different grades. When we are in a position where we must discriminate among students of different ability, we must make sure that the tests or other grading procedures are making the type of discriminations that we want. One of the ways that we can check to see that our tests are making the proper distinctions among students of different ability is to determine the interquartile range. If the interquartile range is very small, we know that our test is not discriminating among the students in the middle range of ability. It may be, of course, that the students are not really that different. If that is the case, however, and the interquartile range is small, we should be very wary about giving these students different grades. Thus the interquartile range may also be used to give us some indication of the degree to which our tests are detecting differences in the ability of our students. The higher the interquartile range, the greater the discriminability; the lower the interquartile range, the smaller the discriminability.

As you can see, then, a measure of variability adds useful information to our measures of typical performance. The measures of variability that have thus far been introduced, however, are not the only measures of variability that are used. The range, the interquartile range, and the semi-interquartile range are used when the measure of typical performance that is reported is either the mode or the median. When we have the kind of data for which the mean is the appropriate measure of typical performance, the measure of variability that is reported is the standard deviation.

The Standard Deviation

The *standard deviation* is a measure of variability that gives us a relative measure of the degree to which each score differs from the mean. Whereas the range and the interquartile range did not take into account every score in the distribution but merely indicated the number of score points between various points on the distribution, the standard deviation is influenced by every single score.

Consider, once again, the distribution of scores in the previously mentioned science classes. As noted, although the range of scores in the biology and chemistry classes was the same, the interquartile range in the chemistry class was larger than that of the biology class. This difference in the interquartile range reflected the fact that the scores in the biology class were, for the most part, closer together than were those in the chemistry class. Similarly, since so many of the scores in the biology class were near the mean, and only a few differed to any extent, the standard deviation of the biology class also is smaller than that of the chemistry class. Since the standard deviation is sensitive to every score in the distribution, however, the standard deviation of the biology class is much larger than that of the physics class. To illustrate this point, let us start by computing the standard deviation of the biology class. We will assume that each of our classes represents a population and, therefore, we will use the formula for a population standard deviation. As with the mean of a population, the standard deviation of a population is also represented by a Greek letter, σ, (the lower-case letter sigma).

In calculating the standard deviation, since we are looking for the degree to which each of the scores differs from the mean, the first step is to determine the deviation between the mean and each of the scores. When we have a grouped distribution as we do in Table 5.5, however, we do not know the value of each of the scores. Therefore, we follow the same procedure we used in calculating the mean, and let the midpoint of each of the intervals represent all of the scores within the interval. The next step, as indicated in Table 5.5, is to find the difference between each midpoint and the mean.

Table 5.5. Computing the Standard Deviation of the Biology Class
(Basic Formula)

Score Interval	Fre-quency (f)	Mid-point (X)	Deviation from the Mean ($X - \bar{X}$)	Squared Deviations ($X - \bar{X}$)²	Deviations Multiplied by Frequencies $f(X - \bar{X})^2$
95-99	2	97	15	225	450
90-94	0	92	10	100	0
85-89	0	87	5	25	0
80-84	26	82	0	0	0
75-79	0	77	−5	25	0
70-74	0	72	−10	100	0
65-69	2	67	−15	225	450
			Sum = 0		Sum = 900

$$\text{Standard deviation } (\sigma) = \sqrt{\frac{\Sigma f(X - \bar{X})^2}{N}} = \sqrt{\frac{900}{30}} = 5.5$$

Since we want to average these differences in some way, it would seem that the next step should be to sum these differences, and to divide by the total number of scores. If we perform this operation, however, we find that the sum of the differences is always equal to zero. In order to overcome this problem, then, we must do something to our deviation scores. If, for example, we eliminated the minus signs, the sum of the deviations would no longer be equal to zero. Minus signs may be eliminated either by taking the absolute value of each of the numbers, or by squaring each number. Both of these procedures are acceptable, but in determining the standard deviation, we must use the method of squaring our numbers. The next step, therefore, is to square each of the deviations.

Once the deviations have been squared, the next step is to sum each of the squared deviations. We must remember, however, that some of the midpoints represent more than one score. In order to be sure that each student's score is included, then, we multiply each squared deviation by the number of students within the interval. We then sum this column and divide by the total number of students. Since we squared each of the deviations, however, we must now take the square root of our result. This procedure, summarized in the formula given below, yields a standard deviation of 5.5 in this example.

Finding the Standard Deviation

$$\text{Standard deviation } (\sigma) = \sqrt{\frac{\Sigma f(X - \bar{X})^2}{N}}$$

1. Find the deviation between each midpoint and the mean ($X - \bar{X}$):

$97 - 82 = 15$
$92 - 82 = 10$
. . .

2. Square each of the deviations $(X - \overline{X})^2$:

$15^2 = 225$
$10^2 = 100$
. . .

3. Multiply each of the squared deviations by the number of scores within the interval $f(X - \overline{X})^2$:

$225 \times 2 = 450$
$100 \times 0 = \quad 0$
. . .

4. Sum each of the squared deviations multiplied by the interval frequencies:

$$\Sigma f(X - \overline{X})^2 = 450 + 0 + 0 + 0 + 0 + 0 + 450 = 900$$

5. Divide the summed deviations by the total number of scores:

$$\frac{\Sigma f(X - \overline{X})^2}{N} = \frac{900}{30} = 30$$

6. Take the square root of the result:

$$\sqrt{\frac{\Sigma f(X - \overline{X})^2}{N}} = \sqrt{30} = 5.5$$

The standard deviation provides a relative measure of the difference between each score and the mean. Some of the scores differ from the mean by more than 5.5 points, and some are closer than 5.5 points to the mean. When each score in the distribution is considered, however, the standard deviation gives us a relative measure of the amount by which each score differs from the mean. The higher the standard deviation, the greater is the spread of scores around the mean; the lower the standard deviation, the closer the scores are to the mean.

The formula for the standard deviation given above is known as the *definition formula* for the standard deviation. That is, this formula tells us that the standard deviation is the square root of the sum of the differences between each score and the mean divided by the total number of scores. It is sometimes preferable, however, to use different forms of this basic formula. These other forms of the basic formula are called *computational formulas,* and they are algebraically equivalent to the formula given above. The advantage of the computational formulas is that they eliminate some of the computational steps, and they are more convenient for use with a calculator. The two most commonly used computational formulas are given next.

Computational Formulas for the Standard Deviation

1. Standard deviation $(\sigma) = \sqrt{\dfrac{\Sigma fX^2}{N} - \overline{X}^2}$

2. Standard deviation $(\sigma) = \dfrac{1}{N}\sqrt{N \Sigma fX^2 - (\Sigma fX)^2}$

Table 5.6. Computing the Standard Deviation of the Chemistry Class: Computational Formula 1

Score Interval	Frequency (f)	Midpoint (X)	X^2	fX^2
95-99	4	97	9,409	37,636
90-94	4	92	8,464	33,856
85-89	4	87	7,569	30,276
80-84	6	82	6,724	40,344
75-79	4	77	5,929	23,716
70-74	4	72	5,184	20,736
65-69	4	67	4,489	17,956
				Sum = 204,520

$$\text{Standard deviation } (\sigma) = \sqrt{\frac{\Sigma fX^2}{N} - \overline{X}^2}$$

$$= \sqrt{\frac{204,520}{30} - (82)^2} = \sqrt{6,817.33 - 6,724}$$

$$= \sqrt{93.33}$$

$$= 9.66$$

To illustrate the use of these formulas, let us now use them to find the standard deviation of the chemistry and physics classes mentioned earlier. In finding the standard deviation of the chemistry class, let us use the first of these formulas. When this formula is used, we do not have to find the difference between each score and the mean. Instead of squaring the deviation between each score and the mean, as illustrated in Table 5.6, we square each of the midpoints. We then multiply each of these squared midpoints by the interval frequencies, and we sum these products. Dividing the sum of these products by the total number of students, we then have the first term under the radical. We subtract the square of the mean from this term, and, to complete the computation, we take the square root of the result. As outlined below, this procedure yields a standard deviation of 9.66.

Finding the Standard Deviation

$$\text{Standard deviation } (\sigma) = \sqrt{\frac{\Sigma fX^2}{N} - \overline{X}^2}$$

1. Square each midpoint (X^2):

   $97^2 = 9,409$
   $92^2 = 8,464$
   . . .

2. Multiply each squared midpoint by the interval frequency (fX^2):

   $4 \times 9,409 = 37,636$
   $4 \times 8,464 = 33,856$
   . . .

3. Sum the squared midpoints multiplied by the interval frequencies:

$$\Sigma fX^2 = 37,636 + 33,856 + 30,276 + 40,344$$
$$+ 23,716 + 20,736 + 17,956 = 204,520$$

4. Divide ΣfX^2 by the total number of students:

$$\frac{\Sigma fX^2}{N} = \frac{204,520}{30} = 6,817.33$$

5. Square the mean:

$$\overline{X}^2 = (82)^2 = 6,724$$

6. Subtract the square of the mean from $\frac{\Sigma fX^2}{N}$:

$$\frac{\Sigma fX^2}{N} - \overline{X}^2 = 6,817.33 - 6,724 = 93.33$$

7. Take the square root of the result:

$$\sqrt{\frac{\Sigma fX^2}{N} - \overline{X}^2} = \sqrt{93.33} = 9.66$$

Note that this procedure gives the same result that would be obtained by the method illustrated in Table 5.5. Either method may be used, the choice being dependent upon which method is more convenient.

You can now see that the standard deviation of the chemistry class is somewhat larger than that of the biology class. This discrepancy in the standard deviations reflects the fact that whereas most of the scores in the biology class clustered around the mean, the scores in the chemistry class were more spread out. If we now compare the standard deviation of the biology class with that of the physics class, we will see that the greater homogeneity in the physics class will result in an even smaller standard deviation.

In finding the standard deviation of the physics class, let us use the second of the computational formulas. As illustrated in Table 5.7 (on the following page), we must find two sums: the sum of the frequencies multiplied by the midpoints of the intervals (ΣfX), and the sum of the frequencies multiplied by the squares of the midpoints (ΣfX^2). Once we have these two sums, we then multiply ΣfX^2 by the total number of students, and we square ΣfX. We then subtract $(\Sigma fX)^2$ from $N \Sigma fX^2$, and we divide the square root of the result by the total number of students. As indicated below, this procedure gives us a standard deviation that is equal to zero.

Finding the Standard Deviation

Standard deviation $(\sigma) = \frac{1}{N} \sqrt{N \Sigma fX^2 - (\Sigma fX)^2}$

1. Multiply each midpoint by the frequency of the interval (fX):

97 X 0 = 0
92 X 0 = 0
. . .

Table 5.7. Finding the Standard Deviation of the Physics Class: Computational Formula 2

Score Interval	Frequency (f)	Midpoint (X)	fX	X^2	fX^2
95-99	0	97	0	9,409	0
90-94	0	92	0	8,464	0
85-89	0	87	0	7,569	0
80-84	30	82	2,460	6,724	201,720
75-79	0	77	0	5,929	0
70-74	0	72	0	5,184	0
65-69	0	67	0	4,489	0
			$\Sigma fX = 2,460$		$\Sigma fX^2 = 201,720$

$$\text{Mean} = \frac{\Sigma fX}{N} = \frac{2460}{30} = 82$$

$$\text{Standard deviation } (\sigma) = \frac{1}{N}\sqrt{N \Sigma fX^2 - (\Sigma fX)^2}$$

$$= \frac{1}{30}\sqrt{30(201,720) - (2,460)^2}$$

$$= \frac{1}{30}\sqrt{6,051,600 - 6,051,600}$$

$$= \frac{1}{30}\sqrt{0} = 0$$

2. Sum the products of the midpoints multiplied by the interval frequencies:

$\Sigma fX = 0 + 0 + 0 + 2,460 + 0 + 0 + 0 = 2,460$

3. Square ΣfX:

$(\Sigma fX)^2 = (2,460)^2 = 6,051,600$

4. Square the midpoints of each of the intervals (X^2):

$97^2 = 9,409$
$92^2 = 8,464$
$\cdots$

5. Multiply the squares of each of the midpoints by the interval frequencies (fX^2):

$9,409 \times 0 = 0$
$8,464 \times 0 = 0$
$\cdots$

6. Sum the products of the squared midpoints multiplied by the interval frequencies:

$\Sigma fX^2 = 0 + 0 + 0 + 201,720 + 0 + 0 + 0 = 201,720$

7. Multiply ΣfX^2 by the total number of students:

$N \Sigma fX^2 = 30 \times 201{,}720 = 6{,}051{,}600$

8. Subtract $(\Sigma fX)^2$ from $N \Sigma fX^2$:

$N \Sigma fX^2 - (\Sigma fX)^2 = 6{,}051{,}600 - 6{,}051{,}600 = 0$

9. Take the square root of the result:

$\sqrt{N \Sigma fX^2 - (\Sigma fX)^2} = \sqrt{0} = 0$

10. Divide $\sqrt{N \Sigma fX^2 - (\Sigma fX)^2}$ by the total number of students:

$$\frac{1}{N}\sqrt{N \Sigma fX^2 - (\Sigma fX)^2} = \frac{1}{30}\sqrt{0} = 0$$

A standard deviation of zero indicates that there was no deviation between any of the scores and the mean; that is, all of the scores in the distribution were exactly the same. If you refer back to the distribution, you can see why the standard deviation was equal to zero. All of the scores fell within the same interval, and, in computing the standard deviation, all these scores were represented by the midpoint of that interval. It may have been, of course, that all of the scores within that interval were not exactly equal to the midpoint; some of the scores may have been 82, some may have been 80 or 81, and still others may have been 83 or 84. Since we have a grouped distribution, however, we do not know the exact values of the 30 scores, and consequently we lose some accuracy.

If we had an ungrouped distribution of these scores, the standard deviation might have been slightly higher. In this case we would have represented each of the scores in the interval from 80 to 84 by a single score (which would have been the midpoint of a 1-point interval), and we would have been looking for the difference between each of these scores and the mean. If all of the scores were not exactly equal to the mean, some of the deviations from the mean would have been higher than zero, and the standard deviation would also have been higher than zero. Even if this were the case, however, the standard deviation would not have been as high as in either of the other classes that were observed. Although we may not know the exact values of each of the scores in the class, we do know that all of these values fell within the interval from 79.5 to 84.5, a range substantially smaller than in any of the other groups.

If we now compare the standard deviation in each of the three classes, we can see that the standard deviation provides a relative measure of the degree to which the scores in a distribution differ from the mean. In the physics class, where all the scores were close to the mean, the standard deviation was the smallest; in the biology class, where all but a few of the scores were close to the mean, the standard deviation was the highest. As you can see, the standard deviation is influenced by every score in the distribution. To the extent that the scores are close to the mean, the standard deviation will be relatively small; to the extent that the scores differ from the mean, the standard deviation will be relatively large. The further the scores are from the mean, and the more scores there are that are distant from the mean, the larger will be the standard deviation. Note, however, that the standard deviation is not dependent on the value of the mean per se, but it is dependent on the difference between the mean and each of the other scores. If a constant is added to each of the scores, the standard deviation will not change. As illustrated in Table 5.8, however, the standard deviation will change if the scores are multiplied or divided by a constant.

Adding or subtracting a constant does not change the standard deviation because operations such as these do not change the distance between each score and the mean. As indicated in Table 5.8, for example, the distance between 70 and 90 is the same as the distance between 80 and 100. When one multiplies or divides the scores by a constant, however, the differences between scores are altered. The difference between 140 and 180, for example, is twice the distance between 70 and 90. Thus, since the differences between scores are doubled, the standard deviation is doubled. If the scores are multiplied by a constant, the standard deviation will be multiplied by that constant; similarly, if the scores are divided by a constant, the standard deviation will be divided by that constant. As you can see, then, the standard deviation is directly influenced by the difference between each score and the mean; the standard deviation will increase if these differences are increased, and it will decrease if these differences are decreased. As long as the differences between scores remain constant, the addition or subtraction of a constant from each of the scores will not affect the value of the standard deviation.

In each of the examples we have considered thus far, we have been concerned with the standard deviation of a population. When we have a sample, however, the calculation of the standard deviation is slightly different. As you may remember from Chapter 4, we have a sample when we are considering only a portion of the students in a larger group. In this case, we are usually not interested in the standard deviation of the sample, but want to use the sample standard deviation as an estimate of the standard deviation of the population. However, variability within a sample tends to be less than within the population, and we tend to underestimate the population standard deviation if we use the formula for σ as our estimate. The formula for the standard deviation of a sample, which is represented by the letter s, is thus modified as indicated below:

The Standard Deviation of a Sample

$$\text{Standard Deviation } (s) = \sqrt{\frac{\Sigma f(X - \bar{X})^2}{n - 1}}$$

As you can see, the sum of the squared difference between each of the scores and the mean is divided by $n - 1$. Dividing by $n - 1$, which is 1 less

Table 5.8. Finding the Standard Deviation when a Constant Is Added to Each of the Scores and when Each of the Scores Is Multiplied by a Constant

Score	Frequency	$X - \bar{X}$	$(X - \bar{X})^2$	$f(X - \bar{X})^2$
		Original Distribution		
90	1	20	400	400
80	2	10	100	200
70	3	0	0	0
60	2	10	100	200
50	1	20	400	400
				$\Sigma f(X - \bar{X})^2 = \overline{1,200}$

$$\text{Standard deviation} = \sqrt{\frac{\Sigma f(X - \bar{X})^2}{N}}$$

$$= \sqrt{\frac{1200}{9}}$$

$$= \sqrt{133.3}$$

$$= 11.5$$

Score	Frequency	$X - \bar{X}$	$(X - \bar{X})^2$	$f(X - \bar{X})^2$
		Original Distribution Plus a Constant (10)		
100	1	20	400	400
90	2	10	100	200
80	3	0	0	0
70	2	10	100	200
60	1	20	400	400
				$\Sigma f(X - \bar{X})^2 = \overline{1,200}$

$$\text{Standard deviation} = \sqrt{\frac{\Sigma f(X - \bar{X})^2}{N}}$$

$$= \sqrt{\frac{1200}{9}}$$

$$= \sqrt{133.3}$$

$$= 11.5$$

Score	Frequency	$X - \bar{X}$	$(X - \bar{X})^2$	$f(X - \bar{X})^2$
		Original Scores Multiplied by a Constant (2)		
180	1	40	1,600	1,600
160	2	20	400	800
140	3	0	0	0
120	2	20	400	800
100	1	40	1,600	1,600
				$\Sigma f(X - \bar{X})^2 = \overline{4,800}$

$$\text{Standard deviation} = \sqrt{\frac{\Sigma f(X - \bar{X})^2}{N}}$$

$$= \sqrt{\frac{4800}{9}}$$

$$= \sqrt{533.3}$$

$$= 23.1$$

than the sample size, results in a larger number than would be obtained by dividing by the total number of people in the group and compensates for the tendency of a sample to exhibit less variability than the population from which it comes. In calculating the standard deviation of a sample, then, we follow the same procedure as for a population standard deviation, the only difference being that, in step 5, we divide by $n - 1$ instead of by N.

Similarly, the computational formula for a sample standard deviation is also slightly different from that for a population standard deviation. The most commonly used computational formula for the standard deviation of a sample is given below:

Computational Formula for a Sample Standard Deviation

$$\text{Standard Deviation } (s) = \sqrt{\frac{n \, \Sigma \, fX^2 - (\Sigma \, fX)^2}{n(n - 1)}}$$

Note that this formula is very similar to the second computational formula we considered for the standard deviation of a population. In using the computational formula for the standard deviation of a sample, we follow steps 1 through 8 exactly as in the computational formula for the standard deviation of a population. We then divide $n \, \Sigma \, fX^2 - (\Sigma \, fX)^2$ by $n \, (n - 1)$, and take the square root of the result. We are, in effect, dividing the squared deviations from the mean by 1 less than the size of the sample, and our result will be slightly greater than would be obtained if we used the formula for a population standard deviation. Even though we get slightly different values for a population standard deviation and a sample standard deviation, however, both measures provide us with similar information about the variability of scores within a specified population.

The Variance

Very closely related to the standard deviation is another measure of variability called the *variance*. The variance, like the standard deviation, is directly related to the size of the difference between each score and the mean. The variance is equal to the square of the standard deviation; if the standard deviation is 5, the variance will be 25. The variance of a population is σ^2 and the variance of a sample is s^2. In Table 5.8, for example, the variance of the original distribution would be 133.3 rather than the square root of that number. Where the scores are doubled, the variance is 533.3.

As you may have noticed, the variance does not increase proportionally with the number of times that the scores are increased. Rather, the variance increases proportionally with the square of the factor by which the scores are increased. In this instance, where the scores were doubled, the variance was increased four times. If the scores had been multiplied by three, the variance would have been multiplied by nine. As you can see, then, the variance, like the standard deviation, is determined on the basis of the difference between each score and the mean. In reporting a measure of variability for a distribution, however, it is conventional to report the standard deviation rather than the variance. The variance is used in many of the more complex statistical analyses, and it is frequently referred to in the literature on educational measurement. Although it is not generally reported as a measure of the variability in a group, it is nevertheless important to recognize the term.

Comparing the standard deviation with the range and the interquartile range, now, we can see that the standard deviation is the preferred measure when we want our measure of variability to reflect every score in the distribution. The standard deviation is much more stable than the range; since the standard deviation takes into account the difference between every score and the mean, one extreme score will not affect the standard deviation to the same extent that it will affect the range. In contrast to the interquartile range, however, the standard deviation does not exclude the upper and lower 25 percent of the scores. As you can see, then, the standard deviation gives us the most information about the variability in the scores.

Since the standard deviation is based on the size of the differences between scores, the standard deviation cannot be used for data for which we cannot determine the distance between the score values. The standard deviation is thus limited to use with interval and ratio data; it is incorrect to use the standard deviation with either nominal or ordinal data. As you can see, then, it is appropriate to use the standard deviation as our measure of variability in those situations when it is appropriate to use the mean as our measure of typical performance. When the median or the mode is the appropriate measure of typical performance, the range and the interquartile range are the appropriate measures of variability.

All of our measures of variability give us some information about the way in which the scores were spread out over the distribution. As you have seen, we need this information in order to compare the performance in two or more classes. Even if two classes have the same mean or median, the students in the classes may have performed quite differently. In one of the classes, the students all may have received practically the same grade, whereas the students in the other may have been distributed over a much wider range of scores. Measures of variability are not only important for describing the differences in performance in various classes, however; they are also important in evaluating the relative performance of one student or one class. Knowing that a student has a score of 85 on a test, for example, we do not know whether he has done well or poorly. If all the other students in the class had scores between 90 and 100, a score of 85 would seem to be rather poor. If the other students were evenly spread out between scores of 65 and 90, however, a score of 85 would have a very different meaning. In order to evaluate the performance of any one student, then, we must know something about the scores of the other students in the class. If we have a measure of the typical performance, and a measure of the variability in the performance, we can then determine the relative standing of any one student. Those statistics that tell us the relative standing of a student are called measures of relative performance, and they are introduced in the following chapter.

PRACTICE PROBLEMS

1. Assume that two of your classes received the following scores on a final examination:

Score	Frequency Class A	Class B
100	3	1
95	3	0
90	5	1
85	8	26
80	5	1
75	3	0
70	3	1

   a. Compare the range, the semi-interquartile range, and the standard deviation (σ) of the two groups. Which measure of variability best reflects the difference in performance between the classes?
   b. How would each of the measures of variability change if you added 5 points to each score? If you multiplied each score by 3?
2. Construct a grouped and an ungrouped frequency distribution of the following scores:

   90, 91, 91, 91, 80, 79, 80, 79, 80, 82, 83, 78, 92, 90, 75
   84, 91, 78, 91, 90, 83, 70, 96, 71, 79, 79, 85, 87, 89, 76

   a. Calculate the mean and standard deviation of each of the distributions.
   b. Does the standard deviation of the grouped scores differ from that of the ungrouped scores? Why?
3. A teacher has given a 100-item midterm examination on which the median score was 80 and the interquartile range was 2. How does this test discriminate among the students?
4. Two classes took the same exam in history; one class had a mean of 85 with a standard deviation of 3, and the other had a mean of 83 with a standard deviation of 10. How do the students in the first class compare with those in the second?

5. The following results were obtained on a 100-word spelling test:

	Class A	Class B
Mean	94	98
Standard deviation	1	10

a. Describe the score distributions in each of the classes.
b. In which class were the highest scores found?
c. In which class were the lowest scores found?

MEASURES 6
OF RELATIVE
PERFORMANCE

The statistics that we have thus far discussed are measures that primarily describe the typical performance of a group. Although these measures tell us something about the characteristics of a particular group of scores, these statistics do not provide us with enough information to evaluate the scores. Even if we knew that the mean score in a class was equal to 85, we would not have enough information to determine whether the class was about average in performance, whether the students did much better than average, or whether, in fact, the performance was particularly poor.

In order to make evaluations of this nature, we need a statistic that tells us, specifically, how one particular student or group of students compares with others. Measures of relative performance are the statistics that provide us with this type of information; these statistics may be used to indicate one student's standing in his class, or they may be used to compare the performance of one class with that of another. As with the other statistics that have been discussed, different measures of relative performance are appropriate in different situations. Ranks and percentile ranks, which provide us with an ordinal scale, may be used when we have ordinal, interval, or ratio data. Standard scores, on the other hand, are appropriate for use only with interval and ratio data, and they allow us to make determinations about the extent of the difference between different levels of performance.

Ranks

When one assigns a rank, one is assigning an ordinal position in a group. Assume that we have 10 students who had competed in an archery meet, and that their scores were as indicated in Table 6.1.

The students are ordered from highest to lowest and, as would be expected, the highest scoring student is assigned a rank of 1. Note, however, that the next two students both received the same score. Since they both had the same score, it would seem that they should both have the same rank. The

Table 6.1. Scores of Ten Students in an Archery Competition

Student	Score	Rank
Michael	100	1
John	90	2.5
Robert	90	2.5
Frank	76	4
Lawrence	75	6
Jerome	75	6
Andrew	75	6
Martin	40	8
Barry	20	9.5
Charles	20	9.5

question, then, is what rank to assign. Since a rank is an ordinal position in a group, and this group was composed of ten students, there will be ten positions to fill. Thus there will be one position for each of the students. When more than one student is tied for a rank, however, the positions that would have been occupied by the tied students are averaged, and each of the students is assigned the mean of these positions. In the foregoing example, John and Robert must fill the second and third positions. Thus we find the mean of these two positions, and we assign both students a rank of 2.5. By assigning this rank, we have accounted for both the second and the third positions, and the next student, Frank, is assigned to the fourth position. Note, now, that the next three students are again tied. Since these students must fill the fifth, sixth, and seventh positions, we assign each of them the mean of these positions. Each of these students thus receives a rank of 6. The next student fills the following position, which is the eighth position, and the last two students, who are also tied, are both assigned the mean of the last two positions. These students are thus assigned a rank of 9.5. As you can see then, ranking involves no more than ordering the students along a dimension, and then assigning each successive student to successive ordinal positions. There are as many positions as there are students, and, as we have seen, we must account for each of these positions.

Ranking, then, is one of the techniques that we can use when we want to determine a student's relative position in a group. Although ranking has the advantage of being simple, there are several disadvantages. First, one must remember that ranking results in an ordinal scale. Even though the original data may form an interval or ratio scale, the conversion to ranks results in the loss of the ability to determine the extent of the difference between scores. Referring back to Table 6.1, for example, note that although the difference between Lawrence and Frank was only 1 score point, this one score point corresponds to a difference of two ranks. On the other hand, although there was also a difference of two ranks between Lawrence and Martin, this difference corresponds to a 35-point difference in raw scores. As you can see, then, ranking has the same drawback that is found in all types of ordinal data; equal differences in rank do not necessarily correspond to equal differences on the variable being measured.

A second drawback in the use of ranks is that a person's rank is limited by the number of people who are being ranked. A rank of 10, for example, would have quite a different meaning if we were ranking 15 students than if we were ranking 100. As you can see, then, we really cannot interpret the meaning of a rank unless we know the number of students that were ranked. Furthermore, even when we do know the number of students in the group, we sometimes run into difficulty in comparing the performance of students in classes of different size. What about the student who has ranked 23rd in a class of 35? How does his standing within his class compare with that of the student who is ranked 19th in a class of 26? As you can see, it is very difficult to make comparisons such as these. It is for this reason that ranks generally are not used for making comparisons among different groups. Instead, it is preferable to use percentile ranks. Whereas ranks are based on the number of people who scored at or above a particular person's score, percentile ranks tell us the percentage of people who scored at or below a person's score.

Percentile Ranks

When we determine a student's percentile rank, we find out what percentage of students had scores that were equal to or below the score of the student in whom we are interested. The percentile rank does not tell us the percentage of items on a test that a student answered correctly, nor does it tell us whether a student's knowledge has increased or not. The percentile rank merely tells us where a student stands in relation to a specific group of people.

Assume, for example, that Johnny's parents want to know how his performance on a mathematics test compares with his performance in English. Obviously, the tests taken in math and English are not exactly the same, and it would be meaningless to compare the raw scores, or the number of items that he had correct on the two tests. Furthermore, if both tests were not taken by the same number of students, it might prove difficult to compare his ranks. What we can do, however, is to look at his percentile ranks. For example, if Johnny's math score fell at the twentieth percentile, we can simply check whether his percentile rank in English is greater or less than 20. If his percentile rank is greater than 20, we can say that he has surpassed a higher percentage of his class in English than he did in math, and that his relative standing is better in English.

Assume that the scores on the English test were distributed as indicated in Table 6.2, and that Johnny had a score of 99. As you can see from the

Table 6.2. Scores of 250 Tenth-Grade Students on a Standardized English Test

Score	Frequency	Cumulative Frequency
122-124	5	250
119-121	10	245
116-118	15	235
113-115	20	220
110-112	20	200
107-109	40	180
104-106	50	140
101-103	25	90
98-100	20	65
95-97	15	45
92-94	10	30
89-91	7	20
86-88	5	13
83-85	5	8
80-82	3	3

cumulative frequencies in Table 6.2, Johnny did better than the 45 students who fell below the interval from 98 to 100. We know, therefore, that Johnny surpassed at least $^{45}/_{250}$ or 18 percent of the students. Note, however, that Johnny's score is higher than the lower exact limit of that interval, and we can thus assume that Johnny has also surpassed some of the 20 students that fell within the interval. Since the interval size is 3, and Johnny's score is 1.5 points above the lower exact limit of that interval, Johnny's score falls halfway into the interval. We can assume, therefore, that Johnny surpassed half of the 20 students falling within that interval. In determining Johnny's percentile rank, then, we know that he not only did better than the 18 percent of the class that fell below the interval which included his score, but he also surpassed an additional $^{10}/_{250}$ or 4 percent of the students. In total, then, his performance was equal to or better than that of 22 percent of the students, and he thus has a percentile rank of 22.

Comparing his performance in English and math, now, we can see that Johnny did relatively better in English. In evaluating his performance, however, one might question whether this difference of two percentile ranks represents a significant difference in performance. As with all types of ordinal data, we do not know how much of a difference in performance is reflected by any specified difference in percentile ranks.

To illustrate that equal differences in percentile rank do not reflect equivalent differences in performance, let us now determine the percentile ranks that are equivalent to the scores of 104 and 109 in the distribution given in Table 6.2. In finding these percentile ranks, we will follow the same procedure followed earlier. This procedure is summarized below and, as you can see, results in widely disparate percentile ranks for these two scores.

Procedure for Finding a Percentile Rank

$$\text{Percentile rank} = \frac{cf + \dfrac{X - LL}{i}(f)}{N} \times 100$$

Where cf = the cumulative frequency of the interval below the one that includes the score in question

     X = the score

     LL = the lower exact limit of the interval that includes the score

     i = the interval size

     f = the frequency of the interval that includes the score

     N = the total number of students

Illustrative example:

Finding the percentile rank of scores of 104 and 109

		Score	
		104	109
1. Determine how many students fell below the interval that includes the score in question	cf	$= 90$	$= 140$
2. Determine how many students within the interval had scores equal to or below the score in question	$\dfrac{X - LL}{i}$	$= \dfrac{104 - 103.5}{3}$	$= \dfrac{109 - 106.5}{3}$
a. Determine what fraction of the way into the interval the score fell		$= \dfrac{.5}{3} = .17$	$= \dfrac{2.5}{3} = .83$
b. Take that fraction of the students within the interval	$\dfrac{X - LL}{i}(f) =$	$.17 \times 50$ $= 8.5$	$.83 \times 40$ $= 33.20$

Illustrative example: *(continued)*

Finding the percentile rank of scores of 104 and 109

	Score	
	104	109
3. Divide by N the total number of students who had scores equal to or below the score in question	$\dfrac{cf + \dfrac{X - LL}{i}(f)}{N} = \dfrac{90 + 8.5}{250}$ $= \dfrac{98.5}{250} = .39$	$= \dfrac{140 + 33.20}{250}$ $= \dfrac{173.20}{250} = .69$
4. Multiply by 100 to get the percentile rank	$.39 \times 100 = 39$	$.69 \times 100 = 69$

If we now compare the difference between the percentile ranks, and the difference between the scores that correspond to these percentile ranks, it becomes very clear that one must be very careful in evaluating the change in performance that may accompany large differences in percentile rank. As you can see in Table 6.3, a 17-point difference in percentile ranks may correspond to the same difference in score points as does a 30-point difference in percentile ranks. Furthermore, a 30-point difference in percentile rank may correspond to as little as a 5-point difference in actual score. Given these limitations on percentile ranks, one must be very wary about assuming that large differences in percentile rank correspond to large differences in performance. Certainly, then, if we wish to evaluate a difference of two percentile ranks between a student's performance in two different subjects, we must limit ourselves to merely saying that his relative position in one subject is slightly better than in the other. We have no way of knowing whether this difference in relative position corresponds to a similar difference in actual ability; we know merely that Johnny has surpassed a higher percentage of his classmates in English than he did in math. If we were to find the twentieth percentile on the English test, we would find that Johnny's score was only .75 of a point higher than that of the student with a percentile rank of 20. On the math test, however, the difference between the twentieth and twenty-second percentiles could correspond to a difference of .75 of a score point, 7.5 points, or even 75 points.

Even with their limitations, percentile ranks are somewhat more useful than ranking, since they may be used to compare the relative performance of students in different classes. Whereas a rank of 10 would have quite a different meaning in a group of 15 than it would in a group of 150, a percentile rank of 10 would have the same meaning in either case. Regardless of the number of students in the group, a percentile rank of 10 indicates that

Table 6.3. Comparison of the Differences Between
Percentile Ranks and their Corresponding Scores

Difference in Score Points	Score	Percentile Rank	Difference in Percentile Ranks
	99	22	
5			17
	104	39	
5			30
	109	69	

the particular student in question did equal to or better than 10 percent of his classmates. Nevertheless, we are limited in the interpretation of percentile ranks in the same way as we are in the interpretation of ranks; equal differences in percentile ranks do not necessarily correspond to equal differences on the variable being measured.

In spite of this limitation, percentile ranks are very widely used, particularly in the reporting of standardized test scores. When one is called upon to make decisions based upon these scores, then, it is very important that the limitations of such data are kept in mind. When one is dividing a class into subgroups for specialized instruction, for example, one should be very careful not to arbitrarily assume that large differences in percentile rank necessarily reflect large differences in ability. Particularly in the middle range of scores, large differences in percentile rank may correspond to relatively small differences in performance. At the extremes, however, the reverse is more likely to be true; small differences in percentile rank may correspond to relatively large differences in performance. Whereas a child with a percentile rank of 55 on a test may not have performed much better than a child with a percentile rank of 45, the child with a percentile rank of 95 is more likely to have done considerably better than the child with a percentile rank of 85. Although this relationship does not always hold, it is usually the case when we have a normal distribution of scores.

When we have a normal distribution, most of the students are bunched together at the middle of the distribution, and a jump of a few score points may account for a relatively high percentage of the students. At the extremes, however, the students are more spread out, and more score points have to be covered to account for the same percentage of students. As you can see, then, we have to be very careful in interpreting differences in percentile ranks. It is for this reason that another type of relative measure, the standard score, is preferable to percentile ranks. As a teacher, you may have run across standard scores in the form of IQ scores, T-scores, and stainines. All of these measures are variations of the same basic measure of relative performance, the standard z-score.

Standard Scores

A standard score is a score that tells us how many standard deviations above or below the mean a particular score falls. If we have a distribution of scores with a mean of 80 and a standard deviation of 5, for example, a score of 90 would be two standard deviations above the mean. Similarly, a score of 75 would be one standard deviation below the mean. As opposed to percentile ranks, then, standard scores are not based on the number or the percentage of students that fell below a particular score, but on the distance between that score and the mean.

The basic standard score is the *z-score*, which simply tells us the number of standard deviations between a score and the mean. In calculating the z-score that corresponds to a particular score, we may use the following formula:

$$z = \frac{X - \bar{X}}{SD}$$

Where X = the score in question

         $\bar{X}$ = the mean of the distribution

         SD = the standard deviation of the distribution

Assume, for example, that we had a test on which the mean was 100 and the standard deviation was equal to 15. If we wanted to find the z-scores that were equivalent to scores of 85, 100, and 115, we would follow the procedure outlined below.

Finding a z-Score

Given: $\bar{X} = 100$
            $SD = 15$

FORMULA

$$z = \frac{X - \bar{X}}{SD}$$

SCORE		Z-SCORE
85	$\frac{85 - 100}{15} = \frac{-15}{15}$	-1
100	$\frac{100 - 100}{15} = \frac{0}{15}$	0
115	$\frac{115 - 100}{15} = \frac{+15}{15}$	$+1$

As you can see, a z-score may be positive or negative; a positive z-score indicates that the score is above the mean, and a negative z-score indicates that the score is below the mean. It is thus very important to retain the sign of the z-score; a z-score of +1 is quite different from a z-score of −1.

You may also note that the distance between the z-scores is proportional to the distance between the raw scores. For each 15-point difference between score points, there will be a 1-point difference in z-scores. We know, therefore, that the difference between a z-score of −1 and a z-score of zero reflects the same difference in score points as does the 1-point difference between a z-score of zero and a z-score of +1. Furthermore, a 2-point difference in z-scores will reflect twice as much of a difference in score points as will a 1-point difference in z-scores, and a .2-point difference in z-scores will reflect one-third the difference in score points as will a .6-point difference in z-scores. Unlike percentile ranks, equal differences in z-scores do reflect equal differences in score points.

As you can see, then, z-scores are superior to percentile ranks when we want to make statements about the differences in performance among members of a class. The z-scores tell us not only where the student stands in relation to the mean but also the degree to which he differed from the other students in the class. Note, however, that the use of z-scores is not limited to comparisons of scores on the same test; z-scores may also be used to compare performance on different tests and in different subjects. Consider the mean and standard deviation on a math and an English test indicated below; we are concerned now with a student's relative performance in these two areas.

Mean and Standard Deviation on a Math and an English Test

Math	English
Mean = 75	Mean = 80
SD = 5	SD = 7

If the student received scores of 85 on both tests, our first impression might be that he did equally well in both subjects. If we look more closely at the test statistics, however, we can see that the scores on the math test were somewhat lower than those on the English test and, in addition, the students were grouped more closely around the mean on the math test. A score of 85 in math, then, has quite a different meaning from a score of 85 in English. If we were to use z-scores rather than the raw scores for making our comparison, this difference would be apparent. In math, a score of 85 would be two standard deviations above the mean, and it would be quivalent to a z-score of +2. In English, however, a score of 85 would be only $5/7$ of a standard deviation above the mean, and it would only be equivalent to a z-score of +.71. Even though the raw scores are exactly the same, the z-scores indicate that a score of 85 reflects superior performance in math than it does in English.

Even when using z-scores, however, we must be careful in interpreting differences in performance. Assume, for example, that we had the following statistics for two tests:

**Mean and Standard Deviation on a
Spelling and a Math Test**

Spelling	Math
Mean = 95	Mean = 70
SD = 1	*SD* = 10

A student who has a z-score of +3 in spelling would have scored 1 point higher than the student with a z-score of +2, and he would be only 3 points above the mean. Assuming this was a 100-word spelling test, one can see that the difference between these scores is negligible. In math, on the other hand, a student with a z-score of +3 would have scored 10 points higher than a student with a z-score of +2, and he would be 30 points above the mean. As you can see, then, even z-scores must be carefully evaluated. Although z-scores are preferable to percentile ranks in that, on any one test, equal differences in z-scores correspond to equal differences in score points, each test must itself be evaluated. When we have a test such as the spelling test described here, we have a test that is obviously too easy for discriminatory purposes. The students are bunched too closely together, and differences between scores are practically meaningless. In such instances, however, it is not the statistic but the test itself that is the cause of the problem. Nevertheless, when we are using statistics for the purpose of evaluating test performance, we must be aware that the meaning of our statistics is limited by the limitations in the tests themselves. Given adequate tests, however, z-scores are preferable to percentile ranks.

Not only do z-scores have the advantage of forming an interval scale, but, in those instances where our scores are normally distributed, each z-score can be converted to a corresponding percentile rank. A normal distribution is defined in such a way that a specified percentage of the scores falls between each standard deviation and the mean. As illustrated in Figure 6.1, for example, 34 percent of the scores fall between the mean and one standard

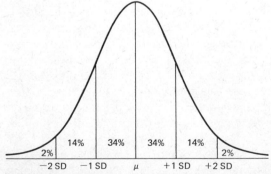

Figure 6.1. Percentage of scores falling between specified points on the normal curve.

deviation above the mean, and another 14 percent fall between the scores that are one and two standard deviations above the mean. Similarly, since the curve is symmetrical, another 34 percent of the scores fall between the mean and one standard deviation below the mean, and another 14 percent fall between one and two standard deviations below the mean. As you can see, a total of 96 percent of the scores fall between the scores that are two standard deviations above and below the mean, and the remaining scores fall further out in the extremes of the distribution.

If we have a normal curve, and we know that a student has a z-score of +1, we know that he has surpassed the 50 percent of the students that fell below the mean, plus the 34 percent that fell between the mean and the score that was one standard deviation above the mean. A student who has a z-score of +1, then, has a percentile rank of 84. Similarly, a student who has a z-score of +2 has a percentile rank of 98, and the student who has a z-score of −1 has a percentile rank of 16. It should be noted, of course, that these conversions are true only when the scores are normally distributed. Although the scores on most classroom tests do not form a normal distribution, most of the commonly used standardized tests are constructed in such a way that the scores are distributed normally. Such conversions can be particularly useful, then, when we want to make comparisons among tests for which the scores are differently reported. Even though the scores on one test are reported as percentile ranks and the scores on another are reported as standard scores, a student's relative performance on the two tests can be compared. If a student has a percentile rank of 86 on one test, for example, and a z-score of +2 on another, we know that he has done relatively better on the test on which his z-score is +2.

Not all standard scores are reported as z-scores, however, and it is useful to recognize some of the other scores that are used. All of these scores have the same properties as z-scores; the forms used are chosen primarily for convenience. With the z-score, for example, it is quite easy to make a clerical error that would confuse two scores. As you know, a z-score of +2 is quite different from a z-score of −2; a simple clerical error involving the omission of the sign could eliminate this difference. For this reason, the z-score is often replaced by the T-score.

As illustrated in Figure 6.2, the mean of the distribution is assigned a T-score of 50, and each standard deviation is equivalent to 10 points on the scale of T values. Thus a student whose score falls at the mean would have a T-score of 50, and a student whose score was one standard deviation above the mean would have a T-score of 60. Similarly, deviation IQ scores are standard scores where the mean is equal to 100, and the standard deviation is equal to 15 IQ points. A student with an IQ of 130, then, would be two standard deviations above the mean, and a student with an IQ of 85 would be one standard deviation below. Knowing the z-score, one can convert to any of the standard scores. As illustrated below, a z-score of +1 would be equivalent

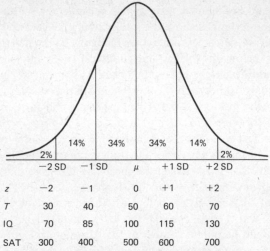

		14%	34%	34%	14%
	2%					2%
	−2 SD	−1 SD	μ	+1 SD	+2 SD
z	−2	−1	0	+1	+2
T	30	40	50	60	70
IQ	70	85	100	115	130
SAT	300	400	500	600	700

Figure 6.2. Conversions of standard scores.

to a T-score of 60, an IQ score of 115, and an SAT score of 600. As you can see, then, standard scores not only can be converted into percentile ranks but can also be converted into other forms of standard scores. It should be remembered, however, that these conversions are appropriate only when the scores are normally distributed. A distribution of z-scores will have the same shape as the original raw score distribution. If the original distribution was normal, the distribution of z-scores will be normal; if the original scores were not normally distributed, neither will be the z-scores.

Formulas for Converting Standard Scores

Type of Standard Score	Conversion Formula
T-score	$T = z(10) + 50$
IQ score	$IQ = z(15) + 100$
SAT score	$SAT = z(100) + 500$

Measures of relative performance thus provide us with tools that can be used in evaluating a student's performance. Whereas a mean score, for example, describes the typical performance of a child, a measure of relative performance tells us how his typical performance compares with that of the other children in his class. A child who has a mean score of 80 in math, for example, is not necessarily doing well. If this performance corresponds to a percentile rank of 10, his performance is relatively poor. On the other hand, if his average performance corresponds to a z-score of +2, we know that he is doing comparatively well. It must be remembered, however, that the final evaluation does not lie in the statistics, but in the teacher's ability to use those statistics intelligently. The statistics do not tell us whether the test was so easy that all the students fell within two points of each other, nor do the statistics tell us that Johnny was absent and missed the work on the test. The statistics are tools that can give us some very useful information but, in order to be truly useful, their uses and limitations must be understood.

PRACTICE PROBLEMS

1. The following mid-semester history grades were obtained by ten students:

Student	Grade
Arthur	95
Bob	90
Carol	90
David	90
Ellen	85
Francine	80
Greg	80
Howard	80
Iris	75
Jane	60

a. Rank each of the students.
b. Find the percentile rank of each of the scores.
c. Find the z-score equivalent to each of the scores.
d. Which of the foregoing ways of describing a student's performance most accurately reflects the difference in performance between Jane and Iris?

2. The following scores were obtained by a class of fifth-graders on an arithmetic and a reading test:

Score Interval	Frequency	
	Reading	Arithmetic
95-99	10	1
90-94	7	5
85-89	5	7
80-84	3	8
75-79	2	5
70-74	2	3
65-69	1	1

a. If a student had a score of 98 on both exams, what would his percentile rank be on each of the exams? His z-score?
b. Compare the student described above with a student who had scores of 93 on both exams. Are the differences in percentile rank equivalent to the differences in the z-scores? Which measure best reflects the difference in performance? Why?

3. The following results were obtained on an English and a science test:

	English	Science
Mean	80	75
Standard deviation	7	4

  a. If a student had an 85 in English and an 80 in science, in which subject was his performance better?

  b. If a student had a z-score of -3 in English, how many points lower did he score than a student who had a z-score of $+1$?

  c. If a student had a z-score of $+1$ in English and $+2$ in science, on which test did he get more items correct?

4. Reviewing the records of a new student, a teacher found the following test results:

Eleventh-Grade Achievement Tests

Math	$T = 70$
English	$z = -1$
Science	Percentile rank = 85
IQ	115
SAT	500 (numerical)
	650 (verbal)

  a. Which of the scores appears to be out of line with the others?

  b. Did the student do relatively better on the science achievement test or the math achievement test?

  c. Was the relative performance better on the numerical portion of the SAT or on the math achievement test?

  d. How does the student's general level of achievement compare with his IQ score?

CORRELATION 7
AND PREDICTION

In the preceding chapters, we dealt with statistics that are used to describe a particular set of scores. There are times, however, when we are not concerned with one particular set of scores but with the relationship between two different sets of scores. We may want to know whether high scores in reading are associated with high scores in arithmetic, or whether the students who do well in the manual arts do poorly in their academic subjects. In order to answer questions such as these, we cannot use a statistic that merely describes the scores on one of our variables; we must turn to a statistic that tells us the degree to which two different variables are related.

The Correlation Coefficient

The correlation coefficient is a statistic that tells us the degree of relationship between two variables. There are different types of correlation coefficients that are appropriate for describing different types of relationships. In this chapter, however, only *linear relationships* are considered. Linear relationships are those in which the graph of the scores on two variables is best described with a straight line.

Unlike the other statistics that have been considered, the values of a correlation coefficient may vary only between +1 and −1. It is impossible to obtain a value of +1.25 or a value of −10. If the value of the correlation coefficient is higher than +1 or lower than −1, an error has been made. In interpreting a linear correlation coefficient, one must consider both the numerical value of the statistic and the sign. The numerical value of the coefficient tells us the strength of the relationship, and the sign tells us the direction of the line representing this relationship. The closer the value is to +1 or −1, the stronger is the relationship between the variables. If the linear correlation coefficient is positive, it means that high scores on one variable are associated with high scores on the other, and low scores on one variable are associated with low scores on the other. If the coefficient is negative, it means that high scores on one variable are associated with low scores on the other. When we have a correlation of +1 between two variables, we have a "perfect" positive correlation; the person who has the highest score on one variable also has the highest score on the other variable, the person with the second highest score on one variable has the second highest score on the other variable, and so forth. Furthermore, the scores of any individual will be equivalent; if John's score is 2.5 standard deviations above the mean on one of the variables, it will be 2.5 standard deviations above the mean of the other. When we have a perfect positive correlation, then every increase in one variable is accompanied by an equivalent increase in the other.

When we have a correlation of −1, on the other hand, we have a "perfect" negative relationship; in this instance, the person with the highest score on one variable would have the lowest score on the other variable, the person with the second highest score on one variable would have next to the lowest score on the other, and so on. In other words, every increase on one variable is accompanied by an equivalent *decrease* in the other. To illustrate this point, let us consider the scores in Table 7.1.

Note first the relationship between the grades in music and in art. As you can see, the scores are exactly alike; the student with the top score in music also had the top score in art, and all students who had grades of 90 in music had grades of 90 in art. The grades in music are perfectly correlated with the grades in art, and the correlation coefficient reflecting this relationship is +1. The relationship between these two variables may also be illustrated in a *scatter diagram,* or a graph in which a point is plotted for each pair of scores. As may be seen in Figure 7.1, the points on the scatter diagram representing the relationship between the scores in music and in art can be connected by a straight line, and the slope of this line is +1. Note that the scatter diagram representing the relationship between the grades in music and in shop also forms a straight line. In this case, however, the line slopes in the opposite

Table 7.1. Midterm Grades of Ten High School Students

Student	Art	Music	Shop	Gym
		Subject		
John	95	95	65	91
Mary	90	90	70	65
Michael	90	90	70	76
Robert	85	85	75	70
Jane	80	80	80	80
Kenneth	80	80	80	90
Susan	75	75	85	90
Anna	70	70	90	70
Charles	70	70	90	85
Dorothy	65	65	95	71

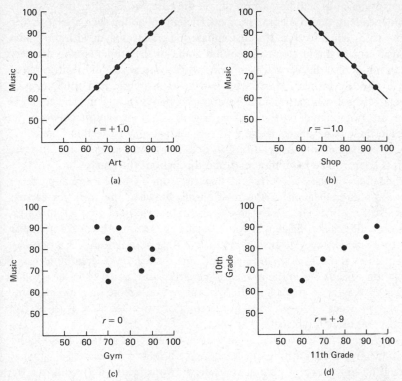

Figure 7.1. Scatter diagrams representing correlation coefficents of +1, −1, 0, and +.9

direction and has a slope of −1, indicating a negative relationship between these two sets of grades. Referring back to Table 7.1, we can see that the relationship between the scores in music and in shop is just the reverse of that between the grades in music and in art. The student with the highest score in music had the lowest score in shop, and the student with the highest score in shop had the lowest score in music. Similarly, the student with the second highest score in music had the second lowest score in shop, and so forth. Note, however, that this relationship is just as strong as the relationship between the scores in music and in art. The only difference is in the direction of the relationship. That is, high scores in music are just as strongly associated with low scores in shop as they are with high scores in art.

When two sets of scores are not related, students who score high in one area do not necessarily do either poorly or well in the other. Some who did well in music, for example, would do equally well in shop, whereas others who did well in music might do extremely poorly in shop. Thus, knowledge of a student's performance in one area would not give us any information about his performance in another. When this is the case, we say that the variables are independent, and the correlation coefficient reflecting such a relationship is close to or equal to zero. If you compare the grades in gym with the grades in music, for example, you can see that some of the students who did very well in music also did very well in gym, while others who did well in music did very poorly in gym. Mary, who had a 90 in music, had a 65 in gym, whereas Michael, who also had a 90 in music, had a 76 in gym. The grades in music are not related to the grades in gym. The correlation between the grades in these two subjects is equal to zero and, as may be seen in Figure 7.1, the scatter diagram of this relationship does not form a straight line. Instead, the dots appear to be randomly scattered throughout the graph.

When the correlation coefficient departs from +1 or −1 and approaches zero, the scatter diagram of the relationship between the variables departs from a straight line. The closer the correlation is to either +1 or −1, however, the closer the scatter diagram is to a straight line. As may be noted in Figure 7.1, for example, the scatter diagram reflecting a correlation of +.9 between two variables is much closer to a straight line than is the diagram reflecting a correlation of zero. When the correlation coefficient is equal to +1 or −1, and the scatter diagram forms a straight line, the person's score on any one of the variables provides us with enough information to determine, with perfect accuracy, his score on the other variable.

Assume that we knew that a particular student had a grade of 90 in art, and we wanted to know his grade in shop. Referring to the scatter diagram of the relationship between the grades in these two subjects, we would find the point on the line that corresponds to a score of 90 on the vertical axis and would see what score on the horizontal axis corresponds to this point. In this case, a grade of 90 in art corresponds to a grade of 70 in shop and, referring back to Table 7.1, you can see that all students who had grades of 90 in art had grades of 70 in shop. As the correlation between two variables approaches zero, the accuracy of such predictions decreases. When this is the case, we find the line that would "best fit" the dots, and we make our predictions based on that line. This line is called a *regression line,* and is drawn in such a way that the distance between each dot and the line is minimized. Since all the dots do not fall on the line, however, there will be some degree of error in our predictions. The higher the absolute value of the correlation, the closer the dots will be to the line, and the less error there will be in our predictions.

As you can see, then, the correlation coefficient tells us the degree of relationship between two variables. If the scores on any one variable are highly associated with the scores on another, then a knowledge of a person's score on one of the variables will give us information about his score on the other. The higher the degree of relationship, the more accurate this information will be. If there is a correlation of +.9 between IQ scores and reading scores, for example, we would be more accurate in predicting that students with high IQ scores would do well in reading than if the correlation was only +.6. Similarly, the higher a negative correlation between two variables, the more certainty we would have that a person scoring high on one of the variables would score low on the other.

Calculating the Correlation Coefficient

There are many methods by which one may obtain a correlation coefficient. As with the other statistics that have been considered, the method to be used in any particular instance depends upon the type of data that are available and the information that is desired. In this chapter, we can consider only the two most common measures of correlation, Spearman's rank-order correlation coefficient and Pearson's product-moment correlation coefficient.

The Product-Moment Correlation Coefficient

When we have interval or ratio data, and we are interested in the relationship between the scores on our two variables, it is appropriate to use the product-moment correlation coefficient. Assume, for example, that we want to determine the extent of agreement between the tenth- and eleventh-grade averages reported in Table 7.2. If we are concerned not only with the relative position of each student, but with their actual grade point average, the statistic to use is as follows:

$$r = \frac{n \, \Sigma \, XY - (\Sigma \, X)(\Sigma \, Y)}{\sqrt{[n \, \Sigma \, X^2 - (\Sigma \, X)^2] \, [n \, \Sigma \, Y^2 - (\Sigma \, Y)^2]}}$$

Where r = the product-moment correlation coefficient

         X = each of the scores on the first variable

         Y = each of the scores on the second variable

         n = the number of pairs of scores

In order to compute the product-moment correlation coefficient, we will need the sum of the scores on each of the variables (ΣX and ΣY), the sum of the squares of the scores on each of the variables (ΣX^2 and ΣY^2), and the sum of the products of the scores on the two variables (ΣXY). Putting these quantities into the formula, as illustrated in Table 7.2, yields a correlation coefficient of +.99.

This value indicates that there was a high degree of relationship between the grade point averages in tenth and eleventh grade. The fact that the coefficient is positive indicates that the relationship was such that high grades in tenth grade were associated with high grades in eleventh grade.

Table 7.2. Grade Point Averages of Ten Students at the End of Tenth and Eleventh Grade

GRADE POINT AVERAGE

Student	Tenth Grade (X)	(X²)	Eleventh Grade (Y)	(Y²)	(XY)
John	90	8,100	95	9,025	8,550
Mary	85	7,225	90	8,100	7,650
Michael	80	6,400	80	6,400	6,400
Robert	75	5,625	70	4,900	5,250
Jane	70	4,900	65	4,225	4,550
Kenneth	70	4,900	65	4,225	4,550
Susan	70	4,900	65	4,225	4,550
Anna	65	4,225	60	3,600	3,900
Charles	60	3,600	55	3,025	3,300
Dorothy	60	3,600	55	3,025	3,300
	$\Sigma X = 725$	$\Sigma X^2 = 53,475$	$\Sigma Y = 700$	$\Sigma Y^2 = 50,750$	$\Sigma XY = 52,000$

$$r = \frac{n\Sigma XY - (\Sigma X)(\Sigma Y)}{\sqrt{[n\Sigma X^2 - (\Sigma X)^2][n\Sigma Y^2 - (\Sigma Y)^2]}}$$

$$= \frac{10(52,000) - (725)(700)}{\sqrt{[10(53,475) - (725)^2][10(50,750) - (700)^2]}}$$

$$= \frac{12,500}{\sqrt{(9,125)(17,500)}} = \frac{12,500}{\sqrt{159,687,500}} = \frac{12,500}{12,636.7}$$

$$= +.99$$

Since the correlation was not equal to +1, we know that there was not a perfect, one-to-one correspondence between the grades. That is, the students did not all have exactly the same average on both occasions. The correlation is quite high, however, and, as may be noted in Table 7.2, the differences between the averages in tenth and eleventh grade were rather small.

If these small differences in grade point average did not concern us, however, and we were really only interested in finding out whether the students maintained the same position in the group, we would not use the product-moment correlation coefficient. In this instance, we would only want to know whether the students maintained their ranks, and we would compute the correlation with the rank-order correlation coefficient.

The Rank-Order Correlation Coefficient

The rank-order correlation coefficient is appropriate when we have ordinal data, or when we are concerned only with the position of the scores on the two variables. Assume, for example, that we are again concerned with the grade point averages in Table 7.2, but we are interested only in whether or not the students were ordered in the same way at the end of the eleventh grade as they were in tenth. Our first step, as indicated in Table 7.3, is to rank the scores in each grade.

Table 7.3. Grade Point Averages of Ten Students at the End of Tenth and Eleventh Grade

Student	Tenth Grade Grade Point Average	Rank	Eleventh Grade Grade Point Average	Rank	D	D^2
John	90	1	95	1	0	0
Mary	85	2	90	2	0	0
Michael	80	3	80	3	0	0
Robert	75	4	70	4	0	0
Jane	70	6	65	6	0	0
Kenneth	70	6	65	6	0	0
Susan	70	6	65	6	0	0
Anna	65	8	60	8	0	0
Charles	60	9.5	55	9.5	0	0
Dorothy	60	9.5	55	9.5	0	0
						$\Sigma D^2 = 0$

$$r = 1 - \frac{6 \Sigma D^2}{n(n^2 - 1)}$$

$$= 1 - \frac{6(0)}{10(100 - 1)} = 1 - 0 = +1$$

Once we have our ranks, we find the difference between the ranks for each of the students, we square these differences, and we find the sum of the squared differences. Then, as illustrated in Table 7.3, we use the following formula to compute the rank-order correlation coefficient:

$$r = 1 - \frac{6 \sum D^2}{n(n^2 - 1)}$$

Where r = the rank-order correlation coefficient
   D = the difference for each individual between his ranks on the two variables
   n = the number of individuals or pairs of ranks

As you can see in Table 7.3, even though the averages were not exactly the same, the ranks on each of the variables are identical. The differences between the ranks are all equal to zero, and, as indicated, the rank-order correlation is equal to +1. We can thus say that there is a perfect positive correlation between a student's standing in tenth and eleventh grade.

It should be noted that even when we do have ordinal data, the correlation between the ranks could be computed with the product-moment correlation coefficient. The rank-order coefficient is preferred, however, because even though the results would be identical, the rank-order correlation is easier to compute. Given the data in Table 7.4, for example, we might want to determine the extent to which speed in typing is related to scores on a test in manual dexterity. Assuming that we are not interested in the correlation between the actual raw scores on the two variables but in the correlation between a student's standing on both skills, we could compute the correlation coefficient using either of the foregoing methods. As you can see, both methods yield a correlation coefficient of +.95, but the computation is much easier when we use the formula for the rank-order correlation coefficient. When using the rank-order formula, we do not have to square each of the ranks, nor do we have to find the products of the ranks. We merely need to find the difference between the ranks on each of the variables and then square these differences. Regardless of the method we use, the correlation coefficient is the same. In this case, the coefficient of +.95 indicates that performance in typing is highly related to manual dexterity, and that the relationship is such that high scores in one skill are associated with high scores in the other.

Referring again to the data in Table 7.4, we can see that those students who did well in typing were indeed the same ones who did well on the test of manual dexterity. Note, though, that the ordering on the two tests was not identical. Whereas Anna ranked eighth in typing, she ranked tenth in manual dexterity, and John, who ranked first in typing, was second in manual dexterity. Similarly, there were slight differences for Mary, Charles, and Dorothy. Note that the differences were all quite small. None of the students

Table 7.4. Ranks of Ten Students on a Speed Typing and a Manual Dexterity Test

	Rank						
Student	Speed Typing	Manual Dexterity	D	D^2	X^2	Y^2	XY
John	1	2	−1	1	1	4	2
Mary	2	1	1	1	4	1	2
Michael	3	3	0	0	9	9	9
Robert	4	4	0	0	16	16	16
Jane	5	5	0	0	25	25	25
Kenneth	6	6	0	0	36	36	36
Susan	7	7	0	0	49	49	49
Anna	8	10	−2	4	64	100	80
Charles	9	8	1	1	81	64	72
Dorothy	10	9	1	1	100	81	90
	$\Sigma X = 55$	$\Sigma Y = 55$		$\Sigma D^2 = 8$	$\Sigma X^2 = 385$	$\Sigma Y^2 = 385$	$\Sigma XY = 381$

Rank-Order Correlation Coefficient

$$r = 1 - \frac{6 \Sigma D^2}{n(n^2 - 1)} = 1 - \frac{6(8)}{10(10^2 - 1)} = 1 - \frac{48}{10(100 - 1)} = 1 - \frac{48}{990} = 1 - .05 = +.95$$

Product-moment Correlation Coefficient

$$r = \frac{n \Sigma XY - (\Sigma X)(\Sigma Y)}{\sqrt{[n \Sigma X^2 - (\Sigma X)^2][n \Sigma Y^2 - (\Sigma Y)^2]}} = \frac{10(381) - (55)(55)}{\sqrt{[10(385) - (55)^2][10(385) - (55)^2]}}$$

$$= \frac{3810 - 3025}{\sqrt{(3850 - 3025)(3850 - 3025)}} = \frac{785}{\sqrt{(825)(825)}} = \frac{785}{825} = +.95$$

who did exceptionally well on one of the tests did poorly on the other. In other words, there were no major reversals and, in general, there was a very close correspondence between the scores on the two tests. Thus, even though we did not have a perfect positive correlation, the value of the correlation coefficient was quite high.

As you can see, a correlation coefficient indicates the degree of relationship between two variables. When the scores on two variables are related as in the preceding example, the correlation coefficient will have a high positive value. When the variables are related in such a way that high scores on one of the variables is associated with low scores on the other, the correlation coefficient will be negative. It is not the sign but the absolute value of the correlation coefficient that tells us the strength of the association. A correlation coefficient of $-.8$ thus indicates a stronger relationship between two variables than does a correlation coefficient of $+.4$.

In interpreting a correlation coefficient, one must remember that even though there may be a strong correlation between two variables, the correlation does not provide evidence of a causal relationship. We know, for example, that there is a very high positive relationship between IQ scores and success in school. It is for this very reason that we often use IQ scores as the basis for grouping our students. Although this high correlation does indicate that school success is associated with high IQ scores, it does not indicate that a high IQ score is the cause of success in school. The correlation merely tells us that, in fact, those children who score well on IQ tests are the same ones who do well in school. This high correlation may very well be due to the fact that those factors that influence a child's performance in school are the same ones that will influence his performance on an IQ test. A child who is not interested in doing well in school, for example, may do poorly merely because he does not pay attention. Similarly, this same child, although he is as intelligent as another child, won't do as well on an IQ test because he doesn't pay attention to the task. As you can see, then, a high correlation does not tell us anything about causality; the fact that two variables are related does not mean that one caused the other.

Another common pitfall one encounters in interpreting correlation coefficients is the assumption that, just because there is a high correlation between two variables, a person who does well on one *must* do well on the other. To use the example of IQ and school success again, one often assumes that if a student does well in school, he must have a high IQ score, or that if a student has a low IQ score, he must do poorly in school. However, a correlation is based upon data for many individuals, and any one particular person may break the pattern. If there was a high negative correlation between anxiety and public speaking, for example, we would know that, *in general,* those individuals who are highly anxious are not good at public speaking; but this correlation does not indicate that we *cannot* find an individual who is high in both or, for that matter, an individual who is a miserable public speaker and not in the least bit anxious. As you can see, then, the correlation coefficient does not provide an infallible tool for determining how a student will do in a particular subject. Rather, the correlation coefficient is a statistic that tells us how much risk we have of being wrong when, given a student's performance in one area, we make assumptions about his performance in another. When the correlation is very high, we know that we have less of a chance of being wrong. If the correlation is low, our chance of error is increased. This information is particularly valuable to the teacher in making decisions about placement and guidance. If a student has scored low on a science aptitude test, for example, and we know that scores on the test are highly correlated with success in science courses, we might advise that student to consider other areas. If a student scores low on a scholastic aptitude test, however, and we know that there is *not* a high correlation between scores on the test and success in academic high school programs, the low score on the test does not necessarily indicate that the student will have trouble in high school.

As you can see, then, a correlation coefficient can give us valuable information as to how we can use the various sources of information that we have on our students. It can tell us how much faith we may put in predictions about future performance. As with all the statistics that have been considered, however, the correlation coefficient is useful only when it is properly interpreted by the teacher.

Regression

Once we have established that a high correlation exists between two variables, we may then want to use performance on one of the variables to predict success in the other. Assume, for example, that scores on a reading achievement test are known to be highly correlated with grades in French. If a student was considering taking French, then, we could use his reading score to predict the likelihood of his success in French. In making such a prediction, we would use a *regression equation,* the equation for the straight line that best fits the relationship between our two sets of scores.

Assume, for example, that the scores in reading and French given in Table 7.5 were obtained by a group of 15 students. If we were to graph these scores, our scatter diagram would be as illustrated in Figure 7.2. Note, however, that we do not have a perfect positive correlation between our two sets of scores and, consequently, our graph does not form a straight line. In order to predict from one variable to the other, then, we must find the equation of the straight line that best fits our dots. This line is the *regression line,* and it is identified by the following formula.

Linear Regression Equation

$Y' = bX + a$

Where Y' = the predicted value

a = the value of Y when $X = 0$

X = the score from which Y is being predicted

b = the slope of the regression line

For any one regression line, the values of a and b are constant; these values identify the line, and they are calculated from the following formulas:

$$b = \frac{\Sigma\,XY - (\Sigma\,X\,\Sigma\,Y/N)}{\Sigma\,X^2 - [(\Sigma\,X)^2/N]}$$

$$a = \frac{\Sigma\,Y - b\,\Sigma\,X}{N}$$

For the scores in Table 7.5, for example, the regression equation for the prediction of success in French would be calculated as follows.

Calculating a Regression Equation

Reading Scores X	French Scores Y	X^2	XY
95	95	9,025	9,025
95	90	9,025	8,550
95	95	9,025	9,025
90	90	8,100	8,100
90	85	8,100	7,650
90	80	8,100	7,200
85	90	7,225	7,650
85	85	7,225	7,225
80	85	6,400	6,800
80	80	6,400	6,400
80	80	6,400	6,400
70	75	4,900	5,250
65	70	4,225	4,550
65	60	4,225	3,900
65	60	4,225	3,900
$\Sigma\,X = 1,230$	$\Sigma\,Y = 1,220$	$\Sigma\,X^2 = 102,600$	$\Sigma\,XY = 101,625$

$$b = \frac{\Sigma\,XY - (\Sigma\,X\,\Sigma\,Y/N)}{\Sigma\,X^2 - [(\Sigma\,X)^2/N]} = \frac{101,625 - [(1,230)(1,220)/15]}{102,600 - 1,230^2/15}$$

$$= \frac{101,625 - 100,040}{102,600 - 100,860} = \frac{1,585}{1,740} = .91$$

$$a = \frac{\Sigma Y - b \Sigma X}{N} = \frac{1,220 - .91(1,230)}{15}$$

$$= \frac{1,220 - 1,119.30}{15} = \frac{100.70}{15} = 6.71$$

$Y' = bX + a$

$Y' = .91X + 6.71$

Once we have the equation of the regression line, we can then use the equation to predict the value of Y for any given value of X. If a student had a score of 90 in reading, we would use our regression equation to predict the student's score in French as follows:

$Y' = .91(90) + 6.71$
$\quad = 81.90 + 6.71$
$\quad = 88.61$

Substituting 90 for the value of X, we find that the predicted value of Y is 88.61. If a student had a reading score of 90, then, our best guess as to his score in French would be 88.61. For any value of X, then, we can predict the value of Y by substituting for X in the regression equation.

For all values of X, however, we know that the predicted value of Y will fall on the regression line. When we wish to make predictions for several students, then, it is easier to draw the regression line and to read our

Table 7.5. Reading and French Scores of Fifteen Students

Student	Scores	
	Reading	French
1	95	95
2	95	90
3	95	95
4	90	90
5	90	85
6	90	80
7	85	90
8	85	85
9	80	85
10	80	80
11	80	80
12	70	75
13	65	70
14	65	60
15	65	60

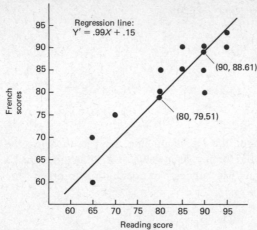

Figure 7.2 Scatter diagram of the relationship between French and reading scores.

predictions directly from the graph. In order to draw a regression line (or any straight line), we must first identify two of the points that fall on the line. Our first step is to select two values of X, and to substitute these values of X in the regression equation. Since we already know that 88.61 is the predicted value of Y for a reading score of 90, we may use the point where $X = 90$ and $Y = 88.61$ as one of our points. For a second point, let us predict the value of Y for a reading score of 80. The predicted value of Y, 79.51, is obtained by substituting in the regression equation as indicated:

$$Y' = .91(80) + 6.71$$
$$= 72.80 + 6.71$$
$$= 79.51$$

We thus have two points that fall on the regression line: (90.0, 88.61) and (80.0, 79.51). If we plot these two points on our graph, as indicated on Figure 7.2 the line running through these points is the regression line. For all other values of X, then, we may determine the predicted value of Y from our graph. If, for example, we wanted to predict the French score of a student who had an 85 in reading, we would find a score of 85 on the X-axis, we would follow this point up to the regression line, and we would read across to the value on the Y-axis. For a reading score of 85, the predicted value of Y would be 84.06.

Referring back to our original scores, now, you may note that even though the predicted value of Y for a reading score of 85 is equal to 84.06, none of the students who actually had an 85 in reading had a score of 84.06 in French. One of these students had a 90 in French, and the other had a score of 85. Similarly, none of the students who scored 90 in reading had French scores of 88.61. As you can see, then, a student with a given score on one of our variables will not necessarily have the predicted score on the other. The predicted score is only an estimate; the better the fit between the regression line and the dots on our scatter diagram, the better will be this estimate. Unless the correlation between our variables is either +1.0 or −1.0, the scatter diagram will not form a straight line, and our estimates will not be perfect. The higher the correlation between our variables, of course, the greater our assurance that the student will perform as predicted; even with a correlation coefficient of +.999, however, a particular student may do either better or worse than expected.

Given that we have two sets of scores that are highly correlated, then, the use of a regression equation can aid us in predicting student performance. Over all, estimates that are based on a regression line will provide the best estimates of the variable being predicted. As you can see, however, our predictions will not be perfect. In predicting performance, then, the teacher's judgment plays an important role. We can use a regression equation to predict performance in a given area, but it is the teacher who must evaluate that prediction. It is the teacher who must decide whether the correlation between two variables is sufficiently high for predictions to be valid, and it is the teacher who must decide whether a student's score is an accurate representation of his ability. Regardless of the correlation between two variables, a student's score on one of the variables may not be predictive of his performance on the other if the student was ill when he took the test, or if he was overanxious or tired. It is up to the teacher to evaluate these factors; the statistic itself merely predicts a score that may or may not be correct.

PRACTICE PROBLEMS

The following scores were obtained on an IQ and a reading test:

| | *Score* | |
Student	IQ	Reading
Alice	115	95
Bob	110	80
Charles	105	90
Donna	100	85
Edward	95	75
Frances	90	70
George	90	65
Howard	80	60

1. Find the product-moment correlation coefficient expressing the relationship between the two sets of scores.
2. Find the rank-order correlation coefficient expressing the relationship between the two sets of scores.

3. Determine the regression equation for predicting reading scores from IQ scores, and graph the regression line.
4. Based on the correlation coefficients determined in the first two problems, which of the following statements are warranted?
   a. Any student who has a high IQ score will do well in reading.
   b. Students who do poorly in reading generally have low IQ scores.
   c. Students who do well in reading always have high IQ scores.
   d. A student who has a low IQ score will definitely have trouble in reading.
   e. A low IQ score is usually the cause of reading problems.

STATISTICAL INFERENCE AND SAMPLING 8

As we have seen, statistics can be used to describe a set of numbers. In the problems we have considered, we have used various statistics to summarize the information in a set of test scores. By summarizing scores in this manner, we have used statistics as a means of succinctly describing classroom performance. There are times, however, when we wish to do more than describe the performance of a specific group of students. Assume, for example, that a school system is considering the purchase of teaching machines and, in order to come to a final decision, the machines are being used on a trial basis in two fourth-grade classes. The school will certainly be interested in describing the performance of the students in these two classes. Note, however, that the school is not going to purchase machines for these particular students, but for future fourth-graders. Thus the performance of these particular students is of concern not because the school wants information about these particular students, but because the administration wants to use this information as a basis for making inferences about other fourth-graders.

Inferential versus Descriptive Statistics

The statistics that we have been using thus far are called *descriptive statistics*. These statistics are used when we have one particular set of data that we wish to describe. The mean and the median, for example, are descriptive statistics that we can use to describe the typical performance of a group of students, all of whom took a particular test. When we wish to go beyond the description of one particular group, however, and we wish to use the performance of one group as a basis for making inferences about groups that include other people, we must then turn to the realm of *inferential statistics*. Inferential statistics tell us the degree of confidence we may put in the statistical inferences we make. Whereas a descriptive statistic, such as the mean, can describe the typical performance of a group of students, an inferential statistic allows us to compare the typical performance of different samples, and to make inferences about the populations from which these samples came. Inferential statistics are concerned with the inferences we make from samples to populations. Before we can deal with inferential statistics, then, we must understand the difference between samples and populations.

Samples and Populations

When we refer to a *population*, we are referring to all instances of a particular category. For example, the population of fourth-graders in the United States would include every fourth-grader in every school in the country. Similarly, the population of boys with blue eyes would include every boy with blue eyes, and the population of Miss Smith's class would include every student in Miss Smith's class. A population is as large or as small as the category defined. The population of boys with blue eyes is immeasurably large, while the population of Miss Smith's class may be no larger than ten. Whereas a population refers to all the instances within a category, a *sample* refers to a portion of the instances within a population. Any one fourth-grade class, for example, would include a sample from the population of all fourth-graders. Similarly, a sample of boys with blue eyes would include only some of the boys with blue eyes, and a sample of students from Miss Smith's class would include only a portion of her students. A sample may be either large or small, but the size of the sample cannot exceed the size of the population.

Usually, our ultimate aim is to describe the characteristics of a population or, in statistical terms, population *parameters*. In the field of education, however, most of our populations are so very large that they are practically impossible to measure. Thus, instead of directly measuring the population, we describe a sample and then make inferences from our sample to the population. We assume that the sample is representative of the population and that, therefore, those characteristics that are displayed in the sample will also be found in the population. However, the sample may not be representative of the population; it may be biased in some way.

For example, assume that we want to determine the average score of fourth-graders on a new reading test that is being developed. It is impossible to give the test to every fourth-grader in every school, so we pick a sample of fourth-graders and, based upon the performance of this sample, we make conclusions about the population of all fourth-graders. If we choose the sample by asking four or five teachers to send some students to take a new test, however, the teachers are likely to select the students from among the best readers in the class. If this is the case, the sample is not a representative sample, and the average performance in this sample is not descriptive of the average performance in the population. The sample is biased, and any inferences based upon the performance of this sample would be similarly biased. As you can see, then, when we are going to draw inferences based upon the performance of a sample, it is most important that the sample be chosen in an unbiased way. In order to eliminate bias of this sort, we select a *random sample.*

Random Sampling

Random sampling is a selection procedure insuring that every member of the population has an equal chance of being included in the sample. To select a random sample of the students in a particular school, for example, we might use one of the following procedures. We could put the name of each student on a piece of paper, combine all the names in a big bowl, mix them up, and ask one of the teachers to pull the desired number of names out of the bowl. Or we could assign each student a number, and select the students by reading numbers from a random numbers table as in the Appendix (Table B). In either case, the sampling procedure would eliminate bias, and we would have a random sample.

There are times, however, when even though we want an unbiased sample, we want to make sure that certain characteristics of the population are reflected in the sample. When this is the case, we pick a *stratified random sample*—a sample that includes random samples from each of the subpopulations that comprise a more inclusive population. Assume, for example, that we want to find the vocational preferences of senior high school students, and we suspect that students from different socioeconomic levels will have different types of aspirations. In this case, we want to be sure that students from all socioeconomic levels are included in the sample, so we select a random sample of the students from within each socioeconomic level. That is, we pick one random sample from among the population of high socioeco-

Table 8.1. IQ Scores of a Population of Five Students

Student	IQ Score
Andrew	140
Barbara	160
Carole	150
Douglas	170
Edward	130
	$\Sigma X = 750$

$$\text{Mean} = \frac{\Sigma X}{N} = \frac{750}{5} = 150$$

Table 8.2. Sample Means Drawn from a Population
Where $\mu = 150$

Sample ($n = 2$)	Sample Mean
Andrew, Barbara	150
Andrew, Carole	145
Andrew, Douglas	155
Andrew, Edward	135
Barbara, Carole	155
Barbara, Douglas	165
Barbara, Edward	145
Carole, Douglas	160
Carole, Edward	140
Douglas, Edward	150

nomic status students, we pick another random sample from among the population of medium socioeconomic status students, and we pick a third random sample from among the population of students from low socioeconomic status homes. The size of each sample should be proportional to the number of students within each socioeconomic level. Combining the three samples, then, we have a stratified random sample of high school seniors.

Even when one has a stratified random sample, however, one can never be sure that the sample is truly representative of the population. To illustrate this point, let's consider the following example. Assume that we have a population of five students in a particular school with IQ scores that are above 130, and that we want to select a sample of two students from this population. If the IQ scores are as indicated in Table 8.1, we can see that the mean IQ score for this population is 150. The means of our samples, however, are not all equal to this population mean. As indicated in Table 8.2, there are ten samples of two students that might be selected from this population and, if the sample is randomly selected, each of these samples is equally likely to occur. Whereas the population mean is equal to 150, however, the sample means vary from 135 to 165. Even when the sample is randomly selected, then, the sample mean may be quite different from the mean of the population. These sample means form a *sampling distribution;* the sample means are distributed around the population mean, with some of the sample means below and some above the mean of the population.

Sampling Distributions

Whenever inferences are made from sample statistics, one must remember that the sample statistic may not exactly describe the population. As indicated previously, the sample mean may not be identical to the mean of

Table 8.3. Sampling Distribution of the Mean (For Data in Table 8.1, $n = 2$)

Sample Mean ($\bar{X}$)	Frequency of Occurrence (f)	Probability of Occurrence (p)
135	1	.10
140	1	.10
145	2	.20
150	2	.20
155	2	.20
160	1	.10
165	1	.10

the population from which the sample comes. Similarly, a sample standard deviation may not be identical to the standard deviation of the population, and a sample proportion may not be identical to the proportion of such items in the population. The distribution of the sample statistic is called a *sampling distribution*; the sampling distribution indicates the frequency with which different sample values will occur if all samples of a particular size are selected from a population.

In Table 8.3, we have a sampling distribution for the mean of the samples selected from the population described earlier. As you can see, sample means that are close to the population mean occur more frequently than those that are further away. One has twice as many chances of selecting a sample with a mean of 150 as one does of selecting a sample with a mean of 135; the probability of selecting a sample with a mean between 145 and 155 is 60 percent, whereas the probability of selecting a sample with a mean between 135 and 145 is only 40 percent. Nevertheless, it is still possible to select a sample with a mean of 135. Note, however, that even though there were students in the population with scores of 130 and 170, it is not possible to select a sample with these values as the mean. Although the mean of the sample means will be exactly the same as the mean of the population, the distribution of sample means is not as spread out as the population. Since each sample mean is an average of two or more of the population values, the extreme values in the population will not appear in the distribution of sample means. As you can see, then, the standard deviation of the distribution of sample means will always be less than the standard deviation of the population. In the previous example, for instance, the standard deviation of the population is equal to 14.14, while the standard deviation of the sample means is only equal to 8.66.

The standard deviation of the sample means indicates the extent to which the sample means vary from the mean of the population. That is, the standard deviation of the sample means tells us the extent of the error that we may expect in using the mean of a sample as an estimate of the population mean. Thus the standard deviation of the sample means is referred to as the *standard error of the mean* or, more simply, as the *standard error*. This term is symbolized as $\sigma_{\bar{X}}$, and plays an important role in statistical inference.

In our example, we were dealing with a rather small population, and the sampling distribution was not difficult to construct. Most often, however, we are concerned with samples where the population is either unavailable or is infinitely large. In such instances, it is practically impossible to construct an actual sampling distribution. In order to determine the probability of obtaining a sample mean that is within a certain distance of the population mean, then, we must turn to a theoretical sampling distribution. Theoretical sampling distributions are based upon considerations of what the sampling distribution would be like if we actually could take all the samples of a particular size. When the population is sufficiently large, these theoretical distributions provide useful representations of the empirical or actual sampling distribution.

Theoretical Sampling Distributions

In considering the various descriptive statistics, we found that different statistics were appropriate in different situations. Similarly, when we deal with theoretical sampling distributions, we will find that the appropriate distribution depends upon the characteristics of the sample, the population from which the sample was selected, and the population parameter in which we are interested. In each instance, the usefulness of the theoretical distribution depends on the closeness of fit between the theoretical distribution and the sampling distribution that would be obtained if we actually could select all possible samples. As we progress to using inferential statistics to test hypotheses about means, proportions, and variability, we will find several theoretical distributions to be useful. Among these are the normal distribution, the Student's (*t*) distribution, the binomial, the chi-square, and the *F* distributions. It is necessary, therefore, to consider the properties of all these distributions.

The Normal Distribution

The normal distribution may be represented as a bell-shaped curve with a specified proportion of the scores falling between various points on the horizontal axis. As illustrated in Figure 8.1, the curve is symmetrical. Fifty percent of the area under the curve falls above the midpoint of the horizontal axis, and fifty percent falls below. The curve is defined in such a way that the mean, the median, and the mode of the distribution all fall at this midpoint and, for each point we move away from the mean, we cover a specified

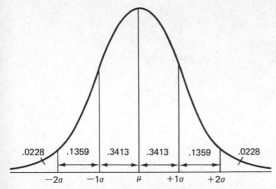

Figure 8.1. Distribution of the area under the normal curve.

proportion of the scores. It is this proportion of scores that defines the normal distribution; that is, a distribution is normal only if the specified proportion of scores falls between specified points on the base of the curve. These proportions are given in Table C of the Appendix, which tells us the proportion of scores, or the area, between the mean and each of the scores in a normal distribution. To illustrate the use of this table, let us assume that we have a population of second-graders whose reading scores are normally distributed with a mean of 80 and a standard deviation of 10.

In order to determine the proportion of scores between any two points in the distribution, we must first determine the distance, in standard deviations, between those points and the mean. In other words, as you may remember from Chapter 6, we must determine the z-scores that are equivalent to the scores in question. Let's say, for example, that we want to determine the proportion of students that had scores between 70 and 90. Our first step is to determine the z values that are equivalent to these two scores. As indicated below, where the mean is equal to 80 and the standard deviation is equal to 10, a score of 90 is equivalent to a z of +1, and a score of 70 is equivalent to a z of −1.

z Values Equivalent to Reading Scores of 90 and 70

READING GRADE	z VALUE
90	$z = \dfrac{X - \overline{X}}{SD} = \dfrac{90 - 80}{10} = +1$
70	$z = \dfrac{X - \overline{X}}{SD} = \dfrac{70 - 80}{10} = -1$

Once we have these z values, we then turn to Table C. We find the absolute value of z (Column 1) in the table and, looking across to the corresponding area, we can see that .3413 of the scores fell between the mean and the score that was one standard deviation away from the mean. Since the normal

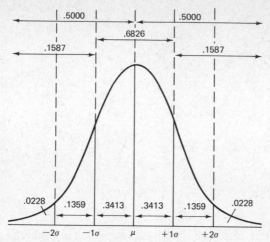

Figure 8.2. Proportion of the area between points on the normal curve.

distribution is symmetrical, we not only know that .3413 of the scores fell between the mean and the score that was equivalent to a z of $+1$, but we also know that .3413 of the scores fell between the mean and the score that was equivalent to a z of -1. As indicated in Figure 8.2, then, .6826 of the scores fell between scores of 70 and 90, this total being composed of the .3413 falling between a score of 70 and the mean, and the .3413 falling between the mean and a score of 90. Similarly, we know that .1587 of the scores fell above a score of 90, and that .8413 of the scores fell above a score of 70.

If we have a normal distribution, then, we can determine the proportion of scores falling between any two z values, the proportion of scores falling above any z-score, and the proportion of scores falling below a particular z-score. If the score is above the mean, we know that at least 50 percent of the scores fell below it; if the score is below the mean, we know that at least 50 percent of the scores fell above it. In order to find the proportion of scores falling above a score that is above the mean, we find the proportion of scores between that score and the mean, and we subtract that proportion from .5000. In order to find the proportion of scores falling below a score that is above the mean, we add .5000 to the proportion of scores between the score and the mean. Similarly, when we have a score that is below the mean, we find the proportion of scores falling below the score by subtracting the proportion of scores between the score and the mean from .5000, and we find the proportion of scores falling above the score by adding .5000 to the proportion of scores between the score and the mean. As you can see, then, once we determine the z value of any two points in a normal distribution, we can then determine the area, or the proportion of scores between those points.

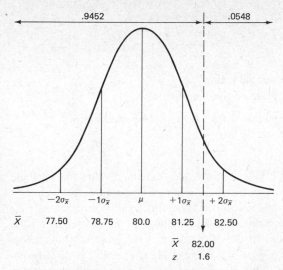

.9452   .0548

$\bar{X}$	$-2\sigma_{\bar{x}}$	$-1\sigma_{\bar{x}}$	μ	$+1\sigma_{\bar{x}}$	$+2\sigma_{\bar{x}}$
	77.50	78.75	80.0	81.25	82.50

$\bar{X}$ 82.00

z 1.6

Figure 8.3. Theoretical sampling distribution of a mean.

Now that we know the properties of a normal distribution, let us see how to use the normal curve as a theoretical sampling distribution. In those instances (which will be described in later chapters) where we can assume that our sample values will be normally distributed, we can treat the normal curve as the sampling distribution for our sample values. Let us assume, for example, that we were randomly selecting samples of 64 students from the population of students who took the reading test described earlier. We can assume that the means of these samples will be normally distributed; as with an empirical sampling distribution, the mean of the sample means will be equal to the population mean, and the standard deviation of the sample means will be equal to the standard error of the mean. In determining the standard error, $\sigma_{\bar{X}}$, we divide the standard deviation of the population by the square root of the sample size. The theoretical sampling distribution is thus as illustrated in Figure 8.3, with a mean of 80 and a standard deviation of $10/\sqrt{64}$ or 1.25.

Let us assume, now, that we want to know the probability of selecting a sample with a mean that is greater than 82. What we must do, then, is to determine the proportion of the area under the normal curve that will fall above the z equivalent of a score of 82. Our first step is to determine the z value that is equivalent to a sample mean of 82. To find this z value, our procedure is similar to that for finding the z value for a score in a normally distributed population. We will find the difference between the sample mean and the mean of the sampling distribution, and we will divide the result by the standard error (the standard deviation of the sampling distribution). The z value will thus tell us the number of standard errors between the sample mean and the mean of the population, and the formula for z would be as follows:

Formula for Finding the z Value for a Sample Mean

$$z_{\overline{X}} = \frac{\overline{X} - \mu_{\overline{X}}}{\sigma / \sqrt{n}}$$

Where $\overline{X}$ = the sample mean

$\mu_{\overline{X}}$ = the mean of the sample means

σ = the standard deviation of the population

n = the sample size

Substituting in our formula, now, we can see that the z value for a sample mean of 82 would be equal to $(82 - 80)/(10/\sqrt{64})$, or $+1.6$. Referring to Table C, we can see that .4452 of the area under the normal curve falls between the mean and the point that is 1.6 standard deviations above the mean. Adding this proportion to the 50 percent of the area that falls below the mean, as illustrated in Figure 8.3, we can see that .9452 of the sample means will be equal to or below a sample mean of 82, and that the remaining samples will have means that are equal to or greater than this value. Subtracting .9452 from 1.0000 (or .4452 from .5000), we thus have a probability of .0548 of obtaining a sample mean that is equal to or greater than 82.

As you can see, the normal distribution may be used for determining the probability of obtaining a particular sample mean. There are times, however, when our sampling distribution cannot be assumed to be normal, and other theoretical distributions are more appropriate. Let us consider, then, some of these other distributions.

The Student's (t) Distribution

Very similar to the normal distribution is the Student's distribution or, as it is also known, the t distribution. As illustrated in Figure 8.4, the shape of the t distribution is very close to that of the normal distribution. In determining the area between different points on the t distribution, however, the distance (or the number of standard deviations) between each score and the mean is expressed as a t instead of a z value. The t values are found in the same way as z values, where $t = (\overline{X} - \mu_{\overline{X}})/(\sigma/\sqrt{n})$, but a different table must be used to determine the area between each t value and the mean.

Unlike the normal distribution, the proportion of the area between any two points in the t distribution will vary with the size of the sample. In order to determine the area between any two points on the curve then, we must have a measure that takes into account the size of the sample; this measure is the *degrees of freedom*, equal to one less than the sample size. When we are selecting samples of size 15, for example, we have 14 degrees of freedom. Similarly, the degree of freedom for a sample of 12 is equal to 11, and the

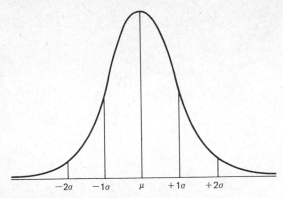

Figure 8.4. The *t* distribution.

degree of freedom for a sample of 8 is equal to 7. Once we have the degree of freedom for our sample, and we have determined the value of *t*, we can then determine the proportion of the area between the mean and that value of *t* by referring to Table D.

To illustrate the use of Table D, consider the following example. Let us assume that we are testing samples of 9 students on an IQ test that has a mean of 100 and a standard deviation of 15, and that we want to know the proportion of times that we can expect our randomly selected samples to have means as low as 90. That is, if we could select all possible samples of 9 students from a population of students with a mean IQ score of 100, what proportion of these samples would have a mean equal to or less than 90? To make this determination, we find the *t* value that is equivalent to a sample mean of 90, and we then turn to Table D to determine the area in the *t* distribution that falls beyond that *t* value. Substituting in our formula for *t*. $(\overline{X} - \mu_{\overline{X}})/(\sigma/\sqrt{n})$, we find that the *t* value that is equivalent to a sample mean of 90 is equal to $(90 - 100)/(15\sqrt{9})$, or −2.00. We now look for the appropriate degree of freedom in Table D, and we read across the row until we find the *t* values in the table between which the absolute value of our *t* value falls. Looking at the row for 8 degrees of freedom, we can see that our value falls between the values of 1.860 and 2.306. Reading the probabilities at the top of the table, then, we can see that 5 percent of the area under the curve falls above the point where *t* is equal to +1.860 and that only 2.5 percent of the area falls above the point where *t* is equal to +2.306. Similarly, 5 percent of the area falls below the point where *t* is equal to −1.860, and 2.5 percent falls below the point where *t* is equal to −2.306. Since the *t* value that is equivalent to a sample mean of 90 lies between the values of −1.860 and −2.306, then, we can expect less than 5 percent and more than 2.5 percent of our samples to have means that are less than or equal to 90.

As you can see, the table for the area between points on the *t* distribution is somewhat different from that for the normal curve. The two tables are

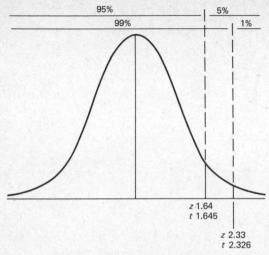

Figure 8.5. Comparison of *t* and *z* values for an infinite degree of freedom.

related, however, as are the curves. Actually, there isn't a single *t* distribution; there is a separate *t* distribution for each degree of freedom and, as the degrees of freedom increase, the *t* distribution approaches the normal distribution. Note, for example, the entries in the *t* table for an infinite degree of freedom; 5 percent of the area under the curve falls beyond a *t* value of 1.645, and 1 percent of the area falls beyond a *t* value of 2.326. Now turn back to Table C, and find the area between the mean and the *z* values of 1.64 and 2.33. As illustrated in Figure 8.5, 47.50 percent of the area under the normal curve lies between the mean and the point that has a *z* value of 1.96. Subtracting 47.50 from 50.0, we can see that, as with the *t* distribution, 5 percent of the area falls beyond this point. Similarly, 49.01 percent of the area under the normal curve falls between the mean and the point where *z* is equal to 2.33, and slightly under 1 percent of the area falls beyond. Thus as the degree of freedom becomes infinitely large, the *t* distribution approaches the shape of the normal distribution. For most practical purposes, therefore, we use the normal distribution in place of the *t* distribution when our sample size is equal to or larger than 30.

As you will see, the *t* distribution is not the only distribution that approaches normality as the sample size increases. Another useful distribution that also has this property is the binomial distribution.

The Binomial Distribution

The binomial distribution represents the sampling distribution of the frequency or the proportion of times one value occurs when sampling from a binomial population, that is, a population so defined that all members of the population may be classified into one of two categories. We would have such a population, for example, if we classified each of our students as being either native-born or foreign-born, as being either short or tall, or as being either male or female. If we assume, now, that we have a population that is 50 percent male and 50 percent female, we may draw samples from this population in which the proportion, or the relative number of males and females may not be the same as in the population. The theoretical distribution of these sample proportions or frequencies will form a binomial sampling distribution with a mean and standard deviation as indicated below. Note that the mean of the distribution of sample proportions is equal to the proportion of times the category occurs in the population, whereas the mean of the theoretical distribution of sample frequencies is equal to the proportion of times the category occurs in the population multiplied by the size of the sample.

Mean and Standard Deviation of a Binomial Sampling Distribution

THE SAMPLING DISTRIBUTION FOR A PROPORTION
Mean: $\qquad \mu_{X/n} = p$
Standard deviation: $\sigma_{X/n} = \sqrt{pq/n}$

THE SAMPLING DISTRIBUTION OF A FREQUENCY
Mean: $\qquad \mu_X = np$
Standard deviation: $\sigma_X = \sqrt{npq}$

Where $\quad p$ = the proportion of times one of the categories occurs in the population

$\qquad q$ = the proportion of times the other category occurs in the population ($q = 1 - p$)

$\qquad n$ = the size of the sample or the number of trials

As may be noted, any sample proportion (X/n) can be transformed into a frequency (X) by multiplying by the size of the sample, and any frequency may be transformed into a proportion by dividing by the size of the sample (n). If we have a sample of 30 students, for example, and we know that 10 percent of the sample has blue eyes, we can very easily determine the frequency of blue eyes by multiplying 30 by .10. Similarly, if we know that blue eyes occurred 3 times in a sample of 30 students, we would divide 3 by 30 to determine the proportion of blue-eyed students.

To illustrate the use of the binomial distribution, let us assume that we are randomly selecting samples of five students from a population that is equally divided between boys and girls, and that we want to know the probability of obtaining a sample that is composed of three or more boys. In order to determine this probability, we must compute the value of the appropriate terms in the binomial expansion, the formula for which follows.

The Binomial Expansion

$$(p + q)^n = p^n + \frac{n}{1} p^{(n-1)}q + \frac{n(n-1)}{(1)(2)} p^{(n-2)}q^2$$

$$+ \frac{n(n-1)(n-2)}{(1)(2)(3)} p^{(n-3)}q^3$$

$$+ \frac{n(n-1)(n-2)(n-3)}{(1)(2)(3)(4)} p^{(n-4)} q^4 + \cdots + q^n$$

Where p = the probability of obtaining one of the values on any one trial

        q = the probability of obtaining the other value on any one trial ($q = 1 - p$)

        n = the size of the sample or the number of trials

and where the value of each term in the expansion gives us the probability of obtaining a specified proportion of p's and q's.

Substituting in the equation, where the probability of selecting either a boy or a girl on any one trial is equal to $\frac{1}{2}$, and where the size of the sample is equal to 5, the probabilities for our example would be as follows.

Values for the Binomial Expansion

$$p = q = \frac{1}{2}$$
$$n = 5$$

$$\left(\frac{1}{2}+\frac{1}{2}\right)^5 = \left(\frac{1}{2}\right)^5 + \frac{5}{1}\left(\frac{1}{2}\right)^4\left(\frac{1}{2}\right) + \frac{(5)(4)}{(1)(2)}\left(\frac{1}{2}\right)^3\left(\frac{1}{2}\right)^2$$

$$+ \frac{(5)(4)(3)}{(1)(2)(3)}\left(\frac{1}{2}\right)^2\left(\frac{1}{2}\right)^3$$

$$+ \frac{(5)(4)(3)(2)}{(1)(2)(3)(4)}\left(\frac{1}{2}\right)\left(\frac{1}{2}\right)^4 + \left(\frac{1}{2}\right)^5$$

The value of the first term in the expansion tells us the probability of obtaining 5 boys and no girls, the value of the second term indicates the probability of obtaining 4 boys and 1 girl, the value of the third term indicates the probability of obtaining 3 boys and 2 girls, and so on. Furthermore, when p is equal to q, the value of the first term is the same as the value of the last term, the value of the second term is the same as the value of the next to the last term, and so forth. Thus the probability of selecting a sample with 4 boys and 1 girl is the same as that of selecting a sample with 4 girls and 1 boy.

To return to the problem at hand, there are three ways in which we may select a sample with 3 or more boys. We would have 3 or more boys if our sample had either 3, 4, or 5 boys. In order to determine the probability of selecting a sample with 3 or more boys, then, we must add together the separate probabilities of selecting a sample with 3 boys, 4 boys, or 5 boys. Referring to our binomial expansion, we can determine the probability of selecting a sample with 5 boys from the value of the first term in the expansion, we can determine the probability of obtaining 4 boys from the second term in the expansion, and we can determine the probability of 3 boys from the third term in the expansion. Adding the value of these terms together, we can see that the probability of selecting a sample with 3 or more boys is equal to

$$\left(\frac{1}{2}\right)^5 + \frac{5}{1}\left(\frac{1}{2}\right)^4\left(\frac{1}{2}\right) + \frac{(5)(4)}{(1)(2)}\left(\frac{1}{2}\right)^3\left(\frac{1}{2}\right)^2$$

which, when worked out, is equal to $\frac{1}{32} + \frac{5}{32} + \frac{10}{32}$, or .5. In other words, if we are selecting samples of 5 students from a population that is evenly divided between boys and girls, the probability is that half of our samples will have at least 3 boys.

As you can see, then, the terms of the binomial expansion can be used to determine the probability of selecting a sample in which the members of one of our binomial categories occur a specific number of times. Note, however, that particularly as our sample size increases, the arithmetic involved in determining our binomial probabilities becomes quite cumbersome. It is for this reason that, when we have large samples, it is more convenient to approximate our binomial probabilities from the normal curve. To illustrate, let us assume that we are now selecting samples of 30 students from a population that is 50 percent male and 50 percent female, and that we want to determine the probability of selecting a sample that has 18 or more boys. We could, of course, work out our binomial probabilities for obtaining 18, 19, 20, 21, . . ., and 30 boys, and we could determine the probability of obtaining 18 or more boys by adding these separate probabilities. It would be much easier, however, to determine this probability from the normal curve.

When we use the normal curve to approximate binomial probabilities, we must express our variable in terms of frequencies rather than proportions. In this case, then, where we are selecting samples of 30 students, the binomial sampling distribution of the number of males in each sample will have a mean, *np*, that is equal to $30 \times .5$, or 15, and a standard deviation, $\sqrt{npq}$, that is equal to $\sqrt{30 \times .5 \times .5}$, or 2.7. Let us assume, however, that this distribution is normal, with a mean of 15 and a standard deviation of 2.7, and that we want to know the proportion of samples in this normal distribution that will have a frequency of 18 or more boys. In order to make this determination, we can now use our formula for *z* to determine the number of standard deviations between the mean frequency of 15 and a sample frequency of 18. Since we are dealing with a distribution of sample frequencies, rather than a distribution of sample means, our formula for *z* will be as follows.

Determining the z Value for a Sample Frequency

$$z = \frac{f - np}{\sqrt{npq}}$$

Where f = the sample frequency

np = the mean of the distribution of frequencies

$\sqrt{npq}$ = the standard deviation of the distribution of frequencies

Note, however, that the formula for z is essentially the same as the formula we used when we were concerned with sample means; in both cases we found the difference between the mean of the distribution and the sample value in question, and we divided by the standard deviation of the distribution. Substituting in our formula, now, we can see that where the sample frequency is equal to 18, z is equal to $(18 - 15)/\sqrt{30}(.5)(.5)$, which is equal to 3/2.7 or 1.11. Referring now to the table of areas under the normal curve, we can see that .3665 of the area lies between the mean and the value that is 1.11 standard deviations above the mean. Subtracting .3665 from .5000, we find that .1335 of the area falls beyond this point. We conclude, therefore, that the probability of selecting a sample from this population which includes 18 or more boys is equal to .1335.

The value is approximately the same as we would get if we worked out the values of the terms in the binomial expansion. As you can see, however, our arithmetic is very much reduced if we use the normal curve to approximate this value. It should be noted, however, that the approximation should be used only with a sample size that is sufficiently large. As a rule of thumb, we usually say that the normal approximation should be used only when either np or nq, whichever is smaller, is greater or equal to 5. If p was equal to .2, therefore, our sample size would have to be as large as 50 for np to be equal to 5. Similarly, if p was equal to .6, q would be equal to .4, and n would have to be as large as 13. As you can see, then, the use of the normal approximation to the binomial is dependent on the size of the sample.

As you have seen, the normal, the t, and the binomial distributions are used to determine the probability of selecting a particular type of sample from a given population. These distributions are referred to as theoretical, rather than empirical, because they are constructed without actually examining the characteristics of every sample of a particular size that could be selected from the population. These distributions simulate the distribution we would get if we could select all possible samples from a particular population. The appropriate theoretical distribution to use in different situations will be discussed in later chapters. For now, however, we must remember that when we use a theoretical distribution such as the normal curve, our probabilities may not be exact. For our purposes, however, the approximations are close enough, and the convenience is certainly worth the loss in accuracy.

Although we have limited ourselves in this chapter to a discussion of the normal, the *t,* and the binomial distributions, these are not the only theoretical distributions that we will find to be useful. We will find that the chi-square and *F* distributions are also useful in certain situations. At this point, however, it will suffice to say that these distributions will be used in the same way as the distributions that have already been discussed. Although the shape of these distributions is somewhat different, we have similar ways of determining the distance between various points on the curve, thereby determining the probability of selecting a particular type of sample.

Regardless of the sampling distribution, however, we now know that even though a population may have certain characteristics, a sample selected from that population may not exhibit these same characteristics. If the mean for a population on a particular measure is 85, for example, a sample selected from that population may have a mean that is as high as 90 or as low as 75. Similarly, if a population is composed of 30 percent redheads and 70 percent brunettes, we may select a sample that is composed of 50 percent brunettes. As you can see, then, when we use sample statistics to indicate population parameters, we are only making estimates about the population.

Estimation

When we are making estimates from a sample to a population, our estimates may take the form of point estimates or interval estimates. We have a point estimate when we use the value of a specific sample statistic, such as the sample mean, as an estimate of a specific population parameter. In this case, we are estimating one particular point on a scale of values. When we make estimates of this nature, however, we know that our estimates may be in error. Rather than estimate a particular point, therefore, we often use our sample statistics to estimate an interval within which the population parameter probably falls. These intervals are called *confidence intervals,* and they indicate the probability of the population parameter falling within the limits of the interval specified. A confidence interval is determined on the basis of the sampling distribution of the statistic upon which the estimate is based. Thus the confidence interval varies for different sample statistics.

The Confidence Interval for a Mean

In determining the confidence interval for a mean, we must first determine the type of sampling distribution that would be formed by our samples.

Large Samples. When we base our interval estimate on the mean of a large sample ($n \geq 30$), we can assume that the distribution of sample means will be normal. When we assume that our distribution of sample means is normal, we can then use the normal curve to determine the proportion of the sample means that will fall within specified distances of the mean of the population. We know, for example, that 68 percent of the sample means will fall within 1 standard deviation above and below the population mean, and we know that 96 percent of the sample means will fall within 2 standard deviations of the population mean. Given any particular sample mean, therefore, we can determine the probability of its being within a specified distance from the mean of the population.

In constructing our confidence interval, then, we first decide upon the level of confidence in which we are interested. That is, we decide upon how much of a chance we want to take that our interval estimate will not include the population mean. We may, of course, decide upon any level of confidence that we desire. In general, however, it is customary to set our level of confidence at either .99 or .95. For purposes of illustration, therefore, let us use the 99 percent level of confidence. Assume that we have selected a sample of 100 students from an infinite population, and the mean of our sample on a particular reading test is equal to 75, with a standard deviation of 10. We know, of course, that the mean of the population is not necessarily equal to exactly 75. Assuming that our sampling distribution is normal, however, we also know, from Table C, that the probability is .99 that a sample mean of 75 is within 2.58 standard deviations of the mean of the population. That is, we know that 99 percent of the sample means are within 2.58 standard deviations of the population mean and that, consequently, we have a 99 percent chance that the particular sample mean that we have obtained will be within 2.58 standard deviations of the mean. In order to determine our confidence interval, then, we must determine the scores that are 2.58 standard deviations above and below the sample mean that we have obtained. Unfortunately, however, the only information that we have about the population is the information that can be obtained from our sample. Not only do we not know the true mean of the population, but neither do we know the standard deviation of the population. How, then, can we determine the standard deviation of the sampling distribution? In instances such as this, where we cannot compute the standard error of the mean, we can estimate the standard deviation of the sampling distribution by substituting the value of the sample standard deviation for the standard deviation of the population. The formula for the estimated standard error of the mean, then, is as indicated below.

Estimated Standard Error of the Mean, $s_{\overline{X}}$

$$s_{\overline{X}} = \frac{s}{\sqrt{n}}$$

Where s = the standard deviation of a particular sample

n = the size of the sample

Once we know how to estimate the standard error of the mean, our 99 percent confidence interval then becomes the interval that extends from the point that is 2.58 estimated standard errors of the mean below the sample mean to the point that is 2.58 estimated standard errors of the mean above. The 99 percent confidence interval for the mean may thus be expressed as follows:

$$P(\overline{X} - 2.58s_{\overline{X}} < \mu < \overline{X} + 2.58s_{\overline{X}}) = .99$$

We can similarly express the 95 percent confidence interval, the 90 percent confidence interval, or even the 80 percent confidence interval. For any specified level of confidence we determine the z values that encompass the specified proportion of sample means, and we go that many standard errors of the mean above and below the sample mean. For the 95 percent, the 90 percent, and the 80 percent confidence intervals, then, our equations are as follows.

Equations for the 95, 90, and 80 Percent Confidence Intervals

$$P(\overline{X} - 1.96s_{\overline{X}} < \mu < \overline{X} + 1.96s_{\overline{X}}) = .95$$
$$P(\overline{X} - 1.64s_{\overline{X}} < \mu < \overline{X} + 1.64s_{\overline{X}}) = .90$$
$$P(\overline{X} - 1.28s_{\overline{X}} < \mu < \overline{X} + 1.28s_{\overline{X}}) = .80$$

To illustrate the calculation of the interval estimate, now, let us return to the sample of 100 students mentioned earlier. If we want to compute the 99 percent confidence interval for the mean, this interval would extend, as indicated, from the point that is 2.58 standard errors below the sample mean to the point that is 2.58 standard errors above the sample mean. In this instance, however, since we do not know the value of σ, we must estimate the standard deviation of the sampling distribution as $s/\sqrt{n}$. In this instance, then, our confidence interval would be as follows.

Calculation of a 99 Percent Confidence Interval

Given: $\overline{X} = 75$
$s = 10$
$n = 100$

$$P\left[\overline{X} - 2.58\left(\frac{s}{\sqrt{n}}\right) < \mu < \overline{X} + 2.58\left(\frac{s}{\sqrt{n}}\right)\right] = .99$$
$$P\left[75 - 2.58\left(\frac{10}{\sqrt{100}}\right) < \mu < 75 + 2.58\left(\frac{10}{\sqrt{100}}\right)\right] = .99$$
$$P\left[75 - 2.58\left(\frac{10}{10}\right) < \mu < 75 + 2.58\left(\frac{10}{10}\right)\right] = .99$$
$$P(75 - 2.58 < \mu < 75 + 2.58) = .99$$
$$P(72.42 < \mu < 77.58) = .99$$

In interpreting our interval estimate, now, we can say that we are 99 percent sure that the population mean falls in the interval from 72.42 to 77.58. We can make this statement because we know that if we constructed confidence intervals for each of the possible sample means, 99 percent of those confidence intervals would include the population mean. Only those 1 percent of the sample means that fell further than 2.58 standard errors of the mean from the mean of the population would yield confidence intervals that did not include the actual mean of the population. Since we have a 99 percent chance of having selected one of the sample means that did fall within 2.58 standard errors of the mean, we have a 99 percent chance of including the true mean of the population within our confidence interval. Similarly, if we had constructed the 95 percent confidence interval, we would have a 95 percent chance of constructing an interval that included the true mean of the population, and if we had constructed the 90 percent confidence interval, we would have had a 90 percent chance of constructing an interval that included the mean of the population.

Note, however, that we are making certain assumptions about the sampling distribution. We are assuming, first, that the form of the sampling distribution will, indeed, be normal, and we are also assuming that the standard deviation of the sample can be substituted for the standard deviation of the population in our equation for the estimated standard error of the mean. To the extent that these assumptions may not be met, our confidence interval may be somewhat incorrect.

Small Samples. When we are estimating the population mean on the basis of the mean of a small sample, our confidence interval will be based on the *t* distribution. The formula for the confidence interval is exactly the same as for a large sample, and the standard error of the mean is again estimated by the standard deviation of the sample divided by the sample size. In determining the upper and lower limits of the confidence interval, however, we must base our distances on the *t* rather than the *z* distribution.

To illustrate the construction of a confidence interval for a small sample, let us assume that we have a sample of 16 students with a mean IQ score of 110, and a standard deviation of 8. In estimating the mean of the population from which this sample was drawn, let us construct the 95 percent confidence interval. Our first step, then, is to determine the points on the *t* distribution that encompass 95 percent of the area under the curve. Remember, however, that in order to use the *t* distribution, we must first determine the degrees of freedom that are associated with our sample size. In this instance, then, since we are dealing with a sample of 16 students, we have $n - 1$, or 15 degrees of freedom. Referring to Table D, now, we can see that for 15 degrees of freedom, 95 percent of the area falls between the points that are equal to *t* values of +2.131 and −2.131. In setting up our confidence interval, then, we know that our 95 percent confidence interval will extend from the point that is 2.13 standard errors of the mean below the sample mean to the point that is 2.13 standard errors of the mean above our sample mean. In determining the value of these points, we construct the 95 percent confidence interval as follows.

Calculating the 95 Percent Confidence Interval

Given: $\overline{X} = 110$
$$s = \quad 8$$
$$n = \quad 16$$

$$P(\overline{X} - 2.13s_{\overline{X}} < \mu < \overline{X} + 2.13s_{\overline{X}}) = .95$$

$$P\left[110 - 2.13\left(\frac{8}{\sqrt{16}}\right) < \mu < 110 + 2.13\left(\frac{8}{\sqrt{16}}\right)\right] = .95$$

$$P\left[110 - 2.13\left(\frac{8}{4}\right) < \mu < 110 + 2.13\left(\frac{8}{4}\right)\right] = .95$$

$$P(110 - 4.26 < \mu < 110 + 4.26) = .95$$

$$P(105.74 < \mu < 114.26) = .95$$

As indicated, the confidence interval extends from a score of 105.74 to a score of 114.26. In interpreting this interval, we can say that there is a 95 percent chance that the mean of the population falls between these two scores.

As you can see, the confidence interval was determined in the same manner as for a large sample. In each case, we determined the points on the appropriate theoretical distribution that cut off the percentage of the scores in which we were interested, and we went that many standard errors of the mean above and below the sample mean. The only difference is in the theoretical distribution to which we refer. For large samples, we refer to the normal distribution; for small samples, we refer to the t distribution. Following this same general method, we may similarly determine the confidence interval for a proportion.

The Confidence Interval for a Proportion

In determining the confidence interval for a proportion, we will consider only the case where the sample is large. When this is the case, as you may remember, the distribution of the sample proportions approaches normality. In determining the confidence interval for a proportion, therefore, we will refer to the normal curve. Our equation for the confidence interval is similar to that used for estimating a mean. Note, however, that we substitute the sample proportion, X/n, for the sample mean, we substitute the standard error of a proportion, $s_{X/n}$, for the standard error of the mean, and we substitute the population proportion, p, for the population mean. Our equations for the 99 and 95 percent confidence intervals are thus as follows.

The 99 and 95 Percent Confidence Intervals for a Proportion

$$P\left(\frac{X}{n} - 2.58s_{X/n} < p < \frac{X}{n} + 2.58s_{X/n}\right) = .99$$

$$P\left(\frac{X}{n} - 1.96s_{X/n} < p < \frac{X}{n} + 1.96s_{X/n}\right) = .95$$

In calculating the confidence interval for a proportion, we must again determine the z values of the points on the theoretical sampling distribution that encompass the proportion of the cases in which we are interested. The confidence interval then extends that many standard errors above and below the proportion of positive instances found in the sample. To illustrate, let us assume that we are concerned with estimating the proportion of students in a particular school district that are reading on or above grade level, and that we are basing our estimate on a sample of 50 randomly selected students. Assuming that .60 of the students in our sample are at least at grade level, we would calculate the 99 percent confidence interval as follows.

Calculating the 99 Percent Confidence Interval for a Proportion

Given: $X = 30, n = 50$

$$\frac{X}{n} = \frac{30}{50} = .6$$

$$s_{X/n} = \sqrt{\frac{(X/n)(1 - X/n)}{n}} = \sqrt{\frac{(.6)(.4)}{50}} = \sqrt{.005} = .07$$

$$P\left[\frac{X}{n} - 2.58s_{X/n} < p < \frac{X}{n} + 2.58s_{X/n}\right] = .99$$

$$P[.6 - 2.58(.07) < p < .6 + 2.58(.07)] = .99$$

$$P[.6 - .18 < p < .6 + .18] = .99$$

$$P[.42 < p < .78] = .99$$

As you can see, we estimate the standard error, $s_{X/n}$, from the characteristics of the sample that was selected, and we then construct the confidence interval to extend 2.58 standard errors above and below the sample proportion. Our 99 percent confidence interval for this sample thus extends from a proportion of .42 to a proportion of .78. We can say, therefore, that the probability is .99 that the proportion of students in the population who are reading on or above grade level is between .42 and .78. We also know, however, that our sample may not be representative of the population, and that the true proportion of such students in the population may not lie within these limits.

As you can see, we can never assume that the characteristics of a sample will be the same as the characteristics of the population from which the sample came. Yet even though our inferences may not be correct, practical considerations force us to rely on sample information. In view of what we know, then, we must be very careful not to overestimate the accuracy of our statistics. Assume, for example, that the mean IQ score of the general population is equal to 100, and we want to know whether the children from one particular ethnic group are above or below average. If we take a random sample of children from the ethnic group in question, and we find that the mean IQ score of this sample is only equal to 95, we must be very careful not to automatically assume that the population of such children is below the general norm. If we constructed a confidence interval for the mean of the minority group, the interval might very well extend above the score that is the mean of the general population, leaving us with the possibility that the mean of the minority population is, in fact, higher than that of the general population.

Similarly, if a random sample of students from two schools have been given an achievement test, and the mean score of one of the samples is 8 points higher than that of the other, we cannot jump to the conclusion that the level of achievement in one of the schools is actually higher than the level of achievement in the other. Before we rush to condemn either the students or the teachers, we must question whether, in fact, the difference wasn't merely due to sampling error. That is, even though the level of achievement may have been identical in the two schools, we may, just by chance, have picked a low sample from one of the schools and a high sample from the other. Many people erroneously assume that as long as our samples are randomly selected, there is no chance for this type of error. We must remember, however, that random sampling merely eliminates bias and does not assure us, even if we select our samples from the same population, that the samples will be equivalent.

When we use the difference between two sample statistics to infer a difference in the populations from which the samples came, we must be very sure that the difference between the samples is large enough so that it is not merely the result of sampling error. How large a difference is sufficient depends on how sure we want to be.

Consider, for example, the ethnic samples mentioned previously. If we construct confidence intervals for each of our sample statistics, we might see that the intervals overlapped to a very great extent. The greater this overlap, the more likely it is that the samples were drawn from equivalent populations. If the mean of the first sample was equal to 80, for example, and the mean of the other was equal to 88, we might find that the 95 percent confidence interval for the first sample extends from 70 to 90, while the 95 percent confidence interval for the second sample extends from 78 to 98. Even though the mean of the second sample is higher than that of the first sample, we have no assurance that the mean of the population from which the first sample came isn't as high as 89. Since the confidence intervals overlap, and the confidence interval for the mean of the lower group extends beyond the sample mean of the higher group, we cannot be sure that, in fact, the poorer sample does not come from a higher achieving population. If the confidence intervals did not overlap, of course, we would be more certain that the populations did actually differ in the same way as the samples. Even then, however, we must remember that there is a chance that the population mean was not included within the confidence interval.

As you can see, then, our confidence intervals provide us with some indication of whether or not we can assume that sample differences do, in fact, reflect real differences in the population. As we progress to the area of hypothesis testing, we must keep these considerations in mind. Almost all hypotheses are tested with sample data and, as you will see, our acceptance or rejection of hypotheses depends on the size of the difference between the sample values that are obtained and the values that were hypothesized.

PRACTICE PROBLEMS

1. The following scores were obtained by a population of students on a midterm examination:

Student	Score
Alice	90
Bob	85
Charles	80
David	80
Edward	75
Francine	70

   a. List all possible samples of two students that could be selected from the population, and find each of the sample means.
   b. List all possible samples of five students that could be selected from the population, and find each of the sample means.
   c. Find the standard error of the mean for each of the sampling distributions. Which is larger? Why? What does this tell you about the relationship between sample size and errors of estimation?
2. If you were sampling from a normal distribution, and you could assume that the distribution of sample means would also be normal, what proportion of your samples would have means that fell:
   a. Above the point where $z = +1.88$.
   b. Below the point where $z = -1.88$.
   c. Between the points where $z = +1.88$ and -1.88.
   d. Below the point where $z = -1.25$.
   e. Above the point where $z = +2.58$.
   f. Between the points where $z = +2.33$ and $+2.58$.
   g. Between the points where $z = -2.58$ and -2.13.
3. In a Student's (t) distribution, what value of t would cut off the upper 5 percent of the curve when the sample size is equal to 10? to 15? to 30?

4. Given the following sample data, find the 95 and 99 percent confidence intervals for the mean.
   a. $\bar{X} = 50, s = 4, n = 16$.
   b. $\bar{X} = 50, s = 4, n = 36$.
   c. $\bar{X} = 80, s = 5, n = 100$.
   d. $\bar{X} = 60, s = 10, n = 64$.

5. Given the following sample data, find the 99 and 95 percent confidence intervals for the population proportions.
   a. $X/n = .6, n = 30$.
   b. $X/n = .3, n = 50$.
   c. $X/n = .4, n = 30$.

HYPOTHESIS TESTING 9

Now that we have considered the problems involved in sampling and estimation, it is time to apply this knowledge to the testing of hypotheses. When one refers to an hypothesis, one is referring to a statement about reality that may or may not be true. In the field of education, for example, one might want to determine the tenability of statements concerning the relative effectiveness of different teaching methods, or statements about the ability of different students. In order to determine the truth of the statement, one must gather evidence and, in view of this evidence, evaluate the tenability of the hypothesis. If the evidence contradicts the hypothesis, it must be rejected. If the evidence is consistent with the hypothesis, it will be retained. To retain an hypothesis, however, is not to say that the hypothesis can be accepted as true. As you will see, our data will never be sufficient to prove the truth of an hypothesis. We will be dealing with probabilities. Based on the probability of obtaining a particular set of data if, in fact, the hypothesis is true, we will decide either to reject or not to reject the hypothesis in question. To illustrate this point, let us now consider a specific hypothesis that might come up in a school setting.

As you may know, the trend in many schools is toward individualized instruction. There are still many educators, however, who question whether individualization is really any more effective for the attainment of curricular goals than are the traditional methods. To shed light on the issue, therefore, one might want to test the hypothesis that traditional and individualized instruction both yield equivalent levels of achievement. In order to test this hypothesis, one would first determine what type of evidence is needed, and then devise a method of collecting the data. For example, half the students in each class could be randomly chosen to receive individualized instruction for one academic year. Then, at the end of the year, the achievement level of the students who received individualized instruction could be compared to that of the students who were taught by the traditional methods. Assume, now, that this experiment was carried out with the following results.

Arithmetic Scores of Students Receiving Individualized and Traditional Instruction

Type of Instruction	Mean Score	Standard Deviation
Individual	83	5
Traditional	80	5

What does this evidence indicate? The mean score of the individualized group is obviously higher than that of the traditional group. One must remember, however, that the groups receiving each type of instruction were randomly chosen samples from a population of students and, as you know, the mean of a sample is not necessarily the same as the mean of the population from which it comes. One must question, therefore, whether this 3-point difference between our two sample means reflects a real difference in the population. We can never know for sure, but in order to help us come to a reasonable decision, we can determine the probability of obtaining these sample results if, in fact, our hypothesis about the population were true. If this probability is high, we would conclude that the evidence does not warrant rejection of our hypothesis. If this probability is low, we would reject the hypothesis in favor of an alternative. In this example, then, we would not reject the hypothesis of equivalence unless it could be shown that a 3-point difference between our sample means would be highly improbable if, in fact, the two methods of instruction were equivalent.

The question may now arise, however, as to how we can determine the probability of obtaining a particular set of results. It is in order to answer this question that we use test statistics in evaluating our sample data. Once we know the theoretical sampling distribution of the values of a statistic, we can then specify the probability of obtaining the particular value that our data yield. When we test an hypothesis, therefore, we must determine an appropriate test statistic, and we must specify the probability of obtaining the value of the statistic that our data yield. Then, in view of this information, we make our decision as to the tenability of our hypothesis. Before we can proceed with these steps, however, we must formulate our hypothesis in statistical terms.

Formulating a Statistical Hypothesis

When formulating an hypothesis to be tested, there are two requirements that must be met. Since our hypotheses are usually statements about populations, our first requirement is that they be stated in terms of a population parameter such as μ or σ. Once the relevant population parameter has been identified, the second requirement is that the hypothesis be exact, that is, that it specify an exact value for the population parameter.

To illustrate, let us consider again the hypothesis concerning the relative merits of traditional and individualized arithmetic instruction, and let us again measure the effects of these different methods by comparing the mean score of the two groups of students on an arithmetic test. In terms of the statistics that will be compared, the hypothesis to be tested is that the mean score of the students receiving individualized instruction will be the same as that of those students receiving traditional instruction. Note, however, that our concern is not only with those students involved in the study, but with the effect of these different methods of instruction on any students that may be exposed to them. Consequently, the hypothesis to be tested is not that the sample means will be equal, but that the population means will be equal. We will have only sample data, of course, but since we will use these data to make inferences about the population, our hypothesis must be stated in terms of μ. In statistical form, our hypothesis would be as follows:

$H_0 : \mu_1 = \mu_2$

or

$H_0 : \mu_1 - \mu_2 = 0$

Where H_0 is read as "the hypothesis to be tested"

$\mu_1 =$ the population mean for students receiving individualized instruction

$\mu_2 =$ the population mean for students receiving traditional instruction.

Note that although the hypothesis is stated in two ways, both the first and the second forms are stated in terms of the population parameter, μ. The second formulation states that the difference between μ_1 and μ_2 will be equal to zero. Obviously, this difference will be zero only if, as stated in the first formulation, μ_1 is exactly equal to μ_2. Both the first and the second forms are equivalent, and either form may be used. It is important to recognize both forms, however, since both may appear in the literature.

Note, now, that not only does this hypothesis make a statement about a population, but it specifies an exact value for the population parameter. It specifies that μ_1 is exactly equal to μ_2. Similarly, the hypothesis would also be exact if it specified an exact numerical value for the population parameter. The hypothesis that μ is equal to 80, for example, is exact in that it specifies that μ must be exactly equal to 80. Neither the hypothesis that μ is greater than 80, or the hypothesis that the mean for individualized instruction will be higher than that for traditional instruction is a specific hypothesis, and neither may be formulated as an hypothesis to be tested. Let us now consider why this is the case.

In deciding whether or not to reject our hypothesis, we examine sample data. Assume, for example, that we were testing the hypothesis that the mean score on a test is equal to 80. We know, of course, that even if μ is equal to 80, the mean of our sample would not necessarily have exactly this value.

Since we assume that the sample means are normally distributed around μ, however, we could give the probability of obtaining any particular sample mean. We know that if μ were equal to 80, for example, a sample mean of 82 would be considerably more likely than a sample mean of 92. What we do, therefore, is specify what range of values would be probable if our hypothesis were true. Then only if our sample mean falls outside this range, would the hypothesis be rejected. In order to specify a range of probable values, however, we must hypothesize a specific value for μ. If our hypothesis was that μ is not equal to 80, then an infinite number of values could satisfy the hypothesis. If this were the case, however, we could not define a specific range of values outside of which we would reject the hypothesis. In order to define this range of values, then, we must have an exact hypothesis.

This exact hypothesis is often referred to as the *null hypothesis,* or the hypothesis of no difference. Consider, for example, our hypothesis about the difference between individualized and traditional teaching instruction. As stated earlier, the hypothesis to be tested was that $\mu_1 = \mu_2$. In other words, it was hypothesized that any difference between the two groups of students would be due not to real differences in the effectiveness of the different teaching methods but to sampling error. Similarly, if one has formulated the hypothesis that μ is equal to a specific value, one is hypothesizing that any difference between the sample mean and the value hypothesized for μ can be attributed to sampling error. In both of these cases, if the difference found is within the range of values that can reasonably be expected to occur as a result of sampling error, the hypothesis would not be rejected. It would be rejected only if the difference is so large as to be unlikely if the sample means do, in fact, come from the population as specified. The hypothesis to be tested is referred to as the *null hypothesis,* therefore, because it states that the difference between one's sample statistic and the hypothesized value of the population parameter is "null."

There are times, however, when an experimenter does not believe that the null hypothesis is true. Furthermore, although we need an exact hypothesis in order to perform a statistical test, most hypotheses arising in the field of education are not exact. A teacher may hypothesize that one teaching method is better than another, or that some children will show better test performance than others. One rarely hypothesizes exactly how much better one method will be than another, or exactly how much difference in performance will be found between two groups of students. Since inexact hypotheses cannot be specified as null hypotheses, however, most null hypotheses do not represent the hypothesis that is believed to be true. Instead, one poses the hypothesis he believes to be true as an alternative to an opposing null hypothesis. Consider, for example, the hypothesis that individualized instruction leads to higher achievement than does traditional instruction. Stated in statistical form, we have:

$$H_a: \mu_1 > \mu_2$$

or

$$H_a: \mu_1 - \mu_2 > 0$$

Where H_a is read as "the alternative hypothesis"

μ_1 = the population mean for students receiving individualized instruction

μ_2 = the population mean for students receiving traditional instruction.

Note first that this hypothesis is stated as an alternative rather than as a null hypothesis. The reason for this is that the hypothesis is not exact. However, as with a null hypothesis, the alternative is stated in terms of a population parameter, and it may be stated in either of the two ways illustrated above. As stated, however, this hypothesis cannot be directly tested. In order to test an hypothesis, we must be able to identify those values of the statistic that would be improbable if the hypothesis were true. Since we have not stated how much greater than μ_2 we expect μ_1 to be, we have no way of finding the probability of obtaining a difference of any particular size. What we must do, therefore, is formulate an exact hypothesis against which our belief may be tested. Then, if the exact hypothesis is rejected, our alternative may be accepted in its place.

In formulating this exact hypothesis, we first ask what possibilities would remain if our alternative were false. Then, from among these possibilities, we choose an exact hypothesis. In this example, for instance, we would ask what possibilities would remain if μ_1, the mean of the individualized group, were not greater than μ_2, the mean for the traditional group. Obviously, if μ_1 is not greater than μ_2, then either (1) μ_1 is equal to μ_2, or (2) μ_1 is less than μ_2. Since (2) is exact, this would be our test hypothesis. In testing this hypothesis, however, we must remember that our primary concern is whether or not this hypothesis may be rejected in favor of the alternative in which we are interested. In evaluating the test hypothesis, then, we limit the values that would lead to rejection. These values are limited so that the test hypothesis will be rejected only if the difference between the groups fell in the direction specified by the alternative.

To illustrate, let us consider the theoretical sampling distribution of the difference between two means. As illustrated in Figure 9.1, we have a z-distribution, where values to the right represent values of z such that μ_1 is greater than μ_2. In testing the hypothesis that $\mu_1 = \mu_2$, we would reject the hypothesis if our sample means were such that the value of z was highly improbable. These improbable values are referred to as the rejection region, and are illustrated in Figure 9.1.

As you can see the rejection region is divided into two parts. When we test an hypothesis against a rejection region of this type, we say that we have a

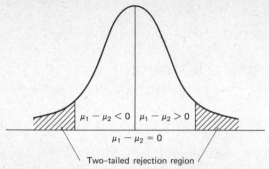

Figure 9.1. Theoretical sampling distribution of the difference between two means.

two-tailed test. If the value of our test statistic fell in either of these areas, the null hypothesis would be rejected. That is, we would reject the hypothesis that the performance of the two groups was equivalent, and we would conclude that there is a difference between them. Merely knowing that the hypothesis was rejected, however, we would not know in which direction the difference fell. In order to support the alternative that not only are μ_1 and μ_2 unequal, but μ_1 is greater than μ_2, we would have to know specifically that the value of the test statistic fell in the right-hand tail of the distribution. What we must do, therefore, is to limit the rejection region. That is, we must specify that the null hypothesis will be rejected only if the sample means are such that the value of the test statistic falls in the right-hand tail of the distribution. With this limitation, then, we know that if the null hypothesis is rejected, we have evidence for the alternative that μ_1 is greater than μ_2.

To review, then, we have limited the values that will lead to rejection of the null hypothesis. The rejection region was defined such that the null hypothesis would be rejected only if the values of the sample means fell in the direction specified in our alternative. Such a procedure is referred to as a *one-tailed test* and, as you can see in Figure 9.2, the rejection region has been limited to the area in only one tail of the distribution. Although results in the opposite direction are equally improbable, such results would not lead to rejection of the null hypothesis because of the way in which we have defined the rejection region. It should be noted that the rejection region may be in either tail of the distribution. The rejection region was placed in the right-hand tail in our illustration merely because we wished to reject the null hypothesis only if the mean of the individualized group was higher than that of the traditional group. If we were interested in the alternative that the mean of the individualized group was *lower* than that of the traditional group, we would have put the rejection region in the left-hand tail. It is the alternative, therefore, that determines where the rejection region will be. In whichever

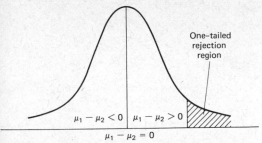

One-tailed
rejection
region

$\mu_1 - \mu_2 < 0$ | $\mu_1 - \mu_2 > 0$

$\mu_1 - \mu_2 = 0$

Figure 9.2. One-tailed rejection region for testing $H_0 : \mu_1 = \mu_2$ against $H_a : \mu_1 > \mu_2$

tail the rejection region lies, however, values of the test statistic falling in the rejection region lead us to reject the null hypothesis in favor of the alternative.

When we have a one-tailed rejection region, then, rejection of the null hypothesis leads to the acceptance of a directional alternative, that is, an alternative that states in which direction the difference will lie. It must be noted, however, that the null hypothesis will be retained not only when the hypothesis of no difference is tenable, but when the difference is in the direction opposite to that specified in the alternative. Retention of the hypothesis of no difference, therefore, does not mean that we have evidence that no difference exists. A decision to retain the null hypothesis merely means that the evidence was not sufficient to warrant acceptance of the alternative against which the hypothesis was tested. Thus when we have a one-tailed test, the null hypothesis is sometimes stated in an inexact fashion. When this is the case, the form of the null hypothesis is determined by the alternative against which it is being tested. To illustrate, several hypotheses are given with their respective alternatives and rejection regions in Figure 9.3. As illustrated in examples 2 and 3, the null hypothesis may state that μ_1 is not only equal to μ_2, but that it is larger or smaller. In other words, the form of the hypothesis indicates that the null hypothesis will be retained not only if no difference exists, but also if a difference exists in the direction opposite to that specified in the alternative.

It is important to note that even though the null hypothesis is sometimes written in this inexact form when we have a directional alternative, it is actually an exact hypothesis. It is an exact hypothesis because we define a theoretical sampling distribution according to an exact value that is hypothesized for the population parameter. In the example cited, for instance, the theoretical sampling distribution was based on the exact hypothesis that $\mu_1 = \mu_2$. It was this hypothesis that was being tested; it was stated in an inexact form only because we had decided to do a one-tailed test.

Test (null) hypothesis	Alternative hypothesis	Rejection region

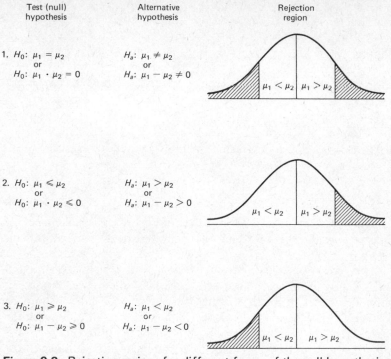

1. $H_0: \mu_1 = \mu_2$
   or
   $H_0: \mu_1 \cdot \mu_2 = 0$

   $H_a: \mu_1 \neq \mu_2$
   or
   $H_a: \mu_1 - \mu_2 \neq 0$

   $\mu_1 < \mu_2$ $\mu_1 > \mu_2$

2. $H_0: \mu_1 \leq \mu_2$
   or
   $H_0: \mu_1 \cdot \mu_2 \leq 0$

   $H_a: \mu_1 > \mu_2$
   or
   $H_a: \mu_1 - \mu_2 > 0$

   $\mu_1 < \mu_2$ $\mu_1 > \mu_2$

3. $H_0: \mu_1 \geq \mu_2$
   or
   $H_0: \mu_1 - \mu_2 \geq 0$

   $H_a: \mu_1 < \mu_2$
   or
   $H_a: \mu_1 - \mu_2 < 0$

   $\mu_1 < \mu_2$ $\mu_1 > \mu_2$

Figure 9.3. Rejection regions for different forms of the null hypothesis.

Choosing the Test Statistic

Once we have formulated the null and alternative hypotheses, our next step is to select the appropriate test statistic. As with the descriptive statistics that we have already considered, test statistics tell us something about a set of numbers. In this case, however, the numbers we are concerned with are usually statistics themselves. Consider, for example, the question of whether a 10-point difference between the means of two groups receiving different methods of instruction is large enough for us to conclude that the two methods have different effects on the population. By using a test statistic, we can determine the probability of obtaining this large a difference between our sample means if, in fact, no difference exists in the population. The value of our test statistic is computed from the sample data collected. Then a probability table, based on the theoretical sampling distribution of the statistic, may be checked in order to determine the probability of obtaining the value in question. When we are concerned with comparing a sample mean with an hypothesized population mean, for instance, our test statistic may be z. We would thus compute the value of z as indicated in Chapter 8, and then check this value against the values in Table C. If z was equal to 2.33, we would know that, if the population was as hypothesized, the probability of obtaining the particular sample mean in question would be less than .01. Similarly, if we were concerned with comparing two sample means, our test statistic might be *t*. In this case we would compute the value of *t*, and check this value against the values in Table D.

We will not at this point go into the problem of selecting the appropriate test statistic. Let it suffice to say that this is a critical step in the testing of hypotheses, and it will be considered more fully in subsequent chapters. At this time, however, we must consider how to determine the values of the test statistic that will lead to rejection of the null hypothesis.

Specifying the Rejection Region

We have stated that the null hypothesis is to be rejected if the value of the test statistic would be highly unlikely if the null hypothesis were true. But how unlikely is unlikely?

The answer to this question is, of course, a matter of judgment. One must make an arbitrary decision as to what probability of occurrence represents unlikelihood. In the field of education, for example, it is conventional to consider an event unlikely if the probability of its occurrence, depending upon the situation, is less than either .05 or .01. The level of probability that one chooses as representing an unlikely event is referred to as the *level of significance* or *alpha,* and the value of alpha determines the proportion of the values in a theoretical sampling distribution that will lie in the rejection region. If alpha is equal to .01, for example, then 1 percent of the values will lie in the rejection region. Similarly, if alpha is equal to .05, then 5 percent of the values will lie in the rejection region. If we have a one-tailed test, these values will all lie in one tail of the distribution. With a two-tailed test, however, half of the critical values will fall in each of the tails.

To illustrate the relationship between the level of alpha and the size of the rejection region, let us consider the hypothesis that μ, the mean on a particular arithmetic test, is equal to 100. In testing this hypothesis, we compute the mean score of a sample of students on the test, and we then determine the difference, if any, between the sample mean and the hypothesized value of μ. If a difference did exist, we would then determine the probability of obtaining such a difference if, in fact, no real difference existed in the population. This probability would be determined from the theoretical sampling distribution of the mean and, depending upon whether we used a one- or a two-tailed test, the rejection region for our different levels of alpha would be as indicated in Figure 9.4.

Comparing the rejection regions where alpha equals .05 and where alpha equals .01, you can see that as alpha increases, the rejection region increases. That is, as we increase alpha, we increase the probability of rejecting the null

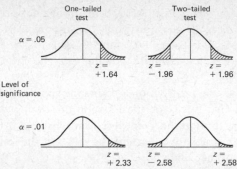

Figure 9.4. Rejection regions for a one- and a two-tailed test at the .01 and .05 levels of significance.

hypothesis. This relationship exists regardless of whether we use a one- or a two-tailed test. For a given level of alpha, however, a two-tailed test is the more stringent test of the alternative. With alpha equal to .05, a two-tailed test of our hypothesis would require that the sample mean be at least 1.96 standard errors from the hypothesized value of μ before the null hypothesis could be rejected in favor of the alternative. With a one-tailed test at the same level of alpha, however, the null hypothesis could be rejected when the sample mean is only 1.64 standard errors from the hypothesized value of μ. One can see, then, that with a two-tailed test, a more extreme value of the sample mean is needed before the alternative can be accepted. At a given level of alpha, therefore, a directional alternative that is correct has a better chance of being accepted when a one-tailed test is used.

However, even though a one-tailed test has more power to detect a correct directional alternative, a one-tailed test does not have the power to detect differences in the opposite direction. For example, consider the one-tailed test of the hypothesis that $\mu = 100$ against the alternative that $\mu > 100$. With alpha equal to .05, we would reject the null hypothesis only for values of our sample mean that were equal to or greater than 1.64 standard errors above 100. For all values of the sample mean that were lower than 100, regardless of how low they might be, the null hypothesis would be retained. That is, the null hypothesis would be retained not only if the mean of the sample was equal to 100, but even if it was as low as 50. When one is considering whether to use a one- or two-tailed test, then, one must first decide how important it is to detect differences in the direction opposite to those hypothesized. If it is important to detect such differences, a two-tailed test must be used. If one is concerned only with detecting differences in the hypothesized direction, however, a one-tailed test will suffice. Remember though, that the decision as to whether to use a one- or two-tailed test must be made before the sample data is evaluated. It is unacceptable to wait and see where the sample value falls, and then decide upon a one-tailed test

Similarly, one must also decide upon the level of alpha before the sample data is evaluated. After it has become apparent that the alternative will be rejected if alpha is equal to .01, it is unacceptable to change alpha to .05. The stringency of the test must be decided upon before the data are evaluated.

In deciding upon the stringency of the test, one must remember that as the rejection region increases, so does the probability of incorrectly rejecting the null hypothesis. That is, even if the null hypothesis is correct, increasing alpha increases the number of values that will lead us to reject this hypothesis. Therefore, in deciding upon our level of significance, we must consider the risk involved in making an error of this nature. Consider a new drug that has been found to be very effective in curing a disease, but which is suspected to have serious side effects. If another equally effective drug is on the market, and this other drug is known to produce these side effects in 30 percent of the patients to which it is administered, then it is of utmost importance to determine whether the new drug effectively reduces the frequency of these side effects. In a one-tailed test of the hypothesis that the new drug has a lower frequency of side effects, the specific null hypothesis would be that p, the proportion of patients in which these side effects are detected, is more than or equal to .30. If this null hypothesis is rejected, the new drug will be assumed to produce these side effects in less than .30 of the patients, and the new drug will then be introduced for use. In this instance, then, one can see that it is very important that the null hypothesis not be rejected unless one is quite certain that the alternative is true. It would be fatal to make the error of using the new drug if, in fact, it produces serious side effects more often than the drug already in use. In situations of this sort, then, one would keep alpha very low. In situations where the consequences of falsely rejecting the null hypothesis are not quite as serious, one can use a higher level of significance.

In the field of education, the risks of rejecting a true hypothesis may not at first seem as serious as in the field of medicine. Serious illness or fatality is certainly not one of the risks that are likely to be involved in the false rejection of an educational hypothesis. Nevertheless, the false rejection of a new teaching method can mean the difference between academic success and failure for many students, and the false rejection of a new diagnostic technique may mean that many children who could be performing better are denied this chance of success because their problems could not be identified. Even in the field of education, then, serious risks may be involved in the rejection of a true hypothesis and, as in all areas of hypothesis testing, these risks must be considered when one decides upon the level of alpha.

There is, of course, no objective way of determining what level of significance to use. This decision is a value judgment that is based on the risks involved if an error is made. Before considering the risks involved, however, one must consider the types of error that can occur. Assume that we are testing the hypothesis that individualized instruction results in superior

Decisions	Conditions	
	H_0 is true	H_a is true
Reject H_0	I	III
Do not reject H_0	IV	II

I Reject H_0 when it is true—Type I error.
II Do not reject H_0 when H_a is true—Type II error.
III Reject H_0 when H_0 is false—Correct decision.
IV Do not reject H_0 when H_0 is true—Correct decision.

Figure 9.5. Possible outcomes in testing an hypothesis.

achievement than does traditional instruction, and that we are testing this hypothesis against the alternative that the two methods are equivalent. In testing this hypothesis, there are four possible outcomes, as illustrated in Figure 9.5.

As you can see, there are two types of errors that can occur. One can reject the null hypothesis when it is true, or one can fail to reject it when it is false. The first type of error is generally called either a Type I or an alpha error, and it is more likely to occur when alpha is relatively large. The second type of error is referred to as either a Type II or a beta error, and it is more likely to occur when alpha is relatively small. In determining the level of alpha, therefore, one must consider which type of error would have the more serious consequences. If an alpha error would be more serious, then alpha must be kept low at the expense of increasing the probability of a beta error. If the consequences of a beta error would be more serious, then it is advisable to increase alpha.

Consider a test designed to identify children in need of remedial instruction in reading. If we already have a test that is efficient in identifying children with reading difficulties, we would be reluctant to change to a new test unless we were certain that the new test was superior. Assume that the currently used test is known, on the average, to identify 80 percent of the children with reading difficulties, while it is claimed that the new test can identify 99 percent of these children. We would prefer to use the more efficient test, of course, but only if we were certain that the increase in efficiency was as great as was claimed. In order to determine whether the test is really this good, we might test the following hypothesis:

$H_0 : p = .80$

$H_a : p > .80$ where p represents the proportion of students with reading difficulties identified by the new test

In this case, we would reject the null hypothesis and adopt the new test only if the proportion of students identified by the new test is significantly higher than 80 percent. Although we certainly do not want to reject the new test if, in fact, it does a better job of identifying students with reading difficulties, neither do we want to go through all the bother and expense of changing tests if the new one is really not much better than the old one. In deciding upon alpha, then, we must weigh the cost involved in needlessly changing tests against the cost of rejecting a test that really is superior. Again, there is no objective way of deciding on alpha, but most people would probably agree that, in a situation of this type, we want to keep alpha quite low. The reason for this decision is that the gains from the new test, even if it is as efficient as claimed, would not be very great; moreover, a good deal of expense would be involved if the new test was to be adopted. One might argue that adopting a measure that would help even a few students is worth the cost, but one must remember that as we increase alpha, we increase the risk of rejecting a test that may, in fact, be no less efficient than the new one. Furthermore, one must consider that the expense involved in a change may result in reduced efficiency in other areas.

Let us consider, however, a slightly different situation. Assume, now, that the old test was not very efficient at all and, as a matter of fact, was much more time-consuming and expensive than the new one. In this case, the risks involved in adopting the new test, even if it is not quite as good as claimed, would not be that great. In this instance, then, we can afford to increase the risk of falsely rejecting the old test, and we may therefore increase alpha.

As you can see, the cost involved in both a Type I and a Type II error must be considered before the alpha level is set. The greater the cost of falsely rejecting the null hypothesis, the lower alpha should be. One must remember, though, that as alpha decreases, so does the risk that we will falsely reject a true alternative.

Evaluating the Results

Once we have defined alpha, we can then go on to define the rejection region and evaluate the results of the statistical test. Assume, for example, that we have a group of culturally deprived youngsters who have been exposed to a preschool enrichment program. If we know that the average IQ score for youngsters from deprived homes is equal to 90, we might want to test the hypothesis that exposure to preschool enrichment will raise these scores. In order to test this hypothesis, we would test the null hypothesis that the mean score is equal to 90 against the alternative that it is greater than 90. If we are concerned only with detecting increases in the mean score of the youngsters, we would have a one-tailed test where the null hypothesis would be rejected for values of $\overline{X}$ significantly higher than 90. Using z as our test statistic, our theoretical sampling distribution is shown in Figure 9.6. In order to determine what values of $\overline{X}$ will fall in the rejection region, we refer to the level of alpha. If alpha is set at .05, the null hypothesis will be rejected for all

Figure 9.6. Rejection region for a one-tailed test with α = .05 and α = .01.

values of $\overline{X}$ falling in the upper 5 percent of the distribution. That is, any value of $\overline{X}$ that would yield a z greater than or equal to +1.68 would lead us to reject the null hypothesis. If alpha is equal to .01, then the null hypothesis will be rejected for all values of $\overline{X}$ such that z would be greater than or equal to +2.33.

Assume, for example, that $\overline{X}$ is such that z is equal to +2.00. If alpha is set at .05, we reject the null hypothesis and conclude that preschool enrichment does serve to raise IQ scores. Note, however, that if alpha is equal to .01, the null hypothesis is retained. With alpha equal to .01, the critical value of z is +2.33, and a z of +2.00 would not lie in the rejection region. It is the level of alpha, therefore, that determines whether the sample value is sufficiently high to warrant rejection of the null hypothesis. Given the same sample mean, the decision will vary for different values of alpha. Note, however, that given the same value of alpha, the decision may not be the same for a one- and a two-tailed test.

Consider testing the same hypothesis with a two-tailed test. In this case, the rejection region is as illustrated in Figure 9.7. Note that if alpha is equal to .05, then 2.5 percent of the area must lie in each tail of the distribution. That is, the area in both rejection regions must sum to 5 percent. With a two-tailed test, therefore, the critical value of z will not be the same as for a one-tailed test. If alpha were set at .05, the critical values of z for a two-tailed test would be +1.96 and −1.96. Whereas a z of +1.68 would lead us to reject the hypothesis with a one-tailed test, this value of z would not be in the rejection region for a two-tailed test. As you can see, then, the decision to reject the null hypothesis is dependent upon both the level of alpha and the type of test. It is not until the type of test and level of significance have been decided upon that we can evaluate the sample data and make a decision as to the fate of the null hypothesis.

Once the decision to reject or not to reject a null hypothesis is made, however, the task of interpretation still lies ahead. What does it mean if we do not reject the null hypothesis? We cannot say that the null hypothesis is true; we can merely state that the evidence was not sufficient to prove its falsity. And what if the null hypothesis is rejected? Can we then state that it is false? No, we can merely state that, in light of the evidence, it is not likely to be true. Even if an hypothesis is unlikely, however, there is still the chance that it may be true. What does it mean, therefore, when someone states that the results of a statistical test are significant?

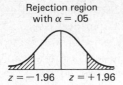
Rejection region
with α = .05

$z = -1.96 \quad z = +1.96$

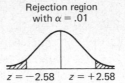
Rejection region
with α = .01

$z = -2.58 \quad z = +2.58$

Figure 9.7. Rejection region for a two-tailed test with α = .01 and α = .05.

When reading journal articles, one often sees statements that the value of a statistic is significant at a specified level of alpha. One may state that z is significant at the .01 level, or that t is significant at the .05 level of significance. To state that a value is statistically significant means merely that this value would be highly improbable if, in fact, the hypothesis being tested were true. To state that a value is significant at the .01 level of alpha means that, if the hypothesis being tested were true, this value would be expected to occur less than 1 percent of the time. Statements of statistical significance, therefore, are statements of probability. Statistical tests provide a uniform procedure by which we may determine the probability of an hypothesis being true. Our decisions are based on probabilities, and they may be wrong. The use of a uniform procedure, however, lessens the chance of bias and provides a common basis for evaluating the tenability of our hypotheses. Note, though, that to state that our results are *statistically* significant is not to state that our results have *educational* significance. The judgment of educational significance is a more subjective decision and must be left to the individual practitioner.

To review, then, hypothesis testing is a procedure whereby one determines the probability of obtaining a particular value for a sample statistic if, in fact, a specified hypothesis about the population is true. If the value of the sample statistic lies within the specified range of probable values, the hypothesis is retained. If the value is not within this range of probable values, the hypothesis is rejected.

This procedure provides a method for evaluating the tenability of educational hypotheses. Knowledge of this procedure provides the teacher with the tools to evaluate hypotheses proposed either by himself or by others in the field. Furthermore, this knowledge enables the teacher to more critically read the research reported in the educational journals. If a research article reports that one method of instruction was shown to be significantly better than another at the .05 level of significance, the teacher may question the significance of these results. He may ask why the level of significance was set at 5 instead of 1 percent. Was it because the risks involved warranted a less stringent test? Or was it because significance could not be obtained if alpha was equal to 1 percent? Was the hypothesis tested by a one- or a two-tailed test? Was the test appropriate? Were the results interpreted properly? Or were statements made that were not supported by the data? These are some of the questions that a critical reader of the journals might raise.

One might also question whether the appropriate statistical test was used. It is obviously impossible to examine the entire range of statistical tests in a text of this nature. In the following chapters, however, we deal with those statistical tests that are most commonly used. For each statistical test, two factors will be examined: (1) the appropriateness of the test for different types of educational hypotheses; and (2) the interpretation of the test results.

PRACTICE PROBLEMS

1. Formulate an appropriate null and alternative hypothesis for each of the following studies:
   a. A study to determine whether the mean age of puberty is higher than 13.
   b. A study to determine whether there is any difference between girls and boys on the Scholastic Aptitude Test.
   c. A study to determine whether students who are in special honors sections do better than students of equal ability who are in regular classes.

   Specify your reasons for choosing a directional or nondirectional test.
2. If you were going to test each of the hypotheses specified in Problem 1, would you set your level of alpha at .01 or .05? Would your level of alpha be the same for each of the hypotheses? Why?
3. If you were testing a null hypothesis against a nondirectional alternative at the .01 level of significance, what would be the critical value of z? Would a z of $+2.63$ fall in the rejection region? A z of -2.63?
4. If you were testing the alternative hypothesis that μ_1 is greater than μ_2, what would be the critical value of z at the .05 level of significance? What values of z would fall in the rejection region?
5. Which of the following is the most stringent test of an alternative hypothesis?
   a. A two-tailed test at the .01 level of significance.
   b. A two-tailed test at the .05 level of significance.
   c. A one-tailed test at the .01 level of significance.
   d. A one-tailed test at the .05 level of significance.

TESTING 10
HYPOTHESES
ABOUT PROPORTIONS

When we wish to test an hypothesis, the test statistic that we use is determined by the nature of the hypothesis. For example, we use a different test statistic to test the hypothesis that 30 percent of our high school seniors are accepted by the college of their choice than for the hypothesis that the mean score on the Scholastic Aptitude Test is equal to 500. In the first instance, we are making an hypothesis about a proportion; in the second, we are hypothesizing about a mean. The first step in selecting our test statistic, then, is to determine the population parameter in which we are interested.

Once the parameter has been identified, we must then consider the number of samples that are being examined. If we wanted to test the hypothesis that 40 percent of qualified females go to graduate school, for example, we use one test; to test the hypothesis that a higher proportion of boys than of girls go to graduate school, we use a different test. In the first instance, we are concerned with a single population, a population of girls, and our test would compare a single sample proportion to the hypothesized population proportion. In the second case, however, we are concerned with two populations, a population of boys and a population of girls, and samples selected from each of these separate populations would be compared to each other. Furthermore, regardless of the hypothesis, a small sample would necessitate the use of a different test statistic than would a large sample.

Before we can test our hypothesis, then, we must consider three things: (1) the population parameter about which we are hypothesizing, (2) the number of samples that will be examined, and (3) the size of the sample. Keeping these factors in mind, let us now consider the appropriate test statistics for hypotheses about proportions.

The z-Test for Proportions

As you remember, a test statistic is the statistic that we use to determine the significance of the difference between two values. Depending, of course, on whether we have a one- or a two-sample test, these values may be either two sample values or a sample value and an hypothesized population value. In either case, it is from the value of the test statistic that we determine the probability of obtaining our sample results if, in fact, our hypothesis is true. In determining the test statistic to be used, we must refer to the sampling distribution of the statistic in which we are interested. When one is testing an hypothesis about a proportion, then, one must refer to the sampling distribution of a proportion. As you may remember from Chapter 8, however, the sampling distribution of a proportion changes with the size of the sample. As the size of the sample increases, the binomial sampling distribution approaches normality, and we may use the normal curve to approximate the sampling distribution. When we have a large sample, then, we may use z to determine the distance between a sample proportion and the mean of the sampling distribution, and z would be the appropriate test statistic for testing hypotheses about proportions. It should be noted, however, that unless we have a very large sample, the sampling distribution of a proportion departs from normality when the mean of the population is very close to either .9 or .1. The use of z should thus be limited to situations where our sample size is sufficiently large so that either np or nq, whichever is smaller, is greater than or equal to 10.

To illustrate the use of z as a test statistic, now, let us consider both a one- and a two-sample test.

One-Sample Tests

To illustrate a one-sample test, let us assume that we have selected a sample of 160 students, and that we wish to test the hypothesis that not more than 50 percent of the students in the population are reading below grade level. If the hypothesis were true, then the sampling distribution of all samples of 160 students would be normal, with a mean of p, the hypothesized population proportion, and a standard deviation of $\sqrt{pq/n}$. Referring to the theoretical sampling distribution, the value of z would represent the distance, in standard deviations, between the sample proportion and the hypothesized population proportion, and would be calculated from the following formula.

The z-Test for Hypotheses about a Single Proportion

$$z = \frac{X/n - p}{\sqrt{pq/n}}$$

Where p = the hypothesized population proportion

X/n = the observed proportion in the sample

$\sqrt{pq/n}$ = the standard deviation of the sampling distribution (the standard error of a proportion)

In testing our hypothesis, now, we follow the procedure outlined in Chapter 9, and evaluate the value of z against the critical value. Before we can determine the critical value, however, we must decide whether to do a one- or a two-tailed test, and we must determine our level of significance. Referring back to our hypothesis, then, let us assume that we are not interested in determining if less than 50 percent of the students are below grade level, but that we are only interested in making sure that no higher than this percentage are below the norm. Given this type of situation, a one-tailed test would be appropriate and, assuming that we want to maximize the probability of detecting a difference, we would test our hypothesis at the .05 level of significance. Assuming, now, that we have examined our sample, and have found 85 students that were reading below grade level, our test is as indicated below.

Testing an Hypothesis about a Single Proportion (Large Sample)

1. Specification of the hypothesis:

$H_0: p = .50$
$H_a: p > .50$

2. Test statistic:

$$z = \frac{X/n - p}{\sqrt{pq/n}}$$

$$= \frac{85/160 - .50}{\sqrt{(.5)(.5)/160}} = \frac{.53 - .50}{\sqrt{.25/160}} = \frac{.03}{\sqrt{.0016}} = \frac{.03}{.04} = +.75$$

3. Level of significance:

$\alpha = .05$

4. Critical value of z:

$z = 1.64$

5. Rejection region:

$z \geqslant 1.64$

6. Decision:

Since the obtained value of z does not fall in the rejection region, we will not reject H_0. We cannot conclude that more than 50 percent of the students in the population are reading below grade level.

As you can see, we tested the null hypothesis, that the proportion of students reading below grade level is equal to .50, against the alternative that more than 50 percent of the students are reading below grade level. By specifying our alternative in this manner, we set up our test so that if the null hypothesis were rejected, we could accept the alternative that more than 50 percent of the students were below grade level. Using z as our test statistic, we then determined the value of z that cuts off the upper 5 percent of the area under the normal curve, and we specified that all values of z falling beyond this value would constitute the rejection region. Substituting our observed and hypothesized values in our formula, we found that the value of z did not fall in the rejection region, and we therefore did not reject the null hypothesis. We must conclude, therefore, that the evidence did not indicate that more than 50 percent of the students were reading below grade level.

When we have a one-sample test, the value of the test statistic tells us the extent of the difference between the sample and hypothesized values. If the difference is so small that the value of the test statistic does not exceed our critical value, as in our example, then we conclude that the difference is merely the result of sampling error. When the difference is so large that the value of the test statistic falls in the rejection region, however, we must reject the null hypothesis and conclude that the population was not as hypothesized.

Two-Sample Tests

When we have a two-sample test, we again compare the value of our test statistic to our critical value. In this case, however, the value of the test statistic will tell us the extent of the difference between two sample values rather than between a sample value and an hypothesized population value. To illustrate this difference, let us now consider a two-sample test.

We have a two-sample test whenever we want to compare two different populations. In such situations, we must draw a sample from each of the populations, and we must compare the characteristics of these two separate samples. For example, consider the hypothesis that the proportion of girls is greater than the proportion of boys that are interested in the fine arts. In order to test this hypothesis, we select a sample of boys and a sample of girls, and we determine the proportion of students interested in the fine arts in each of the samples. Assuming, now, that each of the samples included 100 students, we again use a z-test to determine the significance of the difference between them. In this case, however, z refers to the sampling distribution of the difference between two proportions. If the populations from which the samples were selected are the same, then the difference between the two population proportions is equal to zero. Even if the populations are identical, however, the samples selected from these populations might differ. The sampling distribution of the difference between two proportions thus represents the probability of obtaining a specified difference between our sample proportions if, in fact, the population proportions are the same. When the size of our samples is large, the sampling distribution of the difference between two proportions approaches normality. As indicated in Figure 10.1, the mean of the sampling distribution of the difference between two proportions is equal to the difference between the two population proportions, and the standard error of the difference between proportions is equal to

$$\sqrt{\frac{p_1 q_1}{n_1} + \frac{p_2 q_2}{n_2}}$$

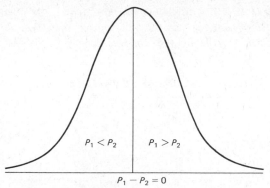

$$P_1 - P_2 = 0$$

Figure 10.1. Theoretical sampling distribution of the difference between two proportions (Large Sample).

Assuming the population proportions are equal, the area to the right of the mean represents those combinations of samples in which X_1/n_1, the first sample proportion, is larger than X_2/n_2, the second sample proportion, and the area to the left of the mean represents those combinations of samples in which X_2/n_2 is larger than X_1/n_1. For a two-tailed test, our rejection region would lie in both tails of the distribution, the critical values being dependent upon the value of alpha. For a one-tailed test, however, the rejection region would depend upon the hypothesis. If our alternative hypothesis specified that X_1/n_1 was larger than X_2/n_2, then the rejection region would lie in the tail to the right. If the alternative specified that X_2/n_2 was greater than X_1/n_1, however, the rejection region would lie in the tail to the left.

Returning to our hypothesis, now, let us refer to the sample of girls as the first sample, and the sample of boys as the second sample. In order to conclude that a greater proportion of girls than of boys are interested in the fine arts, we have to show that X_1/n_1 is significantly greater than X_2/n_2. The value of our test statistic would thus have to fall in the rejection region to the right of the mean. The test statistic is, of course, z. When we are testing an hypothesis about two proportions, however, our formula for z is as follows.

The z-Test for Hypotheses about Two Proportions

$$z = \frac{X_1/n_1 - X_2/n_2}{s_{(X_1/n_1 - X_2/n_2)}}$$

Where

X_1/n_1 = the observed proportion in the first sample

X_2/n_2 = the observed proportion in the second sample

$s_{(X_1/n_1 - X_2/n_2)}$ = the standard error of the difference between proportions

In the formula, the standard error of the difference between two proportions is a pooled estimate, and it takes into account the information that we have from each of the samples. The formula for the standard error is thus computed as follows.

The Estimated Standard Error of the Difference between Proportions

$$s_{(X_1/n_1 - X_2/n_2)} = \sqrt{\frac{X}{n}\left(1 - \frac{X}{n}\right)\left(\frac{1}{n_1} + \frac{1}{n_2}\right)}$$

Where $\dfrac{X}{n} = \dfrac{X_1 + X_2}{n_1 + n_2}$

Let us assume, now, that we will test our hypothesis at the .01 level of significance, and that, even though we think that a higher proportion of girls than of boys is interested in the fine arts, we are interested in detecting a difference in the opposite direction. Given these stipulations, we would have a two-tailed test, and our critical value of z would be equal to 2.58. Assuming, now, that we have examined our samples, and have found 80 girls and 60 boys who have shown an interest in the fine arts, our test is as follows.

Testing an Hypothesis about Two Proportions (Large Sample)

1 Specification of the hypothesis:

$H_0 : p_1 = p_2$
$H_a : p_1 \neq p_2$

2. Test statistic:

$$z = \frac{X_1/n_1 - X_2/n_2}{s_{(X_1/n_1 - X_2/n_2)}} = \frac{80/100 - 60/100}{.065} = \frac{.20}{.065} = +3.08$$

Where $s_{(X_1/n_1 - X_2/n_2)} = \sqrt{\frac{X}{n}\left(1 - \frac{X}{n}\right)\left(\frac{1}{n_1} + \frac{1}{n_2}\right)}$

$$= \sqrt{.7(1 - .7)\left(\frac{1}{100} + \frac{1}{100}\right)}$$

$$= \sqrt{.7(.3)(.02)}$$

$$= \sqrt{.0042} = .065$$

$$\frac{X}{n} = \frac{X_1 + X_2}{n_1 + n_2} = \frac{60 + 80}{100 + 100} = \frac{140}{200} = .7$$

3. Level of significance:

$\alpha = .01$

4. Critical value:

$z = 2.58$

5. Rejection region:

$z = +2.58$ and $z = -2.58$

6. Decision:

Since the value of z falls in the rejection region, we can reject the null hypothesis and conclude that more girls than boys are interested in the fine arts.

As you can see, the form of the test is the same as for testing an hypothesis about a single proportion. The only difference is in the choice of the test statistic. When we were testing an hypothesis about a single proportion, our test statistic was based on the theoretical sampling distribution of a proportion, and the value of the test statistic indicated the number of standard errors between the observed sample proportion and the hypothesized population proportion. When we test an hypothesis about two proportions, however, our test statistic is based on the theoretical sampling distribution of the difference between two proportions. In this case, the mean of the theoretical distribution is equal to zero, and the value of the test statistic indicates the number of standard errors between the observed difference between the samples and a difference of zero. In either case, of course, we are assuming that the normal distribution is a good approximation of the actual sampling distribution. To the extent that this assumption has not been met, our test is not appropriate. When we have small samples, for example, we cannot assume that the sampling distribution of either a proportion or of the difference between two proportions will be normal. In testing hypotheses about proportions with a small sample, therefore, we cannot use z as our test statistic. In its place, we can either use a test that makes no assumptions about the sampling distribution, or we can rely on our binomial expansion.

Using the Binomial Expansion for Testing Hypotheses

Let us assume that we are investigating the dropout rate for children from minority groups, and that we wish to test the hypothesis that 25 percent of these children drop out of school before the completion of high school. Assuming, also, that we are limited to a sample of 10 children, and that 5 of the children in our sample are dropouts, we can test our hypothesis by using the binomial expansion to determine the probability of our outcome if, in fact, the proportion of dropouts in the population were equal to .25.

If our sample size were large, we would determine the proportion of dropouts in our sample, and we would use our z-test to evaluate the extent of the difference between our sample proportion and the hypothesized population proportion. If the value of z were larger than our critical value, we would then conclude that the difference was so large as to be highly improbable if, in fact, the hypothesis were true. If the value of z was less than the critical value, the sample results would then be considered probable, and the null hypothesis would be retained. As you can see, then, we found the value of the test statistic in order to judge the probability of our results.

When we have a small sample, the sampling distribution is not normal, and we do not have a test statistic such as z that will indicate the number of standard errors between the observed and hypothesized results. Instead, we determine the probability of our results directly from our binomial probabilities. If, as in our example, our sample size is 10, and 5 of the 10 students are dropouts, we would have to refer to the terms in our binomial expansion to determine the probability of selecting a sample with 5 or more dropouts. That is, we would have to determine what proportion of our samples would have 5 or more dropouts if, in fact, only 25 percent of the population were dropouts. If the probability of selecting 5 or more dropouts is greater than our level of alpha, we then reject our null hypothesis. If, however, the probability is less than alpha, the hypothesis is retained.

Note, however, that even when we had a large sample, we didn't actually determine the probability of obtaining our sample results. Instead, we specified a level of alpha, and we then determined the critical value of z. We knew that if our observed value of z were more extreme than the critical value, then the probability of our results would be less than the value of alpha. Thus, rather than determine the probability of obtaining our results, we merely compared our observed value of z to the critical value. Similarly, then, when we have a small sample, we can also specify our level of alpha, and we can determine the critical sample proportion. That is, we can determine that sample proportion such that, if our hypothesis were true, the probability of obtaining that extreme a sample porportion would be less than or equal to alpha. Then all sample proportions equal to or more extreme than the critical proportion would then fall in the rejection region.

To illustrate, let us test our hypothesis at the .05 level of significance, using a one-tailed test in which sample proportions significantly higher than .25 will fall in the rejection region. Assuming that we have a sample size of 10, our binomial expansion would be as follows:

$$(.25 + .75)^{10} = (.25)^{10} + 10(.25)^9(.75)$$

$$+ \frac{(10)(9)}{(1)(2)} (.25)^8(.75)^2$$

$$+ \frac{(10)(9)(8)}{(1)(2)(3)} (.25)^7(.75)^3$$

$$+ \frac{(10)(9)(8)(7)}{(1)(2)(3)(4)} (.25)^6(.75)^4$$

$$+ \frac{(10)(9)(8)(7)(6)}{(1)(2)(3)(4)(5)} (.25)^5(.75)^5$$

$$+ \frac{(10)(9)(8)(7)(6)(5)}{(1)(2)(3)(4)(5)(6)} (.25)^4 (.75)^6$$

$$+ \frac{(10)(9)(8)(7)(6)(5)(4)}{(1)(2)(3)(4)(5)(6)(7)} (.25)^3 (.75)^7$$

$$+ \frac{(10)(9)(8)(7)(6)(5)(4)(3)}{(1)(2)(3)(4)(5)(6)(7)(8)} (.25)^2 (.75)^8$$

$$+ \frac{(10)(9)(8)(7)(6)(5)(4)(3)(2)}{(1)(2)(3)(4)(5)(6)(7)(8)(9)} (.25)(.75)^9$$

$$+ (.75)^{10}$$

In specifying the critical sample proportion, we must determine the sample proportion that is so extreme that only 5 percent of the samples will have as high or a higher proportion of dropouts. As you may remember from Chapter 8, the value of the first term in the expansion will tell us the proportion of samples in which 10, or 100 percent of the children will be dropouts. The value of the second term in the expansion will tell us the proportion of samples in which 90 percent of the children will be dropouts, the value of the third term will tell us the proportion of samples in which 80 percent will be dropouts, and the sum of the values of the first three terms will tell us the proportion of samples in which either 80, 90, or 100 percent of the samples will be dropouts. In specifying our critical sample proportion, then, we can sum the values of the successive terms in the expansion until the cumulative sum is equal to .05. If the sum of the values of the first three terms were equal to .05, for example, we would know that the probability of selecting a sample with 8, 9, or 10 dropouts would be equal to .05. Thus $^8/_{10}$ would be the critical value of our sample proportion; the probability of selecting a sample with 8 or more dropouts would be .05, and sample proportions of .8, .9, or 1.0 would lie in the rejection region.

Referring to our expansion, now, let us determine our actual rejection region. Rather than actually calculate the value of each of the terms, however, we can refer to a table that sums the terms for us. Table E of the Appendix is a curtailed version of such a table. Referring to Table E, then, N refers to the size of the sample, m refers to the term in the expansion, and the entries tell us the cumulative sum of the first $m + 1$ terms in the expansion. As you can see, when p is equal to .25 and m is equal to 10, the sum of the first five terms in the expansion is equal to .020, and the sum of the first six terms is equal to .078. Since .020 is thus the highest cumulative sum that is less than .05, the sample proportions represented by the first five terms in the expansion will lie in the rejection region. The critical proportion will thus be equal to .60; if the proportion of dropouts in the sample is equal to or greater than .60, the hypothesis will be rejected.

Using the sample proportion, X/n, in lieu of a test statistic, our test for an hypothesis about a single proportion would be as follows.

Testing an Hypothesis about a Single Proportion (Small Sample)

1. Specification of the hypothesis:

   $H_0 : p = .25$
   $H_a : p \neq .25$

2. Test statistic:

   $$\frac{X}{n} = \frac{5}{10} = .50$$

3. Level of significance:

   $\alpha = .05$

4. Critical value of X/n:

   $$\frac{X}{n} = .60$$

5. Rejection region:

   $$\frac{X}{n} \geqslant .60$$

6. Decision:

   Since the observed sample proportion is less than the critical proportion, the null hypothesis will not be rejected. There is no evidence that more than 25 percent of minority group children are dropouts.

Since the observed sample proportion was less than the critical value, the null hypothesis was not rejected. Note, however, that this was a one-tailed test, and that there was only one rejection region. It is also possible, if it is so desired, to do a two-tailed test. As with the other two-tailed tests that have been discussed, a two-tailed test of this hypothesis would involve two rejection regions. One would therefore have to determine not only the proportions that would be significantly higher than the hypothesized value, but also those that would be significantly lower. If alpha were .05, for example, the proportions that fell at the upper and lower 2.5 percent of the distribution would fall in the rejection region.

As you can see, now, an hypothesis about a proportion may be tested by referring directly to the binomial probability of the possible sample proportions. As mentioned before, however, we may also use a nonparametric test.

The Chi-Square Test

The chi-square test is a test that tells us the extent to which an observed set of frequencies differs from the frequencies that were expected. Chi-square, which is written χ^2, does not make any assumptions about the distribution of a population parameter. When our sample is small, therefore, and we cannot assume normality, the χ^2 test is appropriate. Furthermore, the same statistic can be used for both one- and two-sample tests.

One-Sample Tests

In determining the value of χ^2, we must first specify our expected frequencies. Referring to the hypothesis tested previously, for example, we would expect 25 percent of the sample to be dropouts and 75 percent not to be dropouts. Assuming that our sample consisted of 20 children, the expected frequencies for each of our categories (dropouts and nondropouts) would be 5 and 15. We would then determine the observed frequencies in each of the categories, and we would calculate the value of χ^2 with the following formula.

The Chi-Square Formula

$$\chi^2 = \Sigma \ \frac{(O - E)^2}{E}$$

Where E = the expected frequency for a category

O = the observed frequency for a category

To illustrate the calculation of χ^2, let us now assume that we have selected our sample, and that the observed frequencies were as indicated below.

Calculation of χ^2 for the Significance of the Difference between the Observed and Expected Frequency of Dropouts

	Observed (O)	Expected (E)	$(O - E)$	$(O - E)^2$	$\dfrac{(O - E)^2}{E}$
Dropouts	10	5	5	25	$25/5 = 5.0$
Non-dropouts	10	15	−5	25	$25/15 = 1.67$

$$\chi^2 = \Sigma \ \frac{(O - E)^2}{E} = 6.67$$

As you can see, we first found the difference between our observed and expected frequencies, and then we squared each of these differences, divided by the expected frequency, and summed the resulting values. Following this procedure, χ^2 was found to be equal to 6.67. In evaluating this value of χ^2, we must now refer to Table F to determine the probability of obtaining this high a value of χ^2 if, in fact, the frequencies were not significantly different.

Note, however, that in determining the probability of obtaining a specific value of χ^2, we must first specify the degree of freedom. In determining the degree of freedom, we must consider the number of variables we are interested in and the number of variate values per variable. When we are interested in a single variable, the degree of freedom is equal to one less than the number of variate values. In the foregoing example, for instance, we were concerned with a single variable, the length of time in school, and we had two variate values, dropouts and nondropouts. The degree of freedom associated with the χ^2 test, therefore, is equal to 1. When we are concerned with two variables, however, the degree of freedom for χ^2 is equal to the degree of freedom of one of the variables multiplied by the degree of freedom of the other.

Once we have determined our degree of freedom, we can then determine the critical value of χ^2. As with any test statistic, the critical value will, of course, be dependent upon our level of alpha. Unlike the z-test, however, we do not differentiate, for χ^2, between a one- and a two-tailed rejection region. All values of χ^2 are positive, and the higher the value of χ^2, the more likely it is that a real difference exists between our observed and expected values. In determining the critical value for χ^2, therefore, we need only consider the probability of attaining a value of χ^2 that is greater than a specified value. Referring to Table F, then, we would read across the top of the table for our value of alpha, and we would then go down the corresponding column until we reach our degrees of freedom. If we were testing our hypothesis at the .05 level of significance, for example, you can see that the critical value of χ^2 would be 3.84. In testing our hypothesis at the .05 level, then, we would reject our hypothesis only for values of χ^2 larger than 3.84. The test of our hypothesis would thus be as follows.

The χ^2 Test for an Hypothesis about a Single Proportion

1. Specification of the hypothesis:

$H_0 : p = .25$
$H_a : p \neq .25$

2. Test statistic:

$$\chi^2 = \Sigma \frac{(O - E)^2}{E} = \frac{(10 - 5)^2}{5} + \frac{(10 - 15)^2}{15} = 6.67$$

Degrees of freedom $(df) = 1$

where observed and expected frequencies are as indicated:

	Observed Frequency	Expected Frequency
Dropouts	10	5
Nondropouts	10	15

3. Level of significance:

$\alpha = .05$

4. Critical value of χ^2:

$\chi^2 = 3.84, \qquad df = 1$

5. Rejection region:

$$\chi^2 \geqslant 3.84$$

6. Decision:

Since the obtained value of χ^2 is greater than the critical value, the null hypothesis must be rejected. We may conclude that more than 25 percent of the minority group children are dropouts.

Note that even though our original hypothesis was directional, we actually did a two-tailed test. That is, the value of χ^2 would not only have been significant if the sample proportion were significantly higher than .25, but it would also have been significant if the sample proportion were significantly lower than .25. The value of χ^2 does not tell us whether a sample proportion is higher or lower than what was hypothesized. When χ^2 is significant, we merely know that the observed frequencies were significantly different from what would have been expected if the null hypothesis were true. In order to determine the direction of this difference, one must refer back to the sample data. In this case, then, it was the value of χ^2 that allowed us to reject the null hypothesis, but it was the inspection of the frequencies that allowed us to accept the alternate hypothesis in which we were interested.

You may wonder, now, why the results of our χ^2 test led us to reject the null hypothesis, although the results of our binomial test led us to the opposite decision. In both cases, we hypothesized that 25 percent of the children would be dropouts, and we found that the percentage of dropouts in our sample was equal to 50 percent. Let us consider, then, why our different tests yielded different results. First, let us consider sample size. The power of any test to detect a difference between our observed and hypothesized values is, to a large extent, dependent upon the size of our sample. The larger the sample, up to a point, the greater the probability of finding a difference if, in fact, a difference does exist. Other things being equal, then, the larger the sample, the smaller the difference that is needed for significance. Returning to our binomial test, for example, we found that, with a sample size of 10, the critical sample proportion for our hypothesis was equal to $\frac{6}{10}$. Thus, when our observed sample proportion was .5, we could not reject the hypothesis. Referring to Table E, however, note that, if our sample size were equal to 20, the critical sample proportion would have been equal to $\frac{10}{20}$. Therefore, with a sample size of 20, an observed sample proportion of .5 would have led us to reject our hypothesis. As you can see, if our sample size had been 20 for both the binomial and χ^2 tests, both tests would have led us to the same conclusion. In this case, then, the discrepancy between our tests was due to the discrepancy in the size of our samples.

Even when the size of the sample is the same, however, different tests sometimes yield disparate results. In general, a parametric test, such as the binomial test, is more powerful than a nonparametric test such as χ^2. That is, the parametric test has a better chance of detecting a real difference between the observed and hypothesized values. There are times, however, when the assumptions of a parametric test about the sampling distribution are so violated that only a nonparametric test is appropriate. Nonparametric tests are very versatile and are widely used. The χ^2 test, for example, is not only limited to tests about a single variable, but it can also be used for bi-variate tests. The χ^2 test is also appropriate, when our sample size is small, for testing hypotheses about two proportions.

Two-Sample Tests

To illustrate the use of χ^2 in testing an hypothesis about two proportions, let us test the hypothesis that a higher proportion of boys than of girls have reading difficulties. Assume that we have selected a sample of 30 boys and 20 girls, and that our observed frequencies are as follows.

Observed Frequency of Reading Difficulties for Boys and Girls

	With Reading Difficulties	Without Reading Difficulties	Total
Boys	9	21	30
Girls	1	19	20
Total	10	40	50

As you can see, $^{10}/_{50}$ of the students have reading difficulties. If there were no difference between boys and girls, we would expect $^{10}/_{50}$ of the boys and $^{10}/_{50}$ of the girls to have reading difficulties. In determining our expected frequencies, therefore, the expected frequency of boys with reading difficulties would be $^{10}/_{50}$ of 30, and the expected frequency of girls with reading difficulties would be $^{10}/_{50}$ of 20. Then, in order to determine the expected frequencies of students without reading difficulties, we subtract the expected number of students with reading difficulties from the total number of students within the category. Our expected frequencies would thus be as indicated below.

Expected Frequency of Reading Difficulties for Boys and Girls

	With Reading Difficulties	Without Reading Difficulties	Total
Boys	6	24	30
Girls	4	16	20
Total	10	40	50

In determining our value of χ^2, now, we use the same formula as for a one-sample test. Note, however, that we have four expected and four observed frequencies to consider. In calculating the value of χ^2, then, we have four quantities to sum. Furthermore, since we have bi-variate data, our degree of freedom will be equal to the product of the degree of freedom for each of the variables. The degree of freedom can be represented as the product of one less than the number of rows in the table of expected frequencies $(r - 1)$ multiplied by one less than the number of columns $(c - 1)$. Excluding the totals, our table consists of two rows and two columns, and our degree of freedom is thus equal to $(2 - 1)(2 - 1)$, which is equal to 1.

To test our hypothesis at the .05 level of significance, now, we first find our critical value from Table F for 1 degree of freedom. This value is equal to 3.84, and our test is as follows.

Testing an Hypothesis about Two Proportions (the χ^2 test)

Given:

	Observed Frequencies		Expected Frequencies	
	With Reading Difficulties	Without Reading Difficulties	With Reading Difficulties	Without Reading Difficulties
Boys	9	21	6	24
Girls	1	19	4	16

1. Specification of the hypothesis:

   $H_0 : p_1 = p_2$
   $H_a : p_1 \neq p_2$

2. Test statistic:

$$\chi^2 = \Sigma \ \frac{(O - E)^2}{E} = \frac{(9 - 6)^2}{6} + \frac{(21 - 24)^2}{24} + \frac{(1 - 4)^2}{4} + \frac{(19 - 16)^2}{16}$$

$$= \frac{9}{6} + \frac{9}{24} + \frac{9}{4} + \frac{9}{16}$$

$$= 4.69$$

   Degrees of freedom $(df) = (r-1)(c-1) = (2-1)(2-1) = 1$

3. Level of significance:

   $\alpha = .05$

4. Critical value of χ^2:

   $\chi^2 = 3.84, \qquad df = 1$

5. Rejection region:

   $\chi^2 \geqslant 3.84$

6. Decision:

   Since the observed value of χ^2 falls in the rejection region, we may reject the null hypothesis that the same proportion of boys and of girls have reading difficulties. Referring to the observed frequencies, we can conclude that a higher proportion of boys than of girls have reading difficulties.

As you can see, the value of χ^2 was larger than the critical value, and the null hypothesis was rejected. As in the χ^2 test for a single proportion, this test is also two-sided. A significant χ^2 does not indicate the nature of the difference between the observed and expected frequencies; it merely tells us that differences did exist. To determine which proportion was larger, we must refer to the data.

It should also be noted, now that we have used χ^2 to test hypotheses about proportions, that the χ^2 test is not limited to tests about proportions. Even in the preceding examples, as you may have noted, the value of χ^2 was computed on the basis of *frequencies*. The χ^2 test is actually a test for frequencies, and it is appropriate even when expected frequencies are not determined by an hypothesis about a proportion.

Having considered the z-test, the binomial test, and the χ^2 test, we are now equipped to test hypotheses about either proportions or frequencies. Quite often, however, we are more concerned with hypotheses about means. As with our tests of hypotheses about proportions, our tests for hypotheses about means also depend on the size of the sample and the number of populations about which we are hypothesizing. Regardless of whether our hypothesis is about proportions or means, however, the form of the test will be the same; the only difference will be in the test statistic.

PRACTICE PROBLEMS

1. It was found, over several years, that 50 percent of the students in a particular school were below grade level in reading. After a new method of teaching reading was instituted, many students appeared to be doing much better than before. In order to determine whether, in fact, there was an increase in the reading level of the students, the principal gave a new test to a selected group of students. Of the 50 students that were included in the sample, only 20 were found to be below grade level. Find the significance of these results at the .01 level of significance.
2. In testing the hypothesis that a higher proportion of boys than of girls pose discipline problems, a teacher investigated a sample of 100 girls and 80 boys. She found that 15 of the boys and 5 of the girls had been identified as discipline problems. Test the teacher's hypothesis at the .05 level of significance.
3. The publishers of a new set of curricular materials claim that no more than 25 percent of the students who use their materials are below grade level. Using these materials on a trial basis, however, a school system found that 40 percent of their students were below grade level. Assuming that 20 students were included in the sample, test the publisher's claim at the .05 level of significance. (Do both a binomial and a chi-square test, and compare the results.)

4. In order to test his belief that students prefer discussion classes to lectures, a teacher analyzed the responses of 40 students to a questionnaire. He found that 15 preferred lecture classes and 25 preferred discussion classes. Test the teacher's belief at the .01 level of significance.

5. In testing the hypothesis that social dancing is enjoyed more by girls than by boys, a teacher found that 20 percent of the boys and 15 percent of the girls disliked social dancing. Assuming that 30 boys and 40 girls were included in the sample, test the hypothesis at the .05 level of significance.

TESTING 11
HYPOTHESES
ABOUT MEANS

Now that we know how to test hypotheses about proportions, it is time to consider hypotheses about means. As with hypotheses about proportions, hypotheses about means may be about the mean score of a single population or about the relationship among the mean scores of more than one population. If, for example, we hypothesized that the mean score on a reading test was equal to 70, we would be hypothesizing about the mean score of a single population, and we would test our hypothesis with a one-sample test. If, on the other hand, we had hypothesized that the mean score of the girls taking the test would be higher than that of the boys, we would be hypothesizing about the relationship between two means, and we would test our hypothesis with a two-sample test. It is also possible to hypothesize about more than two means, as when we hypothesize that there is no difference among the mean IQ scores of rural, suburban, and urban children. This chapter, however, is limited to hypotheses about either one or two means. In testing hypotheses about means, as with testing hypotheses about proportions, we again make the distinction between one- and two-sample tests and between large- and small-sample tests.

When our sample size is large, as you may remember from Chapter 8, we may assume that the sampling distribution of a mean is normal. Given an hypothesized population mean, then, we can use z in determining the probability of finding a specified sample mean. Similarly, we may assume that the sampling distribution of the difference between two means is normal, and we can also use z in determining the probability of finding a specified difference between two sample means. When our sample size is small, however, we cannot assume that the sampling distribution will be normal, and z is not appropriate. When this is the case, as you may also remember from Chapter 8, the sampling distribution of the mean is best approximated by the Student's distribution, and t is the appropriate statistic for measuring the distance between the population mean and a given sample mean. In calculating the value of t, however, we use exactly the same formula we use for calculating the value of z. The only difference is that in determining the probability of a specific value of t, we must first determine our degree of freedom, and we then find the probability of our value in Table D rather than Table C. As was previously noted, however, as our sample size increases, and the degrees of freedom similarly increase, the values in Table D approach the values in Table C. When our sample size is large, therefore, either statistic will give the same results. It is when the sample size is small that we must be sure to use t. If we always use t, we will always be correct. The formula for t will vary, however, depending upon whether we have a one- or a two-sample test.

One-Sample Tests

Let us assume, now, that we are testing the hypothesis that the mean score on a national reading test is equal to 70. This is a one-sample test in which we must look at the difference between the mean of our sample and the hypothesized mean of the population. In determining the significance of the difference, we may use t as our test statistic. Our degrees of freedom would be equal to one less than the size of our sample, and the formula for t would be as follows.

The *t*-Test for Hypotheses about a Single Mean

$$t = \frac{\overline{X} - \mu}{s/\sqrt{n}}$$

Degrees of freedom $(df) = n - 1$

Where $\overline{X}$ = the mean of the sample

           μ = the hypothesized mean of the population

    $s/\sqrt{n}$ = the estimated standard error of the mean

In determining the value of t, then, the difference between the sample mean and the hypothesized mean of the population is divided by the estimated standard deviation of the sampling distribution (the standard error of the mean).

To evaluate the difference between the observed and hypothesized means, we compare our value of t with the critical value determined from Table D. Let us assume, for example, that we had a two-tailed test of our hypothesis at the .01 level of significance, and that our sample consisted of 64 students. We would have 63 degrees of freedom and, referring to Table D, our critical value of t would be 2.58. If the mean of our sample is equal to 60, with a standard deviation of 16, we would test our hypothesis as follows.

Testing an Hypothesis about a Single Mean

Given: $\mu = 70, s = 16$

            $\overline{X} = 60, n = 64$

1. Specification of the hypothesis:

    $H_0 : \mu = 70$
    $H_a : \mu \neq 70$

2. Test statistic:

$$t = \frac{\overline{X} - \mu}{s/\sqrt{n}} = \frac{60 - 70}{16/\sqrt{64}} = \frac{-10}{2} = -5.0$$

    $df = 64 - 1 = 63$

3. Level of significance:

    $\alpha = .01$

4. Critical value of t:

    $t = 2.58$

5. Rejection region:

    $t > +2.58$ and $t < -2.58$

6. Decision:

    Since the value of t falls in the rejection region, we will reject H_0 and conclude that the mean score on the test is not equal to 70. Referring to our data, we can conclude that the mean score is significantly less than 70.

As you can see, the results of the t-test led us to reject the null hypothesis. But what if we had used a z-test? Would our results have been the same? As noted previously, the formula for z is exactly the same as the formula for t. The observed value of z would thus be the same as that for t. We know that the t-test does differ from the z-test, however; this difference is in the way that we determine our critical value. Let us consider, then, what our critical value would have been for z. In a two-tailed test at the .01 level of significance, the critical values of z would be the points that cut off the upper and lower .5 percent of the area under the normal curve. Referring to Table C, we can see that the critical value of z would also have been 2.58. Thus a z-test would have led us to the same conclusion as our t-test. It should be noted, however, that this will only be so when the sample size is large. When the sample size is less than 30, the z-test should not be used.

Now that we have considered the tests for hypotheses about a single mean, it is interesting to note their similarities to the tests for hypotheses about a single proportion. Whether we are concerned with proportions or means, our sampling distribution approaches normality as the sample size increases. Where we used a z-test for a large-sample test about a proportion, we may similarly use a z-test for a large-sample test about mean. Furthermore, the z-test for an hypothesis about a proportion is essentially the same as the z-test for an hypothesis about a mean. In either case, we determine the value of z by dividing the difference between our observed and hypothesized values by the standard error of the sampling distribution, and we compare the resulting value of z with the critical value determined from Table C. Similarly, when our sample size is large, we will also find that the test for hypotheses about the difference between two proportions will be essentially the same as the test for hypotheses about the difference between two means.

Two-Sample Tests

When our hypothesis concerns the relationship between two means, our test statistic is no longer based on the sampling distribution of a single mean. Instead, we must consider the sampling distribution of the difference between two means. If, in fact, there is no difference between the means of two populations, then the sampling distribution of the difference between the sample means selected from these populations will approximate either the normal or the Student's distribution and will have a mean of zero. If the difference between our sample means is significantly greater than zero, then, we can reject the null hypothesis that the population means are equal.

When the sample size is large, the sampling distribution of the difference between two means will approach normality, and z will be the appropriate measure of the significance of the difference between our sample means. When the size of the samples is small, however, the sampling distribution will best approximate the Student's distribution, and t will be our test statistic. As for one-sample tests, however, the formulas for t and z are the same, the only difference between the t-test and the z-test being in the determination of the critical value of the test statistic. When the sample size is large, the critical value determined for t will be the same as for z and, of course, either test can be used. When the sample size is less than 30, however, the discrepancy becomes too large, and only the t-test is appropriate. Since the t-test is always appropriate, the illustrations in this section will be limited to t. Remember, though, that when the sample size is large, z can be substituted for t, and the critical value of the test statistic may be determined from our table of the area under the normal curve.

In a two-sample test, however, we must consider more than just the size of the sample. For a two-sample test, the formula will also depend upon whether or not we can assume that the populations from which our samples were selected had equal variances. Before we do our t-test, therefore, we should test the significance of the difference between our population variances. This difference can be tested with the following F-test.

The F-Test for the Difference between Two Variances

$$F = \frac{s_1{}^2}{s_2{}^2}$$

$$df_1 = n_1 - 1, \text{ and } df_2 = n_2 - 1$$

Where s_1^2 = the larger sample variance

s_2^2 = the smaller sample variance

df_1 = the degrees of freedom for the sample with the larger variance

df_2 = the degrees of freedom for the sample with the smaller variance

As you can see, the value of F is determined by dividing the larger of our sample variances by the smaller one. If we have two samples of 50 students, with sample variances of 36 and 25, for example, the value of F would be equal to 36 divided by 25. The value of F would thus be equal to 1.4, with the degrees of freedom for each of the samples equal to 49. In determining the significance of the value of F, we next turn to Table G. We find the degrees of freedom for the sample with the larger variance along the top of the table, and the degrees of freedom for the sample with the smaller variance along the side of the table. Then, by reading across to where the degrees of freedom intersect, we find the critical values of F at the .01 and .05 levels of significance. In this example, the critical values of F are 1.61 and 1.96; since our value of F, 1.4, is less than either of these values, we would conclude that our population variances are not significantly different.

In testing the difference between the means of these samples, then, we would use a test for equal variances. It should be noted, however, that the t-test is not greatly affected by violations of the assumption of equal variances. Thus the t-test for equal variances is often used even when this assumption is not met. If the F-test is performed, however, and the variances are found to be significantly different, it is advisable to use the t-test for unequal variances. Where equal variances can be assumed, our formula for t would be as follows:

The t-Test for Hypotheses about the Difference between Two Means (Equal Variances)

$$t = \frac{\overline{X}_1 - \overline{X}_2}{\sqrt{s^2/n_1 + s^2/n_2}}$$

$$s^2 = \frac{(n_1 - 1)s_1^2 + (n_2 - 1)s_2^2}{n_1 + n_2 - 2}$$

Degrees of freedom $(df) = (n_1 - 1) + (n_2 - 1)$

Where $\overline{X}_1$ = the mean of the first sample

$\overline{X}_2$ = the mean of the second sample

s^2 = the pooled variance of the two samples

s_1^2 = the sample variance of the first sample

s_2^2 = the sample variance of the second sample

n_1 = the size of the first sample

n_2 = the size of the second sample

The value of t represents the difference between the sample means divided by the estimated standard error of the difference between two means. When the population variances can be assumed to be equal, the best estimate of the standard error is based upon s^2, the pooled variance of the two samples. Before we can compute the value of t (or z), then, we must pool our variances as indicated above.

When the population variances cannot be assumed to be equal, however, we do not pool our sample variances, and the formula for t (or z) is as follows:

The t-Test for Hypotheses about the Difference between Two Means (Unequal Variances)

$$t = \frac{\overline{X}_1 - \overline{X}_2}{\sqrt{s_1^2/n_1 + s_2^2/n_2}}$$

The value of t again represents the difference between the sample means divided by the estimated standard error of the difference between two means. When we estimate the standard error, however, each sample variance is divided by the size of that sample. Furthermore, we also have a different way of determing the critical value. When the population variances can be assumed to be equal, the degree of freedom is equal to $(n_1 - 1) + (n_2 - 1) - 2$, and the critical value of t is determined from Table D as usual. When we have unequal variances, however, we must determine the critical value of t from the following formula.

The Critical Value of t (Unequal Variances)

$$t_c = \frac{\dfrac{s_1^2}{n_1}(t_1) + \dfrac{s_2^2}{n_2}(t_2)}{s_1^2/n_1 + s_2^2/n_2}$$

Where t_c = the critical value of t

s_1^2 = the variance of the first sample

s_2^2 = the variance of the second sample

n_1 = the size of the first sample

n_2 = the size of the second sample

t_1 = the critical value of t with $n_1 - 1$ degrees of freedom

t_2 = the critical value of t with $n_2 - 1$ degrees of freedom

As you can see, then, we determine the critical value of t for each of the separate samples, and we then combine those values in the preceding formula.

Now, if we want to test the hypothesis that the mean score on a national reading test is higher for girls than for boys, we would use one of the foregoing formulas for our test statistic. Let us assume that our sample consists of 50 boys and 50 girls, and that the population variances may be assumed to be equal. If our sample data are as indicated below, and if we wish to do a two-tailed test at the .05 level of significance, our test would be as follows:

Testing an Hypothesis about the Difference between Two Means (Equal Variances)

Given:

Girls	Boys
$n_1 = 50$	$n_2 = 50$
$\overline{X}_1 = 85$	$\overline{X}_2 = 78$
$s_1^2 = 36$	$s_2^2 = 25$

$$s^2 = \frac{(n_1 - 1)s_1^2 + (n_2 - 1)s_2^2}{n_1 + n_2 - 2} = \frac{(49)(36) + (49)(25)}{50 + 50 + 2} = \frac{2989}{98} = 30.5$$

1. Specification of the hypothesis:

   $H_0 : \mu_1 - \mu_2 = 0$
   $H_a : \mu_1 - \mu_2 \neq 0$

2. Test statistic:

   $$t = \frac{\overline{X}_1 - \overline{X}_2}{\sqrt{s^2/n_1 + s^2/n_2}} = \frac{85 - 78}{\sqrt{30.5/50 + 30.5/50}} = \frac{7}{\sqrt{1.22}} = \frac{7}{1.1} = 6.4$$

   Degrees of freedom $(df) = n_1 + n_2 - 2 = 98$

3. Level of significance:

   $\alpha = .05$

4. Critical value of t:

   $t = 1.96$

5. Rejection region:

   $t > +1.96$ and $t < -1.96$

6. Decision:

   Since our value of t lies in the rejection region, we will reject the null hypothesis. Referring to our data, we can conclude that girls do better than boys.

Note, now, that a z-test would have yielded the same results. Assuming equal population variances, we would have calculated the value of z from the same formula we used for t. Not only would the obtained value of z have been the same as for t, but the critical values would also have been the same. The sample size was sufficiently large that the critical value of t, 1.96, is the same as the critical value of z for a two-tailed test at the .05 level of significance. As you can see, either z or t can be used for a large-sample test.

Consider now a test in which equal population variances cannot be assumed. Let us assume, for example, that we wish to test the hypothesis that the mean score on a science aptitude test is higher for boys than for girls. Given the following data, a two-tailed test at the .01 level of significance would be as follows:

Testing an Hypothesis about the Difference between Two Means (Unequal Variances)

Given:

Boys	Girls
$n_1 = 10$	$n_2 = 20$
$\overline{X}_1 = 90$	$\overline{X}_2 = 86$
$s_1^2 = 36$	$s_2^2 = 9$

1. Specification of the hypothesis:

   $H_0 : \mu_1 - \mu_2 = 0$
   $H_a : \mu_1 - \mu_2 \neq 0$

2. Test statistic:

   $$t = \frac{\overline{X}_1 - \overline{X}_2}{\sqrt{s_1^2/n_1 + s_2^2/n_2}} = \frac{90 - 86}{\sqrt{36/10 + 9/20}} = \frac{4}{\sqrt{4.05}} = \frac{4}{2.01} = +1.99$$

3. Level of significance:

   $\alpha = .01$

4. Critical value of t:

   $$t_c = \frac{\frac{s_1^2}{n_1}(t_1) + \frac{s_2^2}{n_2}(t_2)}{\sqrt{s_1^2/n_1 + s_2^2/n_2}} = \frac{\frac{36}{10}(3.17) + \frac{9}{20}(2.86)}{\sqrt{36/10 + 9/20}}$$

   $$= \sqrt{12.70/4.05} = 3.13$$

5. Rejection region:

   $t > +3.13$ and $t < -3.13$

6. Decision:

   Since the value of t does not fall in the rejection region, we must conclude that there is no evidence that boys do better than girls.

In this case, an F-test of the difference between our variances would have been significant. Thus, since equal variances could not be assumed, we did not pool the sample variances in our formula for t. Moreover, the critical value of t was not determined directly from Table D. Instead, we determined the critical values for each of our samples at the .01 level of alpha, and we substituted these values in our formula for t_c. Comparing our observed value of t with the critical value, then, we did not reject the null hypothesis, and we concluded that there was no evidence to suggest that boys do better than girls.

Note, now, that because of the sample size, only a t-test would have been appropriate in this example. If our sample size were sufficiently large, we could have substituted z for t, and we could have then determined the critical value of z from Table C. When the sample size is small, however, the critical values of t are not the same as for z. In the foregoing example, for instance, whereas the critical value of t was equal to 3.13, the critical value for z would have been equal to 2.58. As you can see, the sample size was not sufficiently large for the values of t to approximate the values of z. When the sample size is small, then, the z-test is inappropriate.

Reviewing our tests for means, now, our test statistic was determined by three factors: (1) the number of populations about which we were hypothesizing; (2) the size of our sample; and (3) whether we could assume that our samples came from populations with equal variances. Let us now consider another factor, the independence of our samples.

Correlated Samples

Up to this point, our two-sample tests have been limited to the comparison of means of independent samples. That is, the two samples were chosen from separate populations, and the selection of one sample did not have any influence on the selection of the other. There are times, however, when we wish to compare two related samples. For example, we might want to test the hypothesis that the mean score on an arithmetic computation test is higher when taken in the morning than when taken in the afternoon. In order to test this hypothesis, we would take one sample of students and test this same sample in the morning and afternoon. We would then look at the difference between the morning and afternoon scores and determine whether this difference was significantly greater than zero. Although we would be looking at two sets of scores, then, these scores would be for the same sample of students. In fact, we would be looking at a pair of scores for each of the students in the sample. When this is the case, or when we are looking at the difference between the scores of matched pairs of students, we cannot use the previous tests for the difference between two means. Instead, we use the following t-test for correlated samples.

The t-Test for Correlated Samples

$$t = \frac{\overline{D} - d}{s_D/\sqrt{n}}, \qquad df = n - 1$$

Where D = the difference between a pair of scores (a difference score)

$\overline{D}$ = the mean difference between the scores in the sample

d = the mean difference hypothesized for the population ($d = 0$)

$s_D/\sqrt{n}$ = the estimated standard error of the mean difference

As you can see, the formula for t is very similar to the formula we use in a one-sample test. In this case, however, we are concerned with difference scores, D, rather than with single score values. We find the difference between the mean difference score for our sample, $\bar{D}$, and the hypothesized difference, d, of zero and we divide this difference by the estimated standard error.

To illustrate the calculation of t, let us assume that the following data represent the arithmetic computation scores of 10 students. As you can see, we determine $\bar{D}$ by summing the difference between each pair of scores and dividing this sum by the number of pairs. Then, to determine the value of s_D, we use the computational formula for the standard deviation of a sample. Since we are dealing with difference scores, however, we use D in our formula instead of X. Then, to determine the value of t, we substitute the values obtained for $\bar{D}$ and s_D in our formula.

Let us assume now that we want to test our hypothesis with a one-tailed test at the .05 level of significance. Our t-test of the mean population difference, d, between morning and afternoon scores would be as shown in Table 11.1.

Table 11.1. Computation Scores of 10 Students

Student	Morning Score	Afternoon Score	D	D^2
1	74	70	4	16
2	80	75	5	25
3	70	60	10	100
4	80	85	−5	25
5	100	100	0	0
6	95	90	5	25
7	95	85	10	100
8	95	90	5	25
9	79	80	−1	1
10	85	85	0	0
			$\Sigma D = +33$	$\Sigma D^2 = 317$

$$\bar{D} = \frac{\Sigma D}{n} = \frac{+33}{10} = +3.3$$

$$s_D = \sqrt{\frac{n \Sigma D^2 - (\Sigma D)^2}{n(n-1)}} = \sqrt{\frac{(10)(317) - (33)^2}{10(9)}} = \sqrt{\frac{3170 - 1089}{90}}$$

$$= \sqrt{\frac{2081}{90}} = \sqrt{23.12} = 4.81$$

$$t = \frac{\bar{D} - d}{s_D/\sqrt{n}} = \frac{+3.3 - 0}{4.81/\sqrt{10}} = \frac{+3.3}{4.81/3.16} = \frac{+3.3}{1.52} = +2.17$$

Testing an Hypothesis about the Difference between Two Means (Correlated Samples)

1. Specification of the hypothesis:

   $H_0 : d = 0$
   $H_a : d \neq 0$

2. Test statistic:

   $$t = \frac{\overline{D} - d}{s_D / \sqrt{n}} = \frac{3.3 - 0}{4.81 / \sqrt{10}} = +2.17$$

   Degrees of freedom $(df) = n - 1 = 9$

3. Level of significance:

   $\alpha = .05$

4. Critical value of t:

   $t = 1.833$

5. Rejection region:

   $t \geqslant +1.833$

6. Decision:

   Since the value of t does not fall in the rejection region, we cannot conclude that students do better in the morning than in the afternoon.

As you can see, we tested the null hypothesis that d, the mean difference between morning and afternoon scores in the population, would be equal to zero. We used our t-test for correlated samples to evaluate the mean difference between the morning and afternoon scores of our sample, and we found that the sample difference was not significantly greater than zero. We thus concluded that students do not appear to do better in the morning than in the afternoon.

This test, like the previous tests we considered, allowed us to evaluate the difference between two means. Note, however, that all of the tests thus far considered are appropriate only for hypotheses about one or two means. If our hypothesis concerned more than two means, our tests would be inadequate. The following chapter, therefore, will introduce a technique for testing hypotheses about more than two means.

PRACTICE PROBLEMS

1. When a low-income project was built in a school district in which the mean IQ of the students was equal to 110, the principal was concerned that the new students from the project might need extra help to function at the level of the other students in the school. Before assigning the new

students to classes, therefore, he administered an IQ test to a sample of 64 of the new students. Assuming that the mean IQ score of the sample was equal to 105, with a standard deviation of 16, test the significance of the difference between the new and the old students at the .05 level of significance.

2. A sample of 16 third-graders had a mean reading score of 80, with a standard deviation of 8. Using these sample data, test the hypothesis that the mean reading score for all third-graders is equal to 85.

3. A high school history teacher wanted to test the hypothesis that teaching through class discussion results in more learning than does lecturing. He randomly assigned his students to either a discussion or lecture class, and he then compared the mean score of each of the classes on the final examination. Assuming the following results, test the teacher's hypothesis at the .01 level of significance.

	Sample Data	
	Discussion Class	Lecture Class
$\overline{X}$	80	75
SD	6	5
n	30	35

4. A typing teacher found that a double practice period on one day seemed to be more helpful to her students than two short periods on separate days. In order to confirm her suspicion, she randomly assigned a sample of 30 students to the two types of practice periods, and she compared their performance on the mid-term examination. Assuming the following results, test the teacher's hypothesis at the .05 level of significance.

	Sample Data	
	Double Period	Single Period
$\overline{X}$	75	70
SD	4	2
n	15	15

5. A teacher was interested in determining whether or not her students lost their skill in arithmetic over the Christmas vacation. She tested a sample of 12 students before and after vacation, and she obtained the following scores. Test the teacher's hypothesis at the .05 level of significance.

| Student | Arithmetic Scores | |
	Before Vacation	After Vacation
A	95	90
B	95	95
C	92	95
D	90	85
E	85	86
F	83	80
G	82	80
H	80	75
I	78	80
J	75	70
K	70	60
L	70	65

TESTING HYPOTHESES ABOUT MORE THAN TWO MEANS: 12
THE ANALYSIS OF VARIANCE

The analysis of variance is a technique that is used to determine the significance of the difference between more than two means. If, for example, we were investigating three different methods of teaching reading, an analysis of variance would be used in comparing the mean scores of the students receiving each type of instruction. Similarly, an analysis of variance would be used to compare the mean IQ scores of children from low-, middle-, and high-income homes, or to compare the mean scores of students in four different subjects.

Each of these examples involves a comparison of more than two means. In the analysis of variance, however, we do not make a direct comparison of means. Instead, we make an inference about the difference between our means by comparing the variance within our samples to the variance between the sample means. Assume, for example, that the following reading scores were obtained by students being taught by the phonics, "look-say," and ITA methods.

Reading Scores for Phonics, Look-Say, and ITA Methods

Phonics	Look-Say	ITA
79	82	85
77	82	86
80	80	84
79	78	83
80	80	87
	79	85
	79	
$\Sigma X = 395$	$\Sigma X = 560$	$\Sigma X = 510$
$\overline{X} = 79$	$\overline{X} = 80$	$\overline{X} = 85$

$$\text{Grand mean} = \overline{X}_t = \frac{395 + 560 + 510}{5 + 7 + 6} = \frac{1465}{18} = 81.3$$

As you can see, the sample means are not the same. Even if the samples came from identical populations, however, we would expect some differences among the sample means. These differences would be attributed to sampling error and, the larger the standard error of the mean, the larger the sample differences that would be expected. In order to show that our methods differ in effectiveness, then, we would have to show that the variance of the sample means is too great to be attributed to sampling error.

In testing the null hypothesis that the population means are equal, then, we can compare the variance of the sample means, which is referred to as the *between-groups variance,* with an estimate of the variance that can be attributed to sampling error. This estimate is the *within-groups variance,* which is a measure of the differences among the scores within each sample. Assuming, then, that all three samples did come from identical populations, the means should not differ by more than we would expect scores from the same population to differ, and the between-groups variance should not significantly differ from the within-groups variance. If, however, the samples come from populations with different means, then the sample means would differ by a greater amount than the scores within a sample, and the between-groups variance would be significantly greater than the within-groups variance. The ratio of the between-groups variance to the within-groups variance thus provides a test for the significance of the difference between our means. When this ratio is significantly greater than 1.0, the null hypothesis can be rejected.

The *F*-Test

In Chapter 11, as you may remember, we used an *F*-test to determine the significance of the difference between two sample variances. Similarly, in our analysis of variance, we also use an *F*-test. In the analysis of variance, however, *F* is equal to the between-groups variance divided by the within-groups variance, and the degrees of freedom are as indicated below.

The *F*-Test for the Analysis of Variance

$$F = \frac{s_b^2}{s_w^2}, \quad df_{(\text{between})} = k - 1$$

$$df_{(\text{within})} = N - k$$

Where s_b^2 = the between-groups variance

s_w^2 = the within-groups variance

k = the number of samples (the number of sample means being compared)

N = the total number of students in all of the samples

In determining the value of F, then, we must first find the between-groups and within-groups variance.

The Between-Groups Variance

The between-groups variance is the variance of the sample means around the mean of the sample means. In determining the between-groups variance, we follow the usual procedure for finding the variance of a sample. Using the sample means as score values, the formula for the between-groups variance is as follows.

The Between-Groups Variance

$$s_b{}^2 = \frac{\Sigma (\overline{X} - \overline{X}_t)^2}{k - 1}$$

Where $\overline{X}$ = a sample mean

$\overline{X}_t$ = the mean of the sample means (the grand mean)

k = the number of sample means

We sum the squared difference between each of our sample means and the grand mean, and we divide this sum by one less than the number of sample means. That is, we divide the sum of the squared differences by the between-groups degrees of freedom.

If we now apply this formula to the reading scores given earlier, we would calculate our between-groups variance as follows:

$$s_b{}^2 = \frac{(79.0 - 81.3)^2 + (80.0 - 81.3)^2 + (85 - 81.3)^2}{3 - 1}$$

$$= \frac{(2.3)^2 + (1.3)^2 + (3.7)^2}{2}$$

$$= \frac{5.29 + 1.69 + 13.69}{2}$$

$$= \frac{20.67}{2} = 10.34$$

In order to determine the value of F, however, we must also determine our within-groups variance, the procedure for which is described next.

The Within-Groups Variance

The within-groups variance is a measure of the variance of the scores within each sample around the mean of the sample. In determining the within-groups variance, then, we must determine, within each sample, the difference between each score and the sample mean. We then square these differences, sum the squared differences over all of our samples, and divide this sum by the between-groups degrees of freedom.

In finding the within-groups variance of our reading scores, then, we use the following procedure.

Finding the Within-Groups Variance

	Phonics ($\overline{X} = 79$)	
X	$X - \overline{X}$	$(X - \overline{X})^2$
79	0	0
77	−2	4
80	1	1
79	0	0
80	1	1
	$\Sigma(X - \overline{X})^2 = 6$	

	Look-Say ($\overline{X} = 80$)	
X	$X - \overline{X}$	$(X - \overline{X})^2$
82	2	4
82	2	4
80	0	0
78	−2	4
80	0	0
79	−1	1
79	−1	1
	$\Sigma(X - \overline{X})^2 = 14$	

	ITA ($\overline{X} = 85$)	
X	$X - \overline{X}$	$(X - \overline{X})^2$
85	0	0
86	1	1
84	−1	1
83	−2	4
87	2	4
85	0	0
	$\Sigma(X - \overline{X})^2 = 10$	

1. Sum, for all scores in all samples, the squared difference between each score and the mean of the sample:

   $$6 + 14 + 10 = 30$$

2. Divide the sum of the squared differences by the within-groups degree of freedom ($N - k$):

   $$\frac{30}{(5 + 7 + 6) - 3} = \frac{30}{15} = 2.0$$

Now that we have determined both the between-groups and the within-groups variance, let us test the hypothesis that differences do exist in the mean reading scores of the students who receive different types of instruction. We test this hypothesis at the .05 level of significance as follows.

Testing an Hypothesis about the Difference between More than Two Means

1. Specification of the hypothesis:

$H_0 : \mu_1 = \mu_2 = \mu_3$
$H_a : \mu_1 \neq \mu_2 \neq \mu_3$

2. Test statistic:

$$F = \frac{s_b^2}{s_w^2} = \frac{10.34}{2.0} = 5.17$$

$df_b = k - 1 = 3 - 1 = 2$
$df_w = N - k = 18 - 3 = 15$

3. Level of significance:

$\alpha = .05$

4. Critical value of F:

$F = 3.68$

5. Rejection region:

$F \geqslant +3.68$

6. Decision:

Since our value of F falls in the rejection region, we can reject the null hypothesis and conclude that our teaching methods were not equally effective.

Note that in determining the critical value of F in Table G, we look for the between-groups degrees of freedom along the top of the table and the within-groups degrees of freedom along the side of the table. Most of the time, the between-groups variance is the larger variance and, as in our F-test for the difference between two sample variances, we will be looking for the degrees of freedom associated with the larger variance along the top of the table. In rare cases, however, the within-groups variance is larger than the between-groups variance. Usually, though, when we find our within-groups variance to be larger, we have either made an error in our calculations or we have selected samples with widely different variances. When, in fact, the sample variances are widely different, the analysis of variance should not be done. Minor differences in the sample variances do not greatly affect the F-test, however, and should not result in a within-groups variance that is more than the between-groups variance.

Note, also, that since our F-test is always the ratio of the between-groups variance to the within-groups variance, there is only one critical value of F for a given degree of freedom and level of significance. When our F is significant, as in the foregoing example, we know that differences existed among our means, but we do not know which differences were significant. When our F-test is significant, therefore, we should compare our means with another test statistic to determine which differences were significant. One way of testing the means is to use the following t-test:

$$t = \frac{\bar{X}_1 - \bar{X}_2}{\sqrt{s_w^2/n_1 + s_w^2/n_2}}, \qquad df = df_w$$

Note that this is the same t-test that is used for testing the difference between two means when the variances are equal. In this case, however, we substitute the within-groups variance, s_w^2, for the pooled variance, and we use the within-groups degrees of freedom as our degrees of freedom.

If we apply this formula to the example we have been considering, the t-test for the difference between the ITA and phonics methods would be as follows:

$$t = \frac{85.0 - 79.0}{\sqrt{2.0/6 + 2.0/5}} = \frac{6}{\sqrt{.33 + .40}} = \frac{6}{\sqrt{.73}} = \frac{6}{.85} = 7.2$$

$$df = 18 - 3 = 15$$

With 15 degrees of freedom, the critical value of t at the .05 level of significance (for a two-tailed test) would be 2.13. Since our obtained value of t is larger than 2.13, we can now conclude that the mean score for the ITA method is significantly higher than that for the phonics method. Similarly, we could also do t-tests for the significance of the difference between the "look-say" and ITA methods, and between the phonics and "look-say" methods.

It should be noted, however, that this test is not the only method for comparing means after a significant F-test. In reading the literature, you may come across several variations on the t-test, as well as other types of comparisons. Although a description of these methods is beyond the scope of this book, these tests should be recognized as methods for determining the specific differences that cause an analysis of variance to be significant.

It should be also noted that when an analysis of variance has been done, the results of the analysis of variance are reported in a special type of table called a *source table*. Table 12.1, for instance, is a source table for the foregoing example. Note that the between- and within-groups variances are entered in the Mean Square column, and that the variance is obtained by dividing the entry in the Sum of Squares column by the degrees of freedom. As you can see, then, the sum of squares represents the numera-

Table 12.1. Source Table for the Analysis of Variance

Source of Variation	Sum of Squares	Degrees of Freedom	Mean Square	F
Between-groups	20.67	2	10.34	5.17*
Within-groups	30	15	2.0	

*Significant at $\alpha = .05$.

tor of our formula for the variance. For the between-groups variance, the sum of squares represents the sum of the squared deviations between each of the sample means and the grand mean and, for the within-groups variance, the sum of the squares represents the sum, over all samples, of the squared deviations between each of the scores within the sample and the sample mean. Since all the information needed to determine the variance is provided by the sum of squares and degrees of freedom, however, the mean square frequently is omitted from the source table. When this is the case, you can always determine the variance by dividing the sum of squares by the degrees of freedom. The value of F, of course, represents the ratio of the between-groups to the within-groups variance and, if significant, is followed by an asterisk. The footnote at the bottom of the table indicates the level of significance at which F was significant.

The analysis of variance described in this chapter is referred to as a *one-way* or *single classification analysis*; the analysis involved scores on only one variable, and only one F-test was performed. Analyses of variance can be performed, however, even when we are comparing scores on two or three variables. Such analyses are more complex, of course, but the same type of F-test would be performed for each of the variables in which we were interested. The results would be reported in a similar source table, and the F's would be similarly interpreted. Even though the calculations involved in a more complex analysis of variance are beyond the scope of this book, then, the interpretation of these analyses is not. Wherever you have a source table for an analysis of variance, a significant F indicates that there were significant differences among the means that were being compared.

PRACTICE PROBLEMS

1. In order to compare the language performance of the students from three different junior high schools, 10 students from each of the schools were given a modern language achievement test. The scores were as follows:

School A	School B	School C
95	80	83
93	83	84
92	82	85
95	81	87
90	79	86
92	82	85
93	79	83
94	78	86
93	81	85
92	80	86

Test for the significance of the difference between the sample means, and present your results in a source table. Test the hypothesis at the .01 level of significance.

2. The following weights (in pounds) were recorded for samples of ten children from five different countries:

U.S.A.	France	England	Egypt	Peru
70	71	68	68	69
71	70	69	67	67
69	71	70	69	68
70	70	67	67	68
72	72	71	69	69
68	72	69	68	67
69	71	69	68	69
70	71	70	67	67
71	71	68	69	68

With alpha equal to .05, test the hypothesis that the mean weight is the same in each of the countries. Present your results in a source table.

3. The following IQ scores were recorded for a sample of first-, second-, and third-graders in a particular school:

First Grade	Second Grade	Third Grade
101	99	98
100	100	97
100	100	97
99	98	98
101	102	96
99	100	96
100	100	97
99	101	97
100	100	97
101		97
100		

Test the hypothesis that there are no differences between the mean IQ scores in the first, second, and third grades. Test the hypothesis at the .05 level of significance, and present your results in a source table.

To summarize, now, we have considered two types of statistics, descriptive statistics and inferential statistics. When we want to describe a set of scores, we use a descriptive statistic; when we want to use the characteristics of a set of scores to make an inference about other sets of scores, we use an inferential statistic. Regardless of the type of statistic, however, there are two factors that determine the specific statistic to be used: (1) what we want to know, and (2) the type of data we have.

As a review, each of the statistics that we have considered is categorized below in terms of the information it provides and when it should be used. Remember, however, that a statistic itself does not answer a question. A statistic merely provides the information on which an intelligent decision may be based. It is a person who interprets the meaning of a statistic, and who must understand its limitations.

Which Statistic to Use

TO DESCRIBE A SET OF SCORES

	Statistic	Use
	Mode	Identifies the most frequently occurring score in a distribution. Can be used with nominal, ordinal, interval, and ratio data, but is most often used with nominal data
Measures of typical performance	Median	Identifies the middle score of a distribution. Can be used with ordinal, interval or ratio data. Most frequently used with ordinal data and when we don't want extreme scores to affect our measure

Which Statistic to Use *(continued)*

TO DESCRIBE A SET OF SCORES

	Statistic	Use
	Mean	The arithmetic average of a set of scores. Used with interval or ratio data when we want the value of each score in the distribution to affect the measure of typical performance
Measures of variability in performance	Interquartile range and semi-interquartile range	Measures of the number of score points covered by the middle 50 percent of the scores in a distribution
	Standard deviation and variance	Measures of the amount by which scores in a distribution vary from the mean. Used with interval or ratio data.
Measures of relative performance	Ranks	Indicate an ordinal position in a group. May be used with ordinal, interval, or ratio data, but yield ordinal data
	Percentile ranks	Indicate the percentage of people falling below a particular score. Can be used with ordinal, interval, or ratio data, but yield ordinal data
	Standard scores	Indicate the number of standard deviations between a score and a mean. Can be used with interval and ratio data
Measures of relationship	The rank-order correlation coefficient	Indicates the degree of relationship between two sets of ranks
	The product-moment correlation coefficient	Indicates the degree of relationship between two sets of scores. Used with interval or ratio data

TO TEST AN HYPOTHESIS ABOUT A PROPORTION

LARGE SAMPLE

One-Sample Test

$$z = \frac{X/n - p}{\sqrt{pq/n}}$$

Two-Sample Test

$$z = \frac{p_1 - p_2}{\sqrt{p_1 q_1/n_1 + p_2 q_2/n_2}}$$

SMALL SAMPLE

One-Sample Test
Chi-square
or
binomial test

Two-Sample Test
Chi-square

TO TEST AN HYPOTHESIS ABOUT A MEAN

LARGE SAMPLE

One-Sample Test	*Two-Sample Test*	
	Equal Variances	Unequal Variances

One-Sample Test

$$z = \frac{\bar{X} - \mu}{s/\sqrt{n}}$$

Equal Variances

$$z = \frac{\bar{X}_1 - \bar{X}_2}{\sqrt{s^2/n_1 + s^2/n_2}}$$

where

$$s^2 = \frac{(n_1 - 1)s_1^2 + (n_2 - 1)s_2^2}{n_1 + n_2 - 2}$$

Unequal Variances

$$z = \frac{\bar{X}_1 - \bar{X}_2}{\sqrt{s_1^2/n_1 + s_2^2/n_2}}$$

SMALL SAMPLE

Two-Sample Test

One-Sample Test

$$t = \frac{\bar{X} - \mu}{s/\sqrt{n}}$$

$$df = n - 1$$

Equal Variances

$$t = \frac{\bar{X}_1 - \bar{X}_2}{\sqrt{s^2/n_1 + s^2/n_2}}$$

where

$$s_2 = \frac{(n_1 - 1)s_1^2 + (n_2 - 1)s_2^2}{n_1 + n_2 - 2}$$

$$df = n_1 + n_2 - 2$$

Unequal Variances

$$t = \frac{\bar{X}_1 - \bar{X}_2}{\sqrt{s_1^2/n_1 + s_2^2/n_2}}$$

where

$$t_c = \frac{\dfrac{s_1^2}{n_1}(t_1) + \dfrac{s_2^2}{n_2}(t_2)}{s_1^2/n_1 + s_2^2/n_2}$$

TO TEST AN HYPOTHESIS ABOUT MORE THAN TWO MEANS
Analysis of variance: $F = s_b^2/s_w^2$; $df_b = k - 1$, $df_w = N - k$

TO TEST AN HYPOTHESIS ABOUT A VARIANCE
Two-sample variances: $F = s_1^2/s_2^2$; $df_1 = n_1 - 1$, $df_2 = n_2 - 1$

APPENDIX

Table A. Squares and Square Roots of Numbers from 1 to 1000

n	n^2	$\sqrt{n}$	n	n^2	$\sqrt{n}$
1	1	1.0000	43	1849	6.5574
2	4	1.4142	44	1936	6.6332
3	9	1.7321	45	2025	6.7082
4	16	2.0000	46	2116	6.7823
5	25	2.2361	47	2209	6.8557
6	36	2.4495	48	2304	6.9282
7	49	2.6458	49	2401	7.0000
8	64	2.8284	50	2500	7.0711
9	81	3.0000	51	2601	7.1414
10	100	3.1623	52	2704	7.2111
11	121	3.3166	53	2809	7.2801
12	144	3.4641	54	2916	7.3485
13	169	3.6056	55	3025	7.4162
14	196	3.7417	56	3136	7.4833
15	225	3.8730	57	3249	7.5498
16	256	4.0000	58	3364	7.6158
17	289	4.1231	59	3481	7.6811
18	324	4.2426	60	3600	7.7460
19	361	4.3589	61	3721	7.8102
20	400	4.4721	62	3844	7.8740
21	441	4.5826	63	3969	7.9373
22	484	4.6904	64	4096	8.0000
23	529	4.7958	65	4225	8.0623
24	576	4.8990	66	4356	8.1240
25	625	5.0000	67	4489	8.1854
26	676	5.0990	68	4624	8.2462
27	729	5.1962	69	4761	8.3066
28	784	5.2915	70	4900	8.3666
29	841	5.3852	71	5041	8.4261
30	900	5.4772	72	5184	8.4853
31	961	5.5678	73	5329	8.5440
32	1024	5.6569	74	5476	8.6023
33	1089	5.7446	75	5625	8.6603
34	1156	5.8310	76	5776	8.7178
35	1225	5.9161	77	5929	8.7750
36	1296	6.0000	78	6084	8.8318
37	1369	6.0828	79	6241	8.8882
38	1444	6.1644	80	6400	8.9443
39	1521	6.2450	81	6561	9.0000
40	1600	6.3246	82	6724	9.0554
41	1681	6.4031	83	6889	9.1104
42	1764	6.4807	84	7056	9.1652
			85	7225	9.2195

SOURCE: *Descriptive and Sampling Statistics,* by J. G. Peatman. Copyright © 1947 by Harper & Row, New York. Reprinted by permission.

Table A. Squares and Square Roots of Numbers from 1 to 1000 (*Continued*)

n	*n*²	$\sqrt{n}$	*n*	*n*²	$\sqrt{n}$
86	7396	9.2736	136	18496	11.6619
87	7569	9.3274	137	18769	11.7047
88	7744	9.3808	138	19044	11.7473
89	7921	9.4340	139	19321	11.7898
90	8100	9.4868	140	19600	11.8322
91	8281	9.5394	141	19881	11.8743
92	8464	9.5917	142	20164	11.9164
93	8649	9.6437	143	20449	11.9583
94	8836	9.6954	144	20736	12.0000
95	9025	9.7468	145	21025	12.0416
96	9216	9.7980	146	21316	12.0830
97	9409	9.8489	147	21609	12.1244
98	9604	9.8995	148	21904	12.1655
99	9801	9.9499	149	22201	12.2066
100	10000	10.0000	150	22500	12.2474
101	10201	10.0499	151	22801	12.2882
102	10404	10.0995	152	23104	12.3288
103	10609	10.1489	153	23409	12.3693
104	10816	10.1980	154	23716	12.4097
105	11025	10.2470	155	24025	12.4499
106	11236	10.2956	156	24336	12.4900
107	11449	10.3441	157	24649	12.5300
108	11664	10.3923	158	24964	12.5698
109	11881	10.4403	159	25281	12.6095
110	12100	10.4881	160	25600	12.6491
111	12321	10.5357	161	25921	12.6886
112	12544	10.5830	162	26244	12.7279
113	12769	10.6301	163	26569	12.7671
114	12996	10.6771	164	26896	12.8062
115	13225	10.7238	165	27225	12.8452
116	13456	10.7703	166	27556	12.8841
117	13689	10.8167	167	27889	12.9228
118	13924	10.8628	168	28224	12.9615
119	14161	10.9087	169	28561	13.0000
120	14400	10.9545	170	28900	13.0384
121	14641	11.0000	171	29241	13.0767
122	14884	11.0454	172	29584	13.1149
123	15129	11.0905	173	29929	13.1529
124	15376	11.1355	174	30276	13.1909
125	15625	11.1803	175	30625	13.2288
126	15876	11.2250	176	30976	13.2665
127	16129	11.2694	177	31329	13.3041
128	16384	11.3137	178	31684	13.3417
129	16641	11.3578	179	32041	13.3791
130	16900	11.4018	180	32400	13.4164
131	17161	11.4455	181	32761	13.4536
132	17424	11.4891	182	33124	13.4907
133	17689	11.5326	183	33489	13.5277
134	17956	11.5758	184	33856	13.5647
135	18225	11.6190	185	34225	13.6015

Table A. Squares and Square Roots of Numbers from 1 to 1000 (*Continued*)

n	n²	√n	n	n²	√n
186	34596	13.6382	236	55696	15.3623
187	34969	13.6748	237	56169	15.3948
188	35344	13.7113	238	56644	15.4272
189	35721	13.7477	239	57121	15.4596
190	36100	13.7840	240	57600	15.4919
191	36481	13.8203	241	58081	15.5242
192	36864	13.8564	242	58564	15.5563
193	37249	13.8924	243	59049	15.5885
194	37636	13.9284	244	59536	15.6205
195	38025	13.9642	245	60025	15.6525
196	38416	14.0000	246	60516	15.6844
197	38809	14.0357	247	61009	15.7162
198	39204	14.0712	248	61504	15.7480
199	39601	14.1067	249	62001	15.7797
200	40000	14.1421	250	62500	15.8114
201	40401	14.1774	251	63001	15.8430
202	40804	14.2127	252	63504	15.8745
203	41209	14.2478	253	64009	15.9060
204	41616	14.2829	254	64516	15.9374
205	42025	14.3178	255	65025	15.9687
206	42436	14.3527	256	65536	16.0000
207	42849	14.3875	257	66049	16.0312
208	43264	14.4222	258	66564	16.0624
209	43681	14.4568	259	67081	16.0935
210	44100	14.4914	260	67600	16.1245
211	44521	14.5258	261	68121	16.1555
212	44944	14.5602	262	68644	16.1864
213	45369	14.5945	263	69169	16.2173
214	45796	14.6287	264	69696	16.2481
215	46225	14.6629	265	70225	16.2788
216	46656	14.6969	266	70756	16.3095
217	47089	14.7309	267	71289	16.3401
218	47524	14.7648	268	71824	16.3707
219	47961	14.7986	269	72361	16.4012
220	48400	14.8324	270	72900	16.4317
221	48841	14.8661	271	73441	16.4621
222	49284	14.8997	272	73984	16.4924
223	49729	14.9332	273	74529	16.5227
224	50176	14.9666	274	75076	16.5529
225	50625	15.0000	275	75625	16.5831
226	51076	15.0333	276	76176	16.6132
227	51529	15.0665	277	76729	16.6433
228	51984	15.0997	278	77284	16.6733
229	52441	15.1327	279	77841	16.7033
230	52900	15.1658	280	78400	16.7332
231	53361	15.1987	281	78961	16.7631
232	53824	15.2315	282	79524	16.7929
233	54289	15.2643	283	80089	16.8226
234	54756	15.2971	284	80656	16.8523
235	55225	15.3297	285	81225	16.8819

Table A. Squares and Square Roots of Numbers from 1 to 1000 (*Continued*)

n	n²	√n	n	n²	√n
286	81796	16.9115	336	112896	18.3303
287	82369	16.9411	337	113569	18.3576
288	82944	16.9706	338	114244	18.3848
289	83521	17.0000	339	114921	18.4120
290	84100	17.0294	340	115600	18.4391
291	84681	17.0587	341	116281	18.4662
292	85264	17.0880	342	116964	18.4932
293	85849	17.1172	343	117649	18.5203
294	86436	17.1464	344	118336	18.5472
295	87025	17.1756	345	119025	18.5742
296	87616	17.2047	346	119716	18.6011
297	88209	17.2337	347	120409	18.6279
298	88804	17.2627	348	121104	18.6548
299	89401	17.2916	349	121801	18.6815
300	90000	17.3205	350	122500	18.7083
301	90601	17.3494	351	123201	18.7350
302	91204	17.3781	352	123904	18.7617
303	91809	17.4069	353	124609	18.7883
304	92416	17.4356	354	125316	18.8149
305	93025	17.4642	355	126025	18.8414
306	93636	17.4929	356	126736	18.8680
307	94249	17.5214	357	127449	18.8944
308	94864	17.5499	358	128164	18.9209
309	95481	17.5784	359	128881	18.9473
310	96100	17.6068	360	129600	18.9737
311	96721	17.6352	361	130321	19.0000
312	97344	17.6635	362	131044	19.0263
313	97969	17.6918	363	131769	19.0526
314	98596	17.7200	364	132496	19.0788
315	99225	17.7482	365	133225	19.1050
316	99856	17.7764	366	133956	19.1311
317	100489	17.8045	367	134689	19.1572
318	101124	17.8326	368	135424	19.1833
319	101761	17.8606	369	136161	19.2094
320	102400	17.8885	370	136900	19.2354
321	103041	17.9165	371	137641	19.2614
322	103684	17.9444	372	138384	19.2873
323	104329	17.9722	373	139129	19.3132
324	104976	18.0000	374	139876	19.3391
325	105625	18.0278	375	140625	19.3649
326	106276	18.0555	376	141376	19.3907
327	106929	18.0831	377	142129	19.4165
328	107584	18.1108	378	142884	19.4422
329	108241	18.1384	379	143641	19.4679
330	108900	18.1659	380	144400	19.4936
331	109561	18.1934	381	145161	19.5192
332	110224	18.2209	382	145924	19.5448
333	110889	18.2483	383	146689	19.5704
334	111556	18.2757	384	147456	19.5959
335	112225	18.3030	385	148225	19.6214

n	n²	√n	n	n²	√n
386	148996	19.6469	436	190096	20.8806
387	149769	19.6723	437	190969	20.9045
388	150544	19.6977	438	191844	20.9284
389	151321	19.7231	439	192721	20.9523
390	152100	19.7484	440	193600	20.9762
391	152881	19.7737	441	194481	21.0000
392	153664	19.7990	442	195364	21.0238
393	154449	19.8242	443	196249	21.0476
394	155236	19.8494	444	197136	21.0713
395	156025	19.8746	445	198025	21.0950
396	156816	19.8997	446	198916	21.1187
397	157609	19.9249	447	199809	21.1424
398	158404	19.9499	448	200704	21.1660
399	159201	19.9750	449	201601	21.1896
400	160000	20.0000	450	202500	21.2132
401	160801	20.0250	451	203401	21.2368
402	161604	20.0499	452	204304	21.2603
403	162409	20.0749	453	205209	21.2838
404	163216	20.0998	454	206116	21.3073
405	164025	20.1246	455	207025	21.3307
406	164836	20.1494	456	207936	21.3542
407	165649	20.1742	457	208849	21.3776
408	166464	20.1990	458	209764	21.4009
409	167281	20.2237	459	210681	21.4243
410	168100	20.2485	460	211600	21.4476
411	168921	20.2731	461	212521	21.4709
412	169744	20.2978	462	213444	21.4942
413	170569	20.3224	463	214369	21.5174
414	171396	20.3470	464	215296	21.5407
415	172225	20.3715	465	216225	21.5639
416	173056	20.3961	466	217156	21.5870
417	173889	20.4206	467	218089	21.6102
418	174724	20.4450	468	219024	21.6333
419	175561	20.4695	469	219961	21.6564
420	176400	20.4939	470	220900	21.6795
421	177241	20.5183	471	221841	21.7025
422	178084	20.5426	472	222784	21.7256
423	178929	20.5670	473	223729	21.7486
424	179776	20.5913	474	224676	21.7715
425	180625	20.6155	475	225625	21.7945
426	181476	20.6398	476	226576	21.8174
427	182329	20.6640	477	227529	21.8403
428	183184	20.6882	478	228484	21.8632
429	184041	20.7123	479	229441	21.8861
430	184900	20.7364	480	230400	21.9089
431	185761	20.7605	481	231361	21.9317
432	186624	20.7846	482	232324	21.9545
433	187489	20.8087	483	233289	21.9773
434	188356	20.8327	484	234256	22.0000
435	189225	20.8567	485	235225	22.0227

Table A. Squares and Square Roots of Numbers from 1 to 1000 (*Continued*)

n	n^2	$\sqrt{n}$	n	n^2	$\sqrt{n}$
486	236196	22.0454	536	287296	23.1517
487	237169	22.0681	537	288369	23.1733
488	238144	22.0907	538	289444	23.1948
489	239121	22.1133	539	290521	23.2164
490	240100	22.1359	540	291600	23.2379
491	241081	22.1585	541	292681	23.2594
492	242064	22.1811	542	293764	23.2809
493	243049	22.2036	543	294849	23.3024
494	244036	22.2261	544	295936	23.3238
495	245025	22.2486	545	297025	23.3452
496	246016	22.2711	546	298116	23.3666
497	247009	22.2935	547	299209	23.3880
498	248004	22.3159	548	300304	23.4094
499	249001	22.3383	549	301401	23.4307
500	250000	22.3607	550	302500	23.4521
501	251001	22.3830	551	303601	23.4734
502	252004	22.4054	552	304704	23.4947
503	253009	22.4277	553	305809	23.5160
504	254016	22.4499	554	306916	23.5372
505	255025	22.4722	555	308025	23.5584
506	256036	22.4944	556	309136	23.5797
507	257049	22.5167	557	310249	23.6008
508	258064	22.5389	558	311364	23.6220
509	259081	22.5610	559	312481	23.6432
510	260100	22.5832	560	313600	23.6643
511	261121	22.6053	561	314721	23.6854
512	262144	22.6274	562	315844	23.7065
513	263169	22.6495	563	316969	23.7276
514	264196	22.6716	564	318096	23.7487
515	265225	22.6936	565	319225	23.7697
516	266256	22.7156	566	320356	23.7908
517	267289	22.7376	567	321489	23.8118
518	268324	22.7596	568	322624	23.8328
519	269361	22.7816	569	323761	23.8537
520	270400	22.8035	570	324900	23.8747
521	271441	22.8254	571	326041	23.8956
522	272484	22.8473	572	327184	23.9165
523	273529	22.8692	573	328329	23.9374
524	274576	22.8910	574	329476	23.9583
525	275625	22.9129	575	330625	23.9792
526	276676	22.9347	576	331776	24.0000
527	277729	22.9565	577	332929	24.0208
528	278784	22.9783	578	334084	24.0416
529	279841	23.0000	579	335241	24.0624
530	280900	23.0217	580	336400	24.0832
531	281961	23.0434	581	337561	24.1039
532	283024	23.0651	582	338724	24.1247
533	284089	23.0868	583	339889	24.1454
534	285156	23.1084	584	341056	24.1661
535	286225	23.1301	585	342225	24.1868

Table A. Squares and Square Roots of Numbers from 1 to 1000 (*Continued*)

n	n²	√n	n	n²	√n
586	343396	24.2074	636	404496	25.2190
587	344569	24.2281	637	405769	25.2389
588	345744	24.2487	638	407044	25.2587
589	346921	24.2693	639	408321	25.2784
590	348100	24.2899	640	409600	25.2982
591	349281	24.3105	641	410881	25.3180
592	350464	24.3311	642	412164	25.3377
593	351649	24.3516	643	413449	25.3574
594	352836	24.3721	644	414736	25.3772
595	354025	24.3926	645	416025	25.3969
596	355216	24.4131	646	417316	25.4165
597	356409	24.4336	647	418609	25.4362
598	357604	24.4540	648	419904	25.4558
599	358801	24.4745	649	421201	25.4755
600	360000	24.4949	650	422500	25.4951
601	361201	24.5153	651	423801	25.5147
602	362404	24.5357	652	425104	25.5343
603	363609	24.5561	653	426409	25.5539
604	364816	24.5764	654	427716	25.5734
605	366025	24.5967	655	429025	25.5930
606	367236	24.6171	656	430336	25.6125
607	368449	24.6374	657	431649	25.6320
608	369664	24.6577	658	432964	25.6515
609	370881	24.6779	659	434281	25.6710
610	372100	24.6982	660	435600	25.6905
611	373321	24.7184	661	436921	25.7099
612	374544	24.7386	662	438244	25.7294
613	375769	24.7588	663	439569	25.7488
614	376996	24.7790	664	440896	25.7682
615	378225	24.7992	665	442225	25.7876
616	379456	24.8193	666	443556	25.8070
617	380689	24.8395	667	444889	25.8263
618	381924	24.8596	668	446224	25.8457
619	383161	24.8797	669	447561	25.8650
620	384400	24.8998	670	448900	25.8844
621	385641	24.9199	671	450241	25.9037
622	386884	24.9399	672	451584	25.9230
623	388129	24.9600	673	452929	25.9422
624	389376	24.9800	674	454276	25.9615
625	390625	25.0000	675	455625	25.9808
626	391876	25.0200	676	456976	26.0000
627	393129	25.0400	677	458329	26.0192
628	394384	25.0599	678	459684	26.0384
629	395641	25.0799	679	461041	26.0576
630	396900	25.0998	680	462400	26.0768
631	398161	25.1197	681	463761	26.0960
632	399424	25.1396	682	465124	26.1151
633	400689	25.1595	683	466489	26.1343
634	401956	25.1794	684	467856	26.1534
635	403225	25.1992	685	469225	26.1725

Table A. Squares and Square Roots of Numbers from 1 to 1000 (*Continued*)

n	*n²*	*√n*	*n*	*n²*	*√n*
686	470596	26.1916	736	541696	27.1293
687	471969	26.2107	737	543169	27.1477
688	473344	26.2298	738	544644	27.1662
689	474721	26.2488	739	546121	27.1846
690	476100	26.2679	740	547600	27.2029
691	477481	26.2869	741	549081	27.2213
692	478864	26.3059	742	550564	27.2397
693	480249	26.3249	743	552049	27.2580
694	481636	26.3439	744	553536	27.2764
695	483025	26.3629	745	555025	27.2947
696	484416	26.3818	746	556516	27.3130
697	485809	26.4008	747	558009	27.3313
698	487204	26.4197	748	559504	27.3496
699	488601	26.4386	749	561001	27.3679
700	490000	26.4575	750	562500	27.3861
701	491401	26.4764	751	564001	27.4044
702	492804	26.4953	752	565504	27.4226
703	494209	26.5141	753	567009	27.4408
704	495616	26.5330	754	568516	27.4591
705	497025	26.5518	755	570025	27.4773
706	498436	26.5707	756	571536	27.4955
707	499849	26.5895	757	573049	27.5136
708	501264	26.6083	758	574564	27.5318
709	502681	26.6271	759	576081	27.5500
710	504100	26.6458	760	577600	27.5681
711	505521	26.6646	761	579121	27.5862
712	506944	26.6833	762	580644	27.6043
713	508369	26.7021	763	582169	27.6225
714	509796	26.7208	764	583696	27.6405
715	511225	26.7395	765	585225	27.6586
716	512656	26.7582	766	586756	27.6767
717	514089	26.7769	767	588289	27.6948
718	515524	26.7955	768	589824	27.7128
719	516961	26.8142	769	591361	27.7308
720	518400	26.8328	770	592900	27.7489
721	519841	26.8514	771	594441	27.7669
722	521284	26.8701	772	595984	27.7849
723	522729	26.8887	773	597529	27.8029
724	524176	26.9072	774	599076	27.8209
725	525625	26.9258	775	600625	27.8388
726	527076	26.9444	776	602176	27.8568
727	528529	26.9629	777	603729	27.8747
728	529984	26.9815	778	605284	27.8927
729	531441	27.0000	779	606841	27.9106
730	532900	27.0185	780	608400	27.9285
731	534361	27.0370	781	609961	27.9464
732	535824	27.0555	782	611524	27.9643
733	537289	27.0740	783	613089	27.9821
734	538756	27.0924	784	614656	28.0000
735	540225	27.1109	785	616225	28.0179

Table A. Squares and Square Roots of Numbers from 1 to 1000 (*Continued*)

n	n^2	$\sqrt{n}$	n	n^2	$\sqrt{n}$
786	617796	28.0357	836	698896	28.9137
787	619369	28.0535	837	700569	28.9310
788	620944	28.0713	838	702244	28.9482
789	622521	28.0891	839	703921	28.9655
790	624100	28.1069	840	705600	28.9828
791	625681	28.1247	841	707281	29.0000
792	627264	28.1425	842	708964	29.0172
793	628849	28.1603	843	710649	29.0345
794	630436	28.1780	844	712336	29.0517
795	632025	28.1957	845	714025	29.0689
796	633616	28.2135	846	715716	29.0861
797	635209	28.2312	847	717409	29.1033
798	636804	28.2489	848	719104	29.1204
799	638401	28.2666	849	720801	29.1376
800	640000	28.2843	850	722500	29.1548
801	641601	28.3019	851	724201	29.1719
802	643204	28.3196	852	725904	29.1890
803	644809	28.3373	853	727609	29.2062
804	646416	28.3549	854	729316	29.2233
805	648025	28.3725	855	731025	29.2404
806	649636	28.3901	856	732736	29.2575
807	651249	28.4077	857	734449	29.2746
808	652864	28.4253	858	736164	29.2916
809	654481	28.4429	859	737881	29.3087
810	656100	28.4605	860	739600	29.3258
811	657721	28.4781	861	741321	29.3428
812	659344	28.4956	862	743044	29.3598
813	660969	28.5132	863	744769	29.3769
814	662596	28.5307	864	746496	29.3939
815	664225	28.5482	865	748225	29.4109
816	665856	28.5657	866	749956	29.4279
817	667489	28.5832	867	751689	29.4449
818	669124	28.6007	868	753424	29.4618
819	670761	28.6182	869	755161	29.4788
820	672400	28.6356	870	756900	29.4958
821	674041	28.6531	871	758641	29.5127
822	675684	28.6705	872	760384	29.5296
823	677329	28.6880	873	762129	29.5466
824	678976	28.7054	874	763876	29.5635
825	680625	28.7228	875	765625	29.5804
826	682276	28.7402	876	767376	29.5973
827	683929	28.7576	877	769129	29.6142
828	685584	28.7750	878	770884	29.6311
829	687241	28.7924	879	772641	29.6479
830	688900	28.8097	880	774400	29.6648
831	690561	28.8271	881	776161	29.6816
832	692224	28.8444	882	777924	29.6985
833	693889	28.8617	883	779689	29.7153
834	695556	28.8791	884	781456	29.7321
835	697225	28.8964	885	783225	29.7489

Table A. Squares and Square Roots of Numbers from 1 to 1000 (*Continued*)

n	n²	√n	n	n²	√n
886	784996	29.7658	936	876096	30.5941
887	786769	29.7825	937	877969	30.6105
888	788544	29.7993	938	879844	30.6268
889	790321	29.8161	939	881721	30.6431
890	792100	29.8329	940	883600	30.6594
891	793881	29.8496	941	885481	30.6757
892	795664	29.8664	942	887364	30.6920
893	797449	29.8831	943	889249	30.7083
894	799236	29.8998	944	891136	30.7246
895	801025	29.9166	945	893025	30.7409
896	802816	29.9333	946	894916	30.7571
897	804609	29.9500	947	896809	30.7734
898	806404	29.9666	948	898704	30.7896
899	808201	29.9833	949	900601	30.8058
900	810000	30.0000	950	902500	30.8221
901	811801	30.0167	951	904401	30.8383
902	813604	30.0333	952	906304	30.8545
903	815409	30.0500	953	908209	30.8707
904	817216	30.0666	954	910116	30.8869
905	819025	30.0832	955	912025	30.9031
906	820836	30.0998	956	913936	30.9192
907	822649	30.1164	957	915849	30.9354
908	824464	30.1330	958	917764	30.9516
909	826281	30.1496	959	919681	30.9677
910	828100	30.1662	960	921600	30.9839
911	829921	30.1828	961	923521	31.0000
912	831744	30.1993	962	925444	31.0161
913	833569	30.2159	963	927369	31.0322
914	835396	30.2324	964	929296	31.0483
915	837225	30.2490	965	931225	31.0644
916	839056	30.2655	966	933156	31.0805
917	840889	30.2820	967	935089	31.0966
918	842724	30.2985	968	937024	31.1127
919	844561	30.3150	969	938961	31.1288
920	846400	30.3315	970	940900	31.1448
921	848241	30.3480	971	942841	31.1609
922	850084	30.3645	972	944784	31.1769
923	851929	30.3809	973	946729	31.1929
924	853776	30.3974	974	948676	31.2090
925	855625	30.4138	975	950625	31.2250
926	857476	30.4302	976	952576	31.2410
927	859329	30.4467	977	954529	31.2570
928	861184	30.4631	978	956484	31.2730
929	863041	30.4795	979	958441	31.2890
930	864900	30.4959	980	960400	31.3050
931	866761	30.5123	981	962361	31.3209
932	868624	30.5287	982	964324	31.3369
933	870489	30.5450	983	966289	31.3528
934	872356	30.5614	984	968256	31.3688
935	874225	30.5778	985	970225	31.3847

Table A. Squares and Square Roots of Numbers from 1 to 1000 (*Continued*)

n	n^2	$\sqrt{n}$	n	n^2	$\sqrt{n}$
986	972196	31.4006	994	988036	31.5278
987	974169	31.4166	995	990025	31.5436
988	976144	31.4325			
989	978121	31.4484	996	992016	31.5595
990	980100	31.4643	997	994009	31.5753
			998	996004	31.5911
991	982081	31.4802	999	998001	31.6070
992	984064	31.4960	1000	1000000	31.6228
993	986049	31.5119			

Table B. Random Numbers

Row	1	2	3	4	5	6	7	8	9	10	11	12	13	14	15	16	17	18	19
1	9	8	9	6	9	9	0	9	6	3	2	3	3	8	6	8	4	4	2
2	3	5	6	1	7	4	1	3	2	6	8	6	0	4	7	5	2	0	3
3	4	0	6	1	6	9	6	1	5	9	5	4	5	4	8	6	7	4	0
4	6	5	6	3	1	6	8	6	7	2	0	7	2	3	2	1	5	0	9
5	2	4	9	7	9	1	0	3	9	6	7	4	1	5	4	9	6	9	8
6	7	6	1	2	7	5	6	9	4	8	4	2	8	5	2	4	1	8	0
7	8	2	1	3	4	7	4	6	3	0	7	5	0	9	2	9	0	6	1
8	6	9	5	6	5	6	0	9	0	7	7	1	4	1	8	3	1	9	3
9	7	2	1	9	9	8	0	1	6	1	6	2	3	6	9	5	5	8	4
10	2	9	0	7	3	0	8	9	6	3	3	8	5	5	6	5	2	0	9
11	9	3	5	4	5	7	4	0	3	0	1	0	4	3	3	9	5	3	2
12	9	7	5	7	9	4	8	6	8	7	6	1	6	8	2	5	5	5	3
13	4	1	7	8	6	8	1	0	5	8	8	6	1	6	8	2	9	0	4
14	5	0	8	3	3	4	5	4	4	2	5	3	0	4	9	6	1	2	3
15	3	5	0	2	9	4	1	0	0	3	9	0	5	8	6	0	9	9	6
16	0	3	8	2	3	5	1	0	1	0	6	8	5	2	4	8	0	3	8
17	1	7	2	9	1	2	7	8	4	7	0	3	3	1	5	8	2	7	3
18	5	0	5	7	9	5	8	7	8	9	3	5	3	4	4	6	1	1	3
19	7	7	3	3	5	3	6	1	3	2	8	5	4	1	4	8	3	9	0
20	1	0	9	1	3	8	2	5	3	0	3	8	0	9	3	3	0	4	5
21	1	3	8	5	1	8	5	9	4	1	9	3	9	3	6	5	9	8	4
22	8	6	4	7	8	7	5	9	4	1	9	3	9	3	6	5	9	8	4
23	0	6	9	6	5	1	0	3	2	6	7	7	4	9	6	0	3	4	0
24	7	6	7	4	7	0	8	3	8	7	3	2	5	1	2	4	2	9	7
25	3	2	3	8	1	3	1	8	7	4	5	9	0	0	2	4	1	2	1
26	9	2	1	6	4	2	3	8	7	6	2	6	2	6	4	8	1	0	1
27	3	7	4	2	2	8	1	7	8	0	6	0	0	0	3	2	2	9	7
28	0	7	8	0	8	5	1	5	2	6	5	8	7	5	3	0	5	9	6
29	7	4	2	3	3	2	6	0	0	6	5	2	2	3	6	3	9	0	4
30	1	8	2	7	5	9	5	3	6	5	2	9	9	1	1	7	3	4	3
31	4	3	1	8	7	0	6	0	8	6	5	0	1	0	4	0	6	1	5
32	8	5	8	0	6	1	4	1	2	0	4	4	1	4	7	6	3	5	1
33	4	5	8	5	0	4	5	8	3	9	2	8	7	8	9	0	8	4	3
34	5	0	2	5	4	9	2	2	1	1	0	0	5	4	8	7	6	4	0
35	0	8	1	7	0	6	3	3	4	7	6	2	6	8	9	3	4	1	4
36	2	5	9	3	4	6	0	7	5	2	0	0	9	6	0	8	2	2	5
37	2	1	3	1	3	7	8	9	8	4	9	3	8	0	2	2	1	8	1
38	3	8	8	6	8	5	1	3	3	4	6	7	2	6	3	4	8	6	7
39	0	9	9	8	5	9	8	4	4	2	2	1	1	0	1	7	6	1	3
40	2	2	3	5	3	9	7	4	4	2	1	4	0	5	8	2	3	0	8

Table B. Random Numbers (*Continued*)

20	21	22	23	24	25	26	27	28	29	30	31	32	33	34	35	36	37	38	39	40	Row
0	9	7	1	1	9	1	2	7	3	5	1	8	4	0	4	1	0	6	0	3	1
8	3	7	7	9	1	4	9	9	5	9	2	0	1	6	1	2	6	6	7	0	2
2	5	6	3	7	8	3	3	8	4	3	9	3	9	0	0	9	8	3	5	2	3
4	7	0	8	6	6	5	9	6	2	7	3	5	9	0	1	8	0	9	6	9	4
0	9	8	7	3	5	6	8	8	1	2	0	2	3	2	6	4	3	1	9	7	5
5	1	8	8	4	7	0	1	7	6	8	2	1	6	3	2	1	8	1	8	3	6
1	3	7	8	6	9	5	4	1	7	3	8	7	1	5	6	5	6	4	3	6	7
5	9	0	1	5	2	8	6	5	5	7	8	1	8	7	1	2	4	0	4	1	8
2	2	5	5	2	1	8	6	9	8	9	8	0	5	8	9	9	4	1	3	4	9
1	3	4	2	8	5	0	7	9	8	4	3	5	8	0	9	4	6	6	0	5	10
2	6	8	6	6	4	7	1	5	1	6	4	6	7	6	0	8	7	3	5	2	11
8	6	0	1	4	2	9	8	6	8	0	7	6	5	1	9	1	3	7	0	3	12
9	5	7	0	9	8	7	6	9	0	6	5	4	0	3	6	5	6	3	5	0	13
2	2	3	4	7	8	0	2	0	8	0	3	4	9	2	5	7	7	8	6	4	14
2	4	6	1	0	5	0	6	1	4	9	4	7	3	9	1	7	6	4	5	8	15
6	3	4	8	1	6	9	5	6	2	0	4	6	1	6	8	1	9	9	1	1	16
9	0	5	1	3	6	1	9	5	4	1	2	5	4	2	9	5	6	2	4	0	17
3	6	7	0	3	5	3	7	4	1	7	5	4	8	3	7	4	8	5	7	2	18
4	3	6	6	3	6	3	0	0	9	4	2	2	5	1	8	9	5	1	9	7	19
1	0	6	9	0	2	7	3	9	8	4	0	6	9	8	2	3	2	8	0	4	20
9	1	3	5	7	9	6	2	4	3	4	6	4	9	1	3	1	7	5	2	2	21
6	4	2	2	2	1	4	5	2	2	8	3	2	1	2	6	6	0	1	8	9	22
7	2	6	9	0	7	5	3	2	5	6	2	7	6	3	8	1	4	1	5	1	23
8	2	8	2	4	4	4	2	9	1	9	8	3	4	4	1	0	4	6	9	6	24
7	3	1	4	3	0	4	7	1	3	7	4	8	6	7	3	2	6	6	2	0	25
0	6	4	5	8	3	1	4	8	1	8	3	1	6	4	3	0	2	8	7	3	26
4	2	2	8	3	2	1	9	3	0	1	7	5	9	0	9	1	2	5	8	2	27
2	9	8	7	2	0	6	4	0	2	7	1	3	1	6	8	7	0	9	2	5	28
0	8	0	5	6	8	2	4	3	6	1	3	5	2	3	5	9	8	6	2	1	29
0	1	7	6	1	5	7	9	0	3	5	3	4	2	4	8	5	6	4	0	6	30
5	1	9	8	5	2	4	5	1	7	5	3	2	4	6	7	9	9	6	7	2	31
0	3	6	6	3	7	8	6	9	7	2	8	9	0	7	2	9	4	0	8	6	32
5	0	0	0	2	0	8	9	0	1	0	6	2	0	4	6	9	6	5	4	9	33
1	9	4	4	2	6	4	2	4	1	0	2	7	9	6	8	7	5	6	9	3	34
0	0	5	3	8	3	2	7	5	0	4	7	6	4	6	3	0	4	7	5	3	35
6	2	6	2	0	6	0	1	4	8	9	6	5	9	7	3	6	7	6	5	4	36
6	3	9	0	3	5	0	9	1	2	0	5	9	7	3	2	5	9	3	0	2	37
9	7	3	3	5	4	0	6	4	9	4	7	9	1	4	3	9	7	7	1	8	38
1	9	6	2	9	4	2	9	7	0	3	8	9	5	7	0	6	9	7	2	5	39
5	9	4	5	8	6	2	3	0	6	2	9	8	6	3	0	4	1	0	7	6	40

Table C. Areas and Ordinates of the Normal Curve in Terms of x/σ

(1) z Standard Score $\left(\dfrac{x}{\sigma}\right)$	(2) A Area from Mean to $\dfrac{x}{\sigma}$	(3) B Area in Larger Portion	(4) C Area in Smaller Portion	(5) y Ordinate at $\dfrac{x}{\sigma}$
0.00	.0000	.5000	.5000	.3989
0.01	.0040	.5040	.4960	.3989
0.02	.0080	.5080	.4920	.3989
0.03	.0120	.5120	.4880	.3988
0.04	.0160	.5160	.4840	.3986
0.05	.0199	.5199	.4801	.3984
0.06	.0239	.5239	.4761	.3982
0.07	.0279	.5279	.4721	.3980
0.08	.0319	.5319	.4681	.3977
0.09	.0359	.5359	.4641	.3973
0.10	.0398	.5398	.4602	.3970
0.11	.0438	.5438	.4562	.3965
0.12	.0478	.5478	.4522	.3961
0.13	.0517	.5517	.4483	.3956
0.14	.0557	.5557	.4443	.3951
0.15	.0596	.5596	.4404	.3945
0.16	.0636	.5636	.4364	.3939
0.17	.0675	.5675	.4325	.3932
0.18	.0714	.5714	.4286	.3925
0.19	.0753	.5753	.4247	.3918
0.20	.0793	.5793	.4207	.3910
0.21	.0832	.5832	.4168	.3902
0.22	.0871	.5871	.4129	.3894
0.23	.0910	.5910	.4090	.3885
0.24	.0948	.5948	.4052	.3876
0.25	.0987	.5987	.4013	.3867
0.26	.1026	.6026	.3974	.3857
0.27	.1064	.6064	.3936	.3847
0.28	.1103	.6103	.3897	.3836
0.29	.1141	.6141	.3859	.3825
0.30	.1179	.6179	.3821	.3814
0.31	.1217	.6217	.3783	.3802
0.32	.1255	.6255	.3745	.3790
0.33	.1293	.6293	.3707	.3778
0.34	.1331	.6331	.3669	.3765
0.35	.1368	.6368	.3632	.3752
0.36	.1406	.6406	.3594	.3739
0.37	.1443	.6443	.3557	.3725
0.38	.1480	.6480	.3520	.3712
0.39	.1517	.6517	.3483	.3697
0.40	.1554	.6554	.3446	.3683
0.41	.1591	.6591	.3409	.3668
0.42	.1628	.6628	.3372	.3653
0.43	.1664	.6664	.3336	.3637
0.44	.1700	.6700	.3300	.3621

SOURCE: *Statistical Methods,* second edition, by Allen L. Edwards. Copyright © 1967 by Allen L. Edwards. First edition copyright 1954 by Allen L. Edwards under the title *Statistical Methods for the Behavioral Sciences.* Reprinted by permission of Holt Rinehart & Winston, Inc.

Table C
215

Table C. Areas and Ordinates of the Normal Curve in Terms of x/σ (Continued)

(1) z Standard Score $\left(\frac{x}{\sigma}\right)$	(2) A Area from Mean to $\frac{x}{\sigma}$	(3) B Area in Larger Portion	(4) C Area in Smaller Portion	(5) y Ordinate at $\frac{x}{\sigma}$
0.45	.1736	.6736	.3264	.3605
0.46	.1772	.6772	.3228	.3589
0.47	.1808	.6808	.3192	.3572
0.48	.1844	.6844	.3156	.3555
0.49	.1879	.6879	.3121	.3538
0.50	.1915	.6915	.3085	.3521
0.51	.1950	.6950	.3050	.3503
0.52	.1985	.6985	.3015	.3485
0.53	.2019	.7019	.2981	.3467
0.54	.2054	.7054	.2946	.3448
0.55	.2088	.7088	.2912	.3429
0.56	.2123	.7123	.2877	.3410
0.57	.2157	.7157	.2843	.3391
0.58	.2190	.7190	.2810	.3372
0.59	.2224	.7224	.2776	.3352
0.60	.2257	.7257	.2743	.3332
0.61	.2291	.7291	.2709	.3312
0.62	.2324	.7324	.2676	.3292
0.63	.2357	.7357	.2643	.3271
0.64	.2389	.7389	.2611	.3251
0.65	.2422	.7422	.2578	.3230
0.66	.2454	.7454	.2546	.3209
0.67	.2486	.7486	.2514	.3187
0.68	.2517	.7517	.2483	.3166
0.69	.2549	.7549	.2451	.3144
0.70	.2580	.7580	.2420	.3123
0.71	.2611	.7611	.2389	.3101
0.72	.2642	.7642	.2358	.3079
0.73	.2673	.7673	.2327	.3056
0.74	.2704	.7704	.2296	.3034
0.75	.2734	.7734	.2266	.3011
0.76	.2764	.7764	.2236	.2989
0.77	.2794	.7794	.2206	.2966
0.78	.2823	.7823	.2177	.2943
0.79	.2852	.7852	.2148	.2920
0.80	.2881	.7881	.2119	.2897
0.81	.2910	.7910	.2090	.2874
0.82	.2939	.7939	.2061	.2850
0.83	.2967	.7967	.2033	.2827
0.84	.2995	.7995	.2005	.2803
0.85	.3023	.8023	.1977	.2780
0.86	.3051	.8051	.1949	.2756
0.87	.3078	.8078	.1922	.2732
0.88	.3106	.8106	.1894	.2709
0.89	.3133	.8133	.1867	.2685

Table C. Areas and Ordinates of the Normal Curve in Terms of x/σ (*Continued*)

(1) z Standard Score $\left(\dfrac{x}{\sigma}\right)$	(2) A Area from Mean to $\dfrac{x}{\sigma}$	(3) B Area in Larger Portion	(4) C Area in Smaller Portion	(5) y Ordinate at $\dfrac{x}{\sigma}$
0.90	.3159	.8159	.1841	.2661
0.91	.3186	.8186	.1814	.2637
0.92	.3212	.8212	.1788	.2613
0.93	.3238	.8238	.1762	.2589
0.94	.3264	.8264	.1736	.2565
0.95	.3289	.8289	.1711	.2541
0.96	.3315	.8315	.1685	.2516
0.97	.3340	.8340	.1660	.2492
0.98	.3365	.8365	.1635	.2468
0.99	.3389	.8389	.1611	.2444
1.00	.3413	.8413	.1587	.2420
1.01	.3438	.8438	.1562	.2396
1.02	.3461	.8461	.1539	.2371
1.03	.3485	.8485	.1515	.2347
1.04	.3508	.8508	.1492	.2323
1.05	.3531	.8531	.1469	.2299
1.06	.3554	.8554	.1446	.2275
1.07	.3577	.8577	.1423	.2251
1.08	.3599	.8599	.1401	.2227
1.09	.3621	.8621	.1379	.2203
1.10	.3643	.8643	.1357	.2179
1.11	.3665	.8665	.1335	.2155
1.12	.3686	.8686	.1314	.2131
1.13	.3708	.8708	.1292	.2107
1.14	.3729	.8729	.1271	.2083
1.15	.3749	.8749	.1251	.2059
1.16	.3770	.8770	.1230	.2036
1.17	.3790	.8790	.1210	.2012
1.18	.3810	.8810	.1190	.1989
1.19	.3830	.8830	.1170	.1965
1.20	.3849	.8849	.1151	.1942
1.21	.3869	.8869	.1131	.1919
1.22	.3888	.8888	.1112	.1895
1.23	.3907	.8907	.1093	.1872
1.24	.3925	.8925	.1075	.1849
1.25	.3944	.8944	.1056	.1826
1.26	.3962	.8962	.1038	.1804
1.27	.3980	.8980	.1020	.1781
1.28	.3997	.8997	.1003	.1758
1.29	.4015	.9015	.0985	.1736
1.30	.4032	.9032	.0968	.1714
1.31	.4049	.9049	.0951	.1691
1.32	.4066	.9066	.0934	.1669
1.33	.4082	.9082	.0918	.1647
1.34	.4099	.9099	.0901	.1626

Table C
217

Table C. Areas and Ordinates of the Normal Curve in Terms of x/σ (Continued)

(1) z Standard Score $\left(\frac{x}{\sigma}\right)$	(2) A Area from Mean to $\frac{x}{\sigma}$	(3) B Area in Larger Portion	(4) C Area in Smaller Portion	(5) y Ordinate at $\frac{x}{\sigma}$
1.35	.4115	.9115	.0885	.1604
1.36	.4131	.9131	.0869	.1582
1.37	.4147	.9147	.0853	.1561
1.38	.4162	.9162	.0838	.1539
1.39	.4177	.9177	.0823	.1518
1.40	.4192	.9192	.0808	.1497
1.41	.4207	.9207	.0793	.1476
1.42	.4222	.9222	.0778	.1456
1.43	.4236	.9236	.0764	.1435
1.44	.4251	.9251	.0749	.1415
1.45	.4265	.9265	.0735	.1394
1.46	.4279	.9279	.0721	.1374
1.47	.4292	.9292	.0708	.1354
1.48	.4306	.9306	.0694	.1334
1.49	.4319	.9319	.0681	.1315
1.50	.4332	.9332	.0668	.1295
1.51	.4345	.9345	.0655	.1276
1.52	.4357	.9357	.0643	.1257
1.53	.4370	9370	.0630	.1238
1.54	.4382	.9382	.0618	.1219
1.55	.4394	.9394	.0606	.1200
1.56	.4406	.9406	.0594	.1182
1.57	.4418	.9418	.0582	.1163
1.58	.4429	.9429	.0571	.1145
1.59	.4441	.9441	.0559	.1127
1.60	.4452	.9452	.0548	.1109
1.61	.4463	.9463	.0537	.1092
1.62	.4474	.9474	.0526	.1074
1.63	.4484	.9484	.0516	.1057
1.64	.4495	.9495	.0505	.1040
1.65	.4505	.9505	.0495	.1023
1.66	.4515	.9515	.0485	.1006
1.67	.4525	.9525	.0475	.0989
1.68	.4535	.9535	.0465	.0973
1.69	.4545	.9545	.0455	.0957
1.70	.4554	.9554	.0446	.0940
1.71	.4564	.9564	.0436	.0925
1.72	.4573	.9573	.0427	.0909
1.73	.4582	.9582	.0418	.0893
1.74	.4591	.9591	.0409	.0878
1.75	.4599	.9599	.0401	.0863
1.76	.4608	.9608	.0392	.0848
1.77	.4616	.9616	.0384	.0833
1.78	.4625	.9625	.0375	.0818
1.79	.4633	.9633	.0367	.0804

Table C. Areas and Ordinates of the Normal Curve in Terms of x/σ (*Continued*)

(1) z Standard Score $\left(\dfrac{x}{\sigma}\right)$	(2) A Area from Mean to $\dfrac{x}{\sigma}$	(3) B Area in Larger Portion	(4) C Area in Smaller Portion	(5) y Ordinate at $\dfrac{x}{\sigma}$
1.80	.4641	.9641	.0359	.0790
1.81	.4649	.9649	.0351	.0775
1.82	.4656	.9656	.0344	.0761
1.83	.4664	.9664	.0336	.0748
1.84	.4671	.9671	.0329	.0734
1.85	.4648	.9678	.0322	.0721
1.86	.4686	.9686	.0314	.0707
1.87	.4693	.9693	.0307	.0694
1.88	.4699	.9699	.0301	.0681
1.89	.4706	.9706	.0294	.0669
1.90	.4713	.9713	.0287	.0656
1.91	.4719	.9719	.0281	.0644
1.92	.4726	.9726	.0274	.0632
1.93	.4732	.9732	.0268	.0620
1.94	.4738	.9738	.0262	.0608
1.95	.4744	.9744	.0256	.0596
1.96	.4750	.9750	.0250	.0584
1.97	.4756	.9756	.0244	.0573
1.98	.4761	.9761	.0239	.0562
1.99	.4767	.9767	.0233	.0551
2.00	.4772	.9772	.0228	.0540
2.01	.4778	.9778	.0222	.0529
2.02	.4783	.9783	.0217	.0519
2.03	.4788	.9788	.0212	.0508
2.04	.4793	.9793	.0207	.0498
2.05	.4798	.9798	.0202	.0488
2.06	.4803	.9803	.0197	.0478
2.07	.4808	.9808	.0192	.0468
2.08	.4812	.9812	.0188	.0459
2.09	.4817	.9817	.0183	.0449
2.10	.4821	.9821	.0179	.0440
2.11	.4826	.9826	.0174	.0431
2.12	.4830	.9830	.0170	.0422
2.13	.4834	.9834	.0166	.0413
2.14	.4838	.9838	.0162	.0404
2.15	.4842	.9842	.0158	.0396
2.16	.4846	.9846	.0154	.0387
2.17	.4850	.9850	.0150	.0379
2.18	.4854	.9854	.0146	.0371
2.19	.4857	.9857	.0143	.0363
2.20	.4861	.9861	.0139	.0355
2.21	.4864	.9864	.0136	.0347
2.22	.4868	.9868	.0132	.0339
2.23	.4871	.9871	.0129	.0332
2.24	.4875	.9875	.0125	.0325

Table C
219

Table C. Areas and Ordinates of the Normal Curve in Terms of x/σ (*Continued*)

(1) z Standard Score $\left(\frac{x}{\sigma}\right)$	(2) A Area from Mean to $\frac{x}{\sigma}$	(3) B Area in Larger Portion	(4) C Area in Smaller Portion	(5) y Ordinate at $\frac{x}{\sigma}$
2.25	.4878	.9878	.0122	.0317
2.26	.4881	.9881	.0119	.0310
2.27	.4884	.9884	.0116	.0303
2.28	.4887	.9887	.0113	.0297
2.29	.4890	.9890	.0110	.0290
2.30	.4893	.9893	.0107	.0283
2.31	.4896	.9896	.0104	.0277
2.32	.4898	.9898	.0102	.0270
2.33	.4901	.9901	.0099	.0264
2.34	.4904	.9904	.0096	.0258
2.35	.4906	.9906	.0094	.0252
2.36	.4909	.9909	.0091	.0246
2.37	.4911	.9911	.0089	.0241
2.38	.4913	.9913	.0087	.0235
2.39	.4916	.9916	.0084	.0229
2.40	.4918	.9918	.0082	.0224
2.41	.4920	.9920	.0080	.0219
2.42	.4922	.9922	.0078	.0213
2.43	.4925	.9925	.0075	.0208
2.44	.4927	.9927	.0073	.0203
2.45	.4929	.9929	.0071	.0198
2.46	.4931	.9931	.0069	.0194
2.47	.4932	.9932	.0068	.0189
2.48	.4934	.9934	.0066	.0184
2.49	.4936	.9936	.0064	.0180
2.50	.4938	.9938	.0062	.0175
2.51	.4940	.9940	.0060	.0171
2.52	.4941	.9941	.0059	.0167
2.53	.4943	.9943	.0057	.0163
2.54	.4945	.9945	.0055	.0158
2.55	.4946	.9946	.0054	.0154
2.56	.4948	.9948	.0052	.0151
2.57	.4949	.9949	.0051	.0147
2.58	.4951	.9951	.0049	.0143
2.59	.4952	.9952	.0048	.0139
2.60	.4953	.9953	.0047	.0136
2.61	.4955	.9955	.0045	.0132
2.62	.4956	.9956	.0044	.0129
2.63	.4957	.9957	.0043	.0126
2.64	.4959	.9959	.0041	.0122
2.65	.4960	.9960	.0040	.0119
2.66	.4961	.9961	.0039	.0116
2.67	.4962	.9962	.0038	.0113
2.68	.4963	.9963	.0037	.0110
2.69	.4964	.9964	.0036	.0107

Table C. Areas and Ordinates of the Normal Curve in Terms of x/σ *(Continued)*

(1) z Standard Score $\left(\dfrac{x}{\sigma}\right)$	(2) A Area from Mean to $\dfrac{x}{\sigma}$	(3) B Area in Larger Portion	(4) C Area in Smaller Portion	(5) y Ordinate at $\dfrac{x}{\sigma}$
2.70	.4965	.9965	.0035	.0104
2.71	.4966	.9966	.0034	.0101
2.72	.4967	.9967	.0033	.0099
2.73	.4968	.9968	.0032	.0096
2.74	.4969	.9969	.0031	.0093
2.75	.4970	.9970	.0030	.0091
2.76	.4971	.9971	.0029	.0088
2.77	.4972	.9972	.0028	.0086
2.78	.4973	.9973	.0027	.0084
2.79	.4974	.9974	.0026	.0081
2.80	.4974	.9974	.0026	.0079
2.81	.4975	.9975	.0025	.0077
2.82	.4976	.9976	.0024	.0075
2.83	.4977	.9977	.0023	.0073
2.84	.4977	.9977	.0023	.0071
2.85	.4978	.9978	.0022	.0069
2.86	.4979	.9979	.0021	.0067
2.87	.4979	.9979	.0021	.0065
2.88	.4980	.9980	.0020	.0063
2.89	.4981	.9981	.0019	.0061
2.90	.4981	.9981	.0019	.0060
2.91	.4982	.9982	.0018	.0058
2.92	.4982	.9982	.0018	.0056
2.93	.4983	.9983	.0017	.0055
2.94	.4984	.9984	.0016	.0053
2.95	.4984	.9984	.0016	.0051
2.96	.4985	.9985	.0015	.0050
2.97	.4985	.9985	.0015	.0048
2.98	.4986	.9986	.0014	.0047
2.99	.4986	.9986	.0014	.0046
3.00	.4987	.9987	.0013	.0044
3.01	.4987	.9987	.0013	.0043
3.02	.4987	.9987	.0013	.0042
3.03	.4988	.9988	.0012	.0040
3.04	.4988	.9988	.0012	.0039
3.05	.4989	.9989	.0011	.0038
3.06	.4989	.9989	.0011	.0037
3.07	.4989	.9989	.0011	.0036
3.08	.4990	.9990	.0010	.0035
3.09	.4990	.9990	.0010	.0034
3.10	.4990	.9990	.0010	.0033
3.11	.4991	.9991	.0009	.0032
3.12	.4991	.9991	.0009	.0031
3.13	.4991	.9991	.0009	.0030
3.14	.4992	.9992	.0008	.0029

Table C
221

Table C. Areas and Ordinates of the Normal Curve in Terms of x/σ *(Continued)*

(1) z Standard Score $\left(\frac{x}{\sigma}\right)$	(2) A Area from Mean to $\frac{x}{\sigma}$	(3) B Area in Larger Portion	(4) C Area in Smaller Portion	(5) y Ordinate at $\frac{x}{\sigma}$
3.15	.4992	.9992	.0008	.0028
3.16	.4992	.9992	.0008	.0027
3.17	.4992	.9992	.0008	.0026
3.18	.4993	.9993	.0007	.0025
3.19	.4993	.9993	.0007	.0025
3.20	.4993	.9993	.0007	.0024
3.21	.4993	.9993	.0007	.0023
3.22	.4994	.9994	.0006	.0022
3.23	.4994	.9994	.0006	.0022
3.24	.4994	.9994	.0006	.0021
3.30	.4995	.9995	.0005	.0017
3.40	.4997	.9997	.0003	.0012
3.50	.4998	.9998	.0002	.0009
3.60	.4998	.9998	.0002	.0006
3.70	.4999	.9999	.0001	.0004

Table D. t Values

Probability for a One-Tailed Test

Probability for a Two-Tailed Test

df	.45	.40	.35	.30	.25	.20	.15	.1	.05	.025	.01	.005	.0005
	.9	.8	.7	.6	.5	.4	.3	.2	.1	.05	.02	.01	.001
1	.158	.325	.510	.727	1.000	1.376	1.963	3.078	6.314	12.706	31.821	63.657	636.619
2	.142	.289	.445	.617	.816	1.061	1.386	1.886	2.920	4.303	6.965	9.925	31.598
3	.137	.277	.424	.584	.765	.978	1.250	1.638	2.353	3.182	4.541	5.841	12.924
4	.134	.271	.414	.569	.741	.941	1.190	1.533	2.132	2.776	3.747	4.604	8.610
5	.132	.267	.408	.559	.727	.920	1.156	1.476	2.015	2.571	3.365	4.032	6.869
6	.131	.265	.404	.553	.718	.906	1.134	1.440	1.943	2.447	3.143	3.707	5.959
7	.130	.263	.402	.549	.711	.896	1.119	1.415	1.895	2.365	2.998	3.499	5.408
8	.130	.262	.399	.546	.706	.889	1.108	1.397	1.860	2.306	2.896	3.355	5.041
9	.129	.261	.398	.543	.703	.883	1.100	1.383	1.833	2.262	2.821	3.250	4.781
10	.129	.260	.397	.542	.700	.879	1.093	1.372	1.812	2.228	2.764	3.169	4.587
11	.129	.260	.396	.540	.697	.876	1.088	1.363	1.796	2.201	2.718	3.106	4.437
12	.128	.259	.395	.539	.695	.873	1.083	1.356	1.782	2.179	2.681	3.055	4.318
13	.128	.259	.394	.538	.694	.870	1.079	1.350	1.771	2.160	2.650	3.012	4.221
14	.128	.258	.393	.537	.692	.868	1.076	1.345	1.761	2.145	2.624	2.977	4.140
15	.128	.258	.393	.536	.691	.866	1.074	1.341	1.753	2.131	2.602	2.947	4.073
16	.128	.258	.392	.535	.690	.865	1.071	1.337	1.746	2.120	2.583	2.921	4.015
17	.128	.257	.392	.534	.689	.863	1.069	1.333	1.740	2.110	2.567	2.898	3.965
18	.127	.257	.392	.534	.688	.862	1.067	1.330	1.734	2.101	2.552	2.878	3.922
19	.127	.257	.391	.533	.688	.861	1.066	1.328	1.729	2.093	2.539	2.861	3.883
20	.127	.257	.391	.533	.687	.860	1.064	1.325	1.725	2.086	2.528	2.845	3.850
21	.127	.257	.391	.532	.686	.859	1.063	1.323	1.721	2.080	2.518	2.831	3.819
22	.127	.256	.390	.532	.686	.858	1.061	1.321	1.717	2.074	2.508	2.819	3.792
23	.127	.256	.390	.532	.685	.858	1.060	1.319	1.714	2.069	2.500	2.807	3.767
24	.127	.256	.390	.531	.685	.857	1.059	1.318	1.711	2.064	2.492	2.797	3.745
25	.127	.256	.390	.531	.684	.856	1.058	1.316	1.708	2.060	2.485	2.787	3.725

SOURCE: *Statistical Tables for Biological, Agricultural and Medical Research* by R. A. Fisher and F. Yates. Published 1963 by Oliver & Boyd, Edinburgh. Reprinted by permission of the authors and publishers.

Table D. t Values (Continued)

	Probability for a One-Tailed Test												
df	.45	.40	.35	.30	.25	.20	.15	.1	.05	.025	.01	.005	.0005
	Probability for a Two-Tailed Test												
	.9	.8	.7	.6	.5	.4	.3	.2	.1	.05	.02	.01	.001
26	.127	.256	.390	.531	.684	.856	1.058	1.315	1.706	2.056	2.479	2.779	3.707
27	.127	.256	.389	.531	.684	.855	1.057	1.314	1.703	2.052	2.473	2.771	3.690
28	.127	.256	.389	.530	.683	.855	1.056	1.313	1.701	2.048	2.467	2.763	3.674
29	.127	.256	.389	.530	.683	.854	1.055	1.311	1.699	2.045	2.462	2.756	3.659
30	.127	.256	.389	.530	.683	.854	1.055	1.310	1.697	2.042	2.457	2.750	3.646
40	.126	.255	.388	.529	.681	.851	1.050	1.303	1.684	2.021	2.423	2.704	3.551
60	.126	.254	.387	.527	.679	.848	1.046	1.296	1.671	2.000	2.390	2.660	3.460
120	.126	.254	.386	.526	.677	.845	1.041	1.289	1.658	1.980	2.358	2.617	3.373
∞	.126	.253	.385	.524	.674	.842	1.036	1.282	1.645	1.960	2.326	2.576	3.291

Table E. Cumulative Binomial Probabilities: Sum of First $(m + 1)$ Terms in Expansion of $(Q + P)^N$ (Decimal points omitted to save space)

$$\sum_{r=0}^{m} \binom{N}{r} Q^{N-r} P^r$$

A. $Q = .25$ and $P = .75$

N \ m	0	1	2	3	4	5	6	7	8	9	10	11	12	13	14	15
5	001	016	104	367	763	*										
6		005	038	169	466	822	*									
7		001	013	071	244	555	867	*								
8			004	027	114	321	633	900	*							
9			001	010	049	166	399	700	925	*						
10				004	020	078	224	474	756	944	*					
11				001	008	034	115	287	545	803	958	*				
12					003	014	054	158	351	609	842	968	*			
13					001	006	024	080	206	416	667	873	976	*		
14						002	010	038	112	258	479	719	899	982	*	
15						001	004	017	057	148	314	539	764	920	987	*
16							002	007	027	080	190	370	595	803	937	990
17							001	003	012	040	107	235	426	647	836	950
18								001	005	019	057	139	283	481	694	865
19									002	009	029	077	175	332	535	737
20									001	004	014	041	102	214	383	585
21										002	006	021	056	130	256	433
22										001	003	010	030	075	162	301
23											001	005	015	041	096	196
24											001	002	007	021	055	121
25												001	003	011	030	071

*1.0 or approximately 1.0.

SOURCE: *Statistical Inference* by Helen M. Walker and Joseph Lev. Copyright © 1953 by Holt, Rinehart and Winston, Inc., New York. Reprinted by permission of Holt, Rinehart and Winston, Inc.

Table E. Cumulative Binomial Probabilities (*Continued*)

B. Q = P = .5

N \ m	0	1	2	3	4	5	6	7	8	9	10	11	12	13	14	15
5	031	188	500	812	969	*										
6	016	109	344	656	891	984	*									
7	008	062	227	500	773	938	992	*								
8	004	035	145	363	637	855	965	996	*							
9	002	020	090	254	500	746	910	980	998	*						
10	001	011	055	172	377	623	828	945	989	999	*					
11		006	033	113	274	500	726	887	967	994	*	*				
12		003	019	073	194	387	613	806	927	981	997	*	*			
13		002	011	046	133	291	500	709	867	954	989	998	*	*		
14		001	006	029	090	212	395	605	788	910	971	994	999	*	*	
15			004	018	059	151	304	500	696	849	941	982	996	*	*	*
16			002	011	038	105	227	402	598	773	895	962	989	998	*	*
17			001	006	025	072	166	315	500	685	834	928	975	994	999	*
18			001	004	015	048	119	240	407	593	760	881	952	985	996	999
19				002	010	032	084	180	324	500	676	820	916	968	990	998
20				001	006	021	058	132	252	412	588	748	868	942	979	994
21				001	004	013	039	095	192	332	500	668	808	905	961	987
22					002	008	026	067	143	262	416	584	738	857	933	974
23					001	005	017	047	105	202	339	500	661	798	895	953
24					001	003	011	032	076	154	271	419	581	729	846	924
25						002	007	022	054	115	212	345	500	655	788	885

*1.0 or approximately 1.0.

Table E. Cumulative Binomial Probabilities (*Continued*)

C. $Q = .75$ and $P = .25$

N \ m	0	1	2	3	4	5	6	7	8	9	10	11	12	13
5	237	633	896	984	999	*								
6	178	534	831	962	995	*	*							
7	133	445	756	929	987	999	*	*						
8	100	367	679	886	973	996	*	*	*					
9	075	300	601	834	951	990	999	*	*	*				
10	056	244	526	776	922	980	996	999	*	*	*			
11	042	197	455	713	885	966	992	999	*	*	*	*		
12	032	158	391	649	842	946	986	997	999	*	*	*	*	
13	024	127	333	584	794	920	976	994	998	*	*	*	*	*
14	018	101	281	521	742	888	962	990	998	999	*	*	*	*
15	013	080	236	461	686	852	943	983	996	999	*	*	*	*
16	010	063	197	405	630	810	920	973	993	998	*	*	*	*
17	008	050	164	353	574	765	893	960	988	997	999	*	*	*
18	006	039	135	306	519	717	861	943	981	995	999	*	*	*
19	004	031	111	263	465	668	825	923	971	991	998	*	*	*
20	003	024	091	225	415	617	786	898	959	986	996	999	*	*
21	002	019	075	192	367	567	744	870	944	979	994	998	*	*
22	002	015	061	162	323	517	699	838	925	970	990	997	999	*
23	001	012	049	137	283	468	654	804	904	959	985	995	999	*
24	001	009	040	115	247	422	607	766	879	945	979	993	998	999
25	001	007	032	096	214	378	561	727	851	929	970	989	997	999

*1.0 or approximately 1.0.

Table F. Chi-Square Values

Probability

df	.99	.98	.95	.90	.80	.70	.50	.30	.20	.10	.05	.02	.01	.001
1	.0³157	.0³628	.00393	.0158	.0642	.148	.455	1.074	1.642	2.706	3.841	5.412	6.635	10.827
2	.0201	.0404	.103	.211	.446	.713	1.386	2.408	3.219	4.605	5.991	7.824	9.210	13.815
3	.115	.185	.352	.584	1.005	1.424	2.366	3.665	4.642	6.251	7.815	9.837	11.345	16.266
4	.297	.429	.711	1.064	1.649	2.195	3.357	4.878	5.989	7.779	9.488	11.668	13.277	18.467
5	.554	.752	1.145	1.610	2.343	3.000	4.351	6.064	7.289	9.236	11.070	13.388	15.086	20.515
6	.872	1.134	1.635	2.204	3.070	3.828	5.348	7.231	8.558	10.645	12.592	15.033	16.812	22.457
7	1.239	1.564	2.167	2.833	3.822	4.671	6.346	8.383	9.803	12.017	14.067	16.622	18.475	24.322
8	1.646	2.032	2.733	3.490	4.594	5.527	7.344	9.524	11.030	13.362	15.507	18.168	20.090	26.125
9	2.088	2.532	3.325	4.168	5.380	6.393	8.343	10.656	12.242	14.684	16.919	19.679	21.666	27.877
10	2.558	3.059	3.940	4.865	6.179	7.267	9.342	11.781	13.442	15.987	18.307	21.161	23.209	29.588
11	3.053	3.609	4.575	5.578	6.989	8.148	10.341	12.899	14.631	17.275	19.675	22.618	24.725	31.264
12	3.571	4.178	5.226	6.304	7.807	9.034	11.340	14.011	15.812	18.549	21.026	24.054	26.217	32.909
13	4.107	4.765	5.892	7.042	8.634	9.926	12.340	15.119	16.985	19.812	22.362	25.472	27.688	34.528
14	4.660	5.368	6.571	7.790	9.467	10.821	13.339	16.222	18.151	21.064	23.685	26.873	29.141	36.123
15	5.229	5.985	7.261	8.547	10.307	11.721	14.339	17.322	19.311	22.307	24.996	28.259	30.578	37.697
16	5.812	6.614	7.962	9.312	11.152	12.624	15.338	18.418	20.465	23.542	26.296	29.633	32.000	39.252
17	6.408	7.255	8.672	10.085	12.002	13.531	16.338	19.511	21.615	24.769	27.587	30.995	33.409	40.790
18	7.015	7.906	9.390	10.865	12.857	14.440	17.338	20.601	22.760	25.989	28.869	32.346	34.805	42.312
19	7.633	8.567	10.117	11.651	13.716	15.352	18.338	21.689	23.900	27.204	30.144	33.687	36.191	43.820
20	8.260	9.237	10.851	12.443	14.578	16.266	19.337	22.775	25.038	28.412	31.410	35.020	37.566	45.315
21	8.897	9.915	11.591	13.240	15.445	17.182	20.337	23.858	26.171	29.615	32.671	36.343	38.932	46.797
22	9.542	10.600	12.338	14.041	16.314	18.101	21.337	24.939	27.301	30.813	33.924	37.659	40.289	48.268
23	10.196	11.293	13.091	14.848	17.187	19.021	22.337	26.018	28.429	32.007	35.172	38.968	41.638	49.728
24	10.856	11.992	13.848	15.659	18.062	19.943	23.337	27.096	29.553	33.196	36.415	40.270	42.980	51.179
25	11.524	12.697	14.611	16.473	18.940	20.867	24.337	28.172	30.675	34.382	37.652	41.566	44.314	52.620

SOURCE: *Statistical Tables for Biological, Agricultural and Medical Research*, by R. A. Fisher and F. Yates. Published 1963 by Oliver & Boyd, Edinburgh. Reprinted by permission of the authors and publishers.

NOTE: For odd values of n between 30 and 70 the mean of the tabular values for $n - 1$ and $n + 1$ may be taken. For larger values of n, the expression $\sqrt{2\chi^2} - \sqrt{2n - 1}$ may be used as a normal deviate with unit variance, remembering that the probability for χ^2 corresponds with that of a single tail of the normal curve.

Table F. Chi-Square Values (Continued)

df	\.99	\.98	\.95	\.90	\.80	\.70	\.50	\.30	\.20	\.10	\.05	\.02	\.01	\.001
							Probability							
26	12.198	13.409	15.379	17.292	19.820	21.792	25.336	29.246	31.795	35.563	38.885	42.856	45.642	54.052
27	12.879	14.125	16.151	18.114	20.703	22.719	26.336	30.319	32.912	36.741	40.113	44.140	46.963	55.476
28	13.565	14.847	16.928	18.939	21.588	23.647	27.336	31.391	34.027	37.916	41.337	45.419	48.278	56.893
29	14.256	15.574	17.708	19.768	22.475	24.577	28.336	32.461	35.139	39.087	42.557	46.693	49.588	58.302
30	14.953	16.306	18.493	20.599	23.364	25.508	29.336	33.530	36.250	40.256	43.773	47.962	50.892	59.703
32	16.362	17.783	20.072	22.271	25.148	27.373	31.336	35.665	38.466	42.585	46.194	50.487	53.486	62.487
34	17.789	19.275	21.664	23.952	26.938	29.242	33.336	37.795	40.676	44.903	48.602	52.995	56.061	65.247
36	19.233	20.783	23.269	25.643	28.735	31.115	35.336	39.922	42.879	47.212	50.999	55.489	58.619	67.985
38	20.691	22.304	24.884	27.343	30.537	32.992	37.335	42.045	45.076	49.513	53.384	57.969	61.162	70.703
40	22.164	23.838	26.509	29.051	32.345	34.872	39.335	44.165	47.269	51.805	55.759	60.436	63.691	73.402
42	23.650	25.383	28.144	30.765	34.157	36.755	41.335	46.282	49.456	54.090	58.124	62.892	66.206	76.084
44	25.148	26.939	29.787	32.487	35.974	38.641	43.335	48.396	51.639	56.369	60.481	65.337	68.710	78.750
46	26.657	28.504	31.439	34.215	37.795	40.529	45.335	50.507	53.818	58.641	62.830	67.771	71.201	81.400
48	28.177	30.080	33.098	35.949	39.621	42.420	47.335	52.616	55.993	60.907	65.171	70.197	73.683	84.037
50	29.707	31.664	34.764	37.689	41.449	44.313	49.335	54.723	58.164	63.167	67.505	72.613	76.154	86.661
52	31.246	33.256	36.437	39.433	43.281	46.209	51.335	56.827	60.332	65.422	69.832	75.021	78.616	89.272
54	32.793	34.856	38.116	41.183	45.117	48.106	53.335	58.930	62.496	67.673	72.153	77.422	81.069	91.872
56	34.350	36.464	39.801	42.937	46.955	50.005	55.335	61.031	64.658	69.919	74.468	79.815	83.513	94.461
58	35.913	38.078	41.492	44.696	48.797	51.906	57.335	63.129	66.816	72.160	76.778	82.201	85.950	97.039
60	37.485	39.699	43.188	46.459	50.641	53.809	59.335	65.227	68.972	74.397	79.082	84.580	88.379	99.607
62	39.063	41.327	44.889	48.226	52.487	55.714	61.335	67.322	71.125	76.630	81.381	86.953	90.802	102.166
64	40.649	42.960	46.595	49.996	54.336	57.620	63.335	69.416	73.276	78.860	83.675	89.320	93.217	104.716
66	42.240	44.599	48.305	51.770	56.188	59.527	65.335	71.508	75.424	81.085	85.965	91.681	95.626	107.258
68	43.838	46.244	50.020	53.548	58.042	61.436	67.335	73.600	77.571	83.308	88.250	94.037	98.028	109.791
70	45.442	47.893	51.739	55.329	59.898	63.346	69.334	75.689	79.715	85.527	90.531	96.388	100.425	112.317

Table G. Values of *F* Significant at .05 and .01 Levels

df Associated with the Denominator		df Associated with the Numerator																		
nominator		1	2	3	4	5	6	7	8	9	10	12	14	16	20	30	40	50	100
1	5%	161	200	216	225	230	234	237	239	241	242	244	245	246	248	250	251	252	253
	1%	4052	5000	5403	5625	5764	5859	5928	5982	6022	6056	6106	6142	6169	6208	6258	6286	6302	6334
2	5%	18.5	19.0	19.2	19.2	19.3	19.3	19.4	19.4	19.4	19.4	19.4	19.4	19.4	19.4	19.5	19.5	19.5	19.5
	1%	98.5	99.0	99.2	99.2	99.3	99.3	99.4	99.4	99.4	99.4	99.4	99.4	99.4	99.5	99.5	99.5	99.5	99.5
3	5%	10.1	9.55	9.28	9.12	9.01	8.94	8.89	8.85	8.81	8.78	8.74	8.71	8.69	8.66	8.62	8.60	8.58	8.56
	1%	34.1	30.3	29.5	28.7	28.2	27.9	27.7	27.5	27.3	27.2	27.1	26.9	26.8	26.7	26.5	26.4	26.3	26.2
4	5%	7.71	6.94	6.59	6.39	6.26	6.16	6.09	6.04	6.00	5.96	5.91	5.87	5.84	5.80	5.74	5.71	5.70	5.66
	1%	21.2	18.0	16.7	16.0	15.5	15.2	15.0	14.8	14.7	14.5	14.4	14.2	14.2	14.0	13.8	13.7	13.7	13.6
5	5%	6.61	5.79	5.41	5.19	5.05	4.95	4.88	4.82	4.77	4.74	4.68	4.64	4.60	4.56	4.50	4.46	4.44	4.40
	1%	16.3	13.3	12.1	11.4	11.0	10.7	10.5	10.3	10.2	10.1	9.89	9.77	9.68	9.55	9.38	9.29	9.24	9.13
6	5%	5.99	5.14	4.76	4.53	4.39	4.28	4.21	4.15	4.10	4.06	4.00	3.96	3.92	3.87	3.81	3.77	3.75	3.71
	1%	13.7	10.9	9.78	9.15	8.75	8.47	8.26	8.10	7.98	7.87	7.72	7.60	7.52	7.39	7.23	7.14	7.09	6.99
7	5%	5.59	4.74	4.35	4.12	3.97	3.87	3.79	3.73	3.68	3.63	3.57	3.52	3.49	3.44	3.38	3.34	3.32	3.28
	1%	12.2	9.55	8.45	7.85	7.46	7.19	6.99	6.84	6.72	6.62	6.47	6.35	6.27	6.15	5.98	5.90	5.85	5.75
8	5%	5.32	4.46	4.07	3.84	3.69	3.58	3.50	3.44	3.39	3.34	3.28	3.23	3.20	3.15	3.08	3.05	3.03	2.98
	1%	11.3	8.65	7.59	7.01	6.63	6.37	6.18	6.03	5.91	5.82	5.67	5.56	5.48	5.36	5.20	5.11	5.06	4.96
9	5%	5.12	4.26	3.86	3.63	3.48	3.37	3.29	3.23	3.18	3.13	3.07	3.02	2.98	2.93	2.86	2.82	2.80	2.76
	1%	10.6	8.02	6.99	6.42	6.06	5.80	5.61	5.47	5.35	5.26	5.11	5.00	4.92	4.80	4.64	4.56	4.51	4.41
10	5%	4.96	4.10	3.71	3.48	3.33	3.22	3.14	3.07	3.02	2.97	2.91	2.86	2.82	2.77	2.70	2.67	2.64	2.59
	1%	10.0	7.56	6.55	5.99	5.64	5.39	5.20	5.06	4.94	4.85	4.71	4.60	4.52	4.41	4.25	4.17	4.12	4.01
11	5%	4.84	3.98	3.59	3.36	3.20	3.09	3.01	2.95	2.90	2.86	2.79	2.74	2.70	2.65	2.57	2.53	2.50	2.45
	1%	9.65	7.21	6.22	5.67	5.32	5.07	4.89	4.74	4.63	4.54	4.40	4.29	4.21	4.10	3.94	3.86	3.80	3.70
12	5%	4.75	3.89	3.49	3.26	3.11	3.00	2.91	2.85	2.80	2.76	2.69	2.64	2.60	2.54	2.46	2.42	2.40	2.35
	1%	9.33	6.93	5.95	5.41	5.06	4.82	4.64	4.50	4.39	4.30	4.16	4.05	3.98	3.86	3.70	3.61	3.56	3.46

SOURCE: *Statistical Methods*, fourth edition, by G. W. Snedecor, Copyright © 1946, The Iowa State University Press, Ames, Iowa. Reprinted by permission.

Table G. Values of *F* Significant at .05 and .01 Levels (*Continued*)

df Associated with the Numerator

df Associated with the Denominator		1	2	3	4	5	6	7	8	9	10	12	14	16	20	30	40	50	100
13	5%	4.67	3.81	3.41	3.18	3.03	2.92	2.83	2.77	2.71	2.67	2.60	2.55	2.51	2.46	2.38	2.34	2.32	2.26
	1%	9.07	6.70	5.74	5.21	4.86	4.62	4.44	4.30	4.19	4.10	3.96	3.85	3.78	3.67	3.51	3.42	3.37	3.27
14	5%	4.60	3.74	3.34	3.11	2.96	2.85	2.76	2.70	2.65	2.60	2.53	2.48	2.44	2.39	2.31	2.27	2.24	2.19
	1%	8.86	6.51	5.56	5.04	4.70	4.46	4.28	4.14	4.03	3.94	3.80	3.70	3.62	3.51	3.34	3.26	3.21	3.11
15	5%	4.54	3.68	3.29	3.06	2.90	2.79	2.71	2.64	2.59	2.55	2.48	2.43	2.39	2.33	2.25	2.21	2.18	2.12
	1%	8.68	6.36	5.42	4.89	4.56	4.32	4.14	4.00	3.89	3.80	3.67	3.56	3.48	3.36	3.20	3.12	3.07	2.97
16	5%	4.49	3.63	3.24	3.01	2.85	2.74	2.66	2.59	2.54	2.49	2.42	2.37	2.33	2.28	2.20	2.16	2.13	2.07
	1%	8.53	6.23	5.29	4.77	4.44	4.20	4.03	3.89	3.78	3.69	3.55	3.45	3.37	3.25	3.10	3.01	2.96	2.86
17	5%	4.45	3.59	3.20	2.96	2.81	2.70	2.61	2.55	2.49	2.45	2.38	2.33	2.29	2.23	2.15	2.11	2.08	2.02
	1%	8.40	6.11	5.18	4.67	4.34	4.10	3.93	3.79	3.68	3.59	3.45	3.35	3.27	3.16	3.00	2.92	2.86	2.76
18	5%	4.41	3.55	3.16	2.93	2.77	2.66	2.58	2.51	2.46	2.41	2.34	2.29	2.25	2.19	2.11	2.07	2.04	1.98
	1%	8.29	6.01	5.09	4.58	4.25	4.01	3.84	3.71	3.60	3.51	3.37	3.27	3.19	3.07	2.91	2.83	2.78	2.68
19	5%	4.38	3.52	3.13	2.90	2.74	2.63	2.54	2.48	2.42	2.38	2.31	2.26	2.21	2.15	2.07	2.02	2.00	1.94
	1%	8.18	5.93	5.01	4.50	4.17	3.94	3.77	3.63	3.52	3.43	3.30	3.19	3.12	3.00	2.84	2.76	2.70	2.60
20	5%	4.35	3.49	3.10	2.87	2.71	2.60	2.51	2.45	2.39	2.35	2.28	2.23	2.18	2.12	2.04	1.99	1.96	1.90
	1%	8.10	5.85	4.94	4.43	4.10	3.87	3.70	3.56	3.46	3.37	3.23	3.13	3.05	2.94	2.77	2.69	2.63	2.53
21	5%	4.32	3.47	3.07	2.84	2.68	2.57	2.49	2.42	2.37	2.32	2.25	2.20	2.15	2.09	2.00	1.96	1.93	1.87
	1%	8.02	5.78	4.87	4.37	4.04	3.81	3.64	3.51	3.40	3.31	3.17	3.07	2.99	2.88	2.72	2.63	2.58	2.47
22	5%	4.30	3.44	3.05	2.82	2.66	2.55	2.46	2.40	2.34	2.30	2.23	2.18	2.13	2.07	1.98	1.93	1.91	1.84
	1%	7.95	5.72	4.82	4.31	3.99	3.76	3.59	3.45	3.35	3.26	3.12	3.02	2.94	2.83	2.67	2.58	2.53	2.42
23	5%	4.28	3.42	3.03	2.80	2.64	2.53	2.44	2.37	2.32	2.28	2.20	2.14	2.10	2.04	1.96	1.91	1.88	1.82
	1%	7.88	5.66	4.76	4.26	3.94	3.71	3.54	3.41	3.30	3.21	3.07	2.97	2.89	2.78	2.62	2.53	2.48	2.37
24	5%	4.26	3.40	3.01	2.78	2.62	2.51	2.42	2.36	2.30	2.26	2.18	2.13	2.09	2.02	1.94	1.89	1.86	1.80
	1%	7.82	5.61	4.72	4.22	3.90	3.67	3.50	3.36	3.26	3.17	3.03	2.93	2.85	2.74	2.58	2.49	2.44	2.33

Table G. Values of F Significant at .05 and .01 Levels (Continued)

df Associated with the Denominator		df Associated with the Numerator																	
		1	2	3	4	5	6	7	8	9	10	12	14	16	20	30	40	50	100
25	5%	4.24	3.39	2.99	2.76	2.60	2.49	2.40	2.34	2.28	2.24	2.16	2.11	2.06	2.00	1.92	1.87	1.84	1.77
	1%	7.77	5.57	4.68	4.18	3.86	3.63	3.46	3.32	3.22	3.13	2.99	2.89	2.81	2.70	2.54	2.45	2.40	2.29
26	5%	4.23	3.37	2.98	2.74	2.59	2.47	2.39	2.32	2.27	2.22	2.15	2.10	2.05	1.99	1.90	1.85	1.82	1.76
	1%	7.72	5.53	4.64	4.14	3.82	3.59	3.42	3.29	3.18	3.09	2.96	2.86	2.77	2.66	2.50	2.41	2.36	2.25
27	5%	4.21	3.35	2.96	2.73	2.57	2.46	2.37	2.31	2.25	2.20	2.13	2.08	2.03	1.97	1.88	1.84	1.80	1.74
	1%	7.68	5.49	4.60	4.11	3.78	3.56	3.39	3.26	3.15	3.06	2.93	2.83	2.74	2.63	2.47	2.38	2.33	2.21
28	5%	4.20	3.34	2.95	2.71	2.56	2.45	2.36	2.29	2.24	2.19	2.12	2.06	2.02	1.96	1.87	1.81	1.78	1.72
	1%	7.64	5.45	4.57	4.07	3.75	3.53	3.36	3.23	3.12	3.03	2.90	2.80	2.71	2.60	2.44	2.35	2.30	2.18
29	5%	4.18	3.33	2.93	2.70	2.55	2.43	2.35	2.28	2.22	2.18	2.10	2.05	2.00	1.94	1.85	1.80	1.77	1.71
	1%	7.60	5.42	4.54	4.04	3.73	3.50	3.33	3.20	3.09	3.00	2.87	2.77	2.68	2.57	2.41	2.32	2.27	2.15
30	5%	4.17	3.32	2.92	2.69	2.53	2.42	2.33	2.27	2.21	2.16	2.09	2.04	1.99	1.93	1.84	1.79	1.76	1.69
	1%	7.56	5.39	4.51	4.02	3.70	3.47	3.30	3.17	3.07	2.98	2.84	2.74	2.66	2.55	2.38	2.29	2.24	2.13
40	5%	4.08	3.23	2.84	2.61	2.45	2.34	2.25	2.18	2.12	2.07	2.00	1.95	1.90	1.84	1.74	1.69	1.66	1.59
	1%	7.31	5.18	4.31	3.83	3.51	3.29	3.12	2.99	2.89	2.80	2.66	2.56	2.49	2.37	2.20	2.11	2.05	1.94
60	5%	4.00	3.15	2.76	2.53	2.37	2.25	2.17	2.10	2.04	1.99	1.92	1.86	1.81	1.75	1.65	1.59	1.56	1.48
	1%	7.08	4.98	4.13	3.65	3.34	3.12	2.95	2.82	2.72	2.63	2.50	2.40	2.32	2.20	2.03	1.93	1.87	1.74
125	5%	3.92	3.07	2.68	2.44	2.29	2.17	2.08	2.01	1.95	1.90	1.83	1.77	1.72	1.65	1.55	1.49	1.45	1.36
	1%	6.84	4.78	3.94	3.47	3.17	2.95	2.79	2.65	2.56	2.47	2.33	2.23	2.15	2.03	1.85	1.75	1.68	1.54

BIBLIOGRAPHY

ARDMORE, SIDNEY J. *Introduction to Statistical Analysis and Inference for Psychology and Education*. New York: Wiley, 1966.

DOWNIE, N. M., and HEATH, R. W. *Basic Statistical Methods*, 2nd ed. New York: Harper and Row, 1965.

EDWARDS, ALLEN E. *Statistical Analysis*, 3rd ed. New York: Holt, Rinehart and Winston, 1969.

————*Statistical Methods*, 2nd ed. New York: Holt, Rinehart and Winston, 1967.

FERGUSON, GEORGE A. *Statistical Analysis in Psychology and Education*, 2nd ed. New York: McGraw-Hill, 1966.

GOUREVITCH, VIVIAN. *Statistical Methods: A Problem-Solving Approach*. Boston: Allyn and Bacon, 1965.

HAYS, WILLIAM L. *Statistics for Psychologists*. New York: Holt, Rinehart and Winston, 1963.

LATHROP, RICHARD G. *Introduction to Psychological Research—Logic, Design, Analysis*. New York: Harper and Row, 1969.

SIEGEL, SIDNEY. *Nonparametric Statistics for the Behavioral Sciences*. New York: McGraw-Hill, 1956.

SMITH, MILTON G. *A Simplified Guide to Statistics for Psychology and Education*, 4th ed. New York: Holt, Rinehart and Winston, 1970.

TOWNSEND, EDWARD A., and BURKE, PAUL J. *Statistics for the Classroom Teacher*. New York: Macmillan, 1968.

WALKER, HELEN M., and LEV, JOSEPH. *Elementary Statistical Methods*, 3rd ed. New York: Holt, Rinehart and Winston, 1969.

————*Statistical Inference*. New York: Holt, Rinehart and Winston, 1953.